Stella Grey is a pseudonym

COMMENTS RECEIVED VIA TWITTER, WHILE THE COLUMN WAS RUNNING IN THE *GUARDIAN*

From @RebNew1: It's been a relief knowing it's not just me who's gone through these scenarios.

From @carolineratner: I recently suggested a newly single friend read you from the beginning so she knew what to expect from dating.

From @CharleneWhite, ITV news anchor: This has been one of my fav regular weekend reads. Love it. Thanks for sharing.

From @patriciajrogers: Thank you for all those weeks of laughing, wincing and nodding knowingly to your column. Parallel experiences start to end.

From @caracourage: You've written words I've taken to heart, on the self in dating.

From @gnasherwell: Your column/twitter has made me feel normal.

From @catherineaman1: I feel like you've gone with me into the maelstrom, as an entertaining & kind companion.

From @theflossietp: Sad your column is ending, but at least it won't feel like you've been reading my journal any more!

From (NE
#stillse

From @helwels: Thanks for the reassurance that all the idiots weren't 'just me'.

From @missinformed11: As a woman of a similar age in a similar situation, the IT'S NOT JUST ME Factor was huge!

From @accentdialectuk: I've grown to feel just as ritual-adoring with your column as some people feel about The Archers.

From @adrianalemus: Even as a 20-something I could identify. Stella Grey might not be a typical heroine, but the wit, honesty, and her self-awareness of her own attributes and flaws made me see a woman to aspire to be, in her.

From @NesreenMSalem: I've had to resort to writing satires to make sense of the absurdity of my experience. Yours were less crazy & made me realise that I'm probably not doing it right …

From @SarahABGee: I suspect that many (most?) of us could share similar tales … you were never alone.

From @dellvink: I hope you get a movie rights offer. It would be great. A grown up UK romcom.

THERE WERE ALSO MEN WHO COULD RELATE

From @nickodyson: Highly recommended for the romantically inclined, and believers in hope.

From @GervaseWebb: I loved the final column. It should be printed out and given to everyone; male or female, over 50 or under.

THE
HEARTFIX

An Online Dating Diary

STELLA GREY

4th ESTATE • *London*

4th Estate
An imprint of HarperCollins*Publishers*
1 London Bridge Street
London SE1 9GF
www.4thEstate.co.uk

First published in Great Britain by 4th Estate in 2016
This paperback edition published by 4th Estate in 2017

1

A catalogue record for this book is
available from the British Library

ISBN 978-0-00-820175-3

Printed and bound in Great Britain by
Clays Ltd, St Ives plc

FSC™ is a non-profit international organisation established to promote
the responsible management of the world's forests. Products carrying the
FSC label are independently certified to assure consumers that they come
from forests that are managed to meet the social, economic and
ecological needs of present and future generations,
and other controlled sources.

Find out more about HarperCollins and the environment at
www.harpercollins.co.uk/green

THE
HEARTFIX

Outlandish though some of the following events and conversations may seem, they were real events and conversations, which took place over two years. This is not a work of fiction, nor fictionalised (although I can see why some people might think so). Names have been changed and some other identifying details, so as to protect those involved, including myself. Stella Grey is a pseudonym.

I'd like to thank all the people who have supported me in telling this story: Harriet Green, my editor at *Guardian Family*, who had already heard about some of these events, and who commissioned the original column. Clare, my sub-editor there. Nicholas Pearson, my editor and publisher at 4th Estate, who approached me with an offer to produce a book. The friends who cheered me on, throughout this journey, with unwavering support and love. My family, the thought of whom makes my hand clasp to my heart. My literary agent, who is always steadfastly in my corner. All the women (and men, too) who shared their dating stories – some of them very similar to my own – online and in letters.

Last of all, but by no means least … you'll have to get to the end to see that final dedication.

Introduction

The end of my marriage was an event that came suddenly and unexpectedly. It was rather like that scene in *Alien*, in which John Hurt is sitting contentedly eating spaghetti with the spacecraft crew, and then the infant monster bursts out of his chest, leaving everybody shocked and splattered. My ex-husband fell in love with someone else, and that's that. I can say, 'And that's that,' now, but I'm not going to pretend it didn't take time and a lot of ups and downs to get here, to the point at which I'm able to use three words. At the time it didn't feel real; we'd been married a long time; and then, when I started online dating, hoping to be cheered up, things became even more surreal. Life got quite *Alice in Wonderland*, as you will see. The journey I took – and I do think of it as a journey – was weird, hilarious, difficult, mind-boggling, nerve-racking and ultimately … (but I'm not going to spoil it for you). I online-dated for almost two years, and it isn't an exaggeration to say that it shaped the person I am now, a different person in various ways to the person I was. In many ways I like her better than the old me.

Dating was a strong medicine taken in the hopes of softening the corners of a desperate sadness. It wasn't easy, drawing the line that ended the married years and declaring myself to be single. It wasn't that I bypassed the heavy drinking phase. When somebody announces that they're leaving you, it's a physical shock. It starts in your brain and reverberates through your bones. It might *feel* like being told you have a terminal illness (when in fact it's usually highly treatable, and in time you'll get better). First there is denial, and then there is rage, and then there is acceptance. Denial is parasitical and tries to colonise you, and the rage that follows is like a baby cuckoo, perpetually hungry, and then there's acceptance, when you begin to want to make the best of getting up in the morning and carrying on. Renewal might follow. Renewal is a painful experience. It means being properly alive again, and trusting and vulnerable, and that can hurt.

There came a point, having healed sufficiently, having moved on from the daytime vodka phase – daytime vodka while eating whole tubs of ice cream and crying over property search programmes (it's distressing to be a cliché, but there you are) – at which I thought, So now what? *So now what?* is a good sign. It marks the first day of looking forward, and not back. I'm not saying I stopped harking back, but I began to look ahead and think about what might happen next. I'd always imagined the future would be shared with my husband, and now there were many other roads, forking off, over hill and dale and into the unknown. It occurred to me for the first time that I might not be unhappy for the rest of my life. I realised that it was all in my hands. I ditched the vodka, the dairy products stacked in the freezer and daytime television. I had a haircut and colour, bought a dress and went to the bookshop. I sat on a park bench with my books in a bag (not all of them self-help, either), tilting my face up to the early spring sunshine, and decided that I needed to meet new people, and by people I mean men.

The world was full of couples and I wanted to be half of one of them. That was the mission. It was my own diagnosis of what I needed. I was heartbroken and needed a fix. I needed *a heartfix*. The world was full of couples busy being casually happy with one another. The young ones didn't trouble me, the kind who canoodled in cinema queues. But the midlife ones really bothered me, and particularly the silver-haired, affluent couples holding hands in the street. There was a prime example in the coffee shop where I used to hang out at the weekend, a pair who were just back from holiday. They were talking about how much they were missing island light and their swimming pool. She was wearing the bracelet he'd bought her, and it was turquoise against her tanned arm. The non-affluent retired bothered me too: the world was full of ordinary untanned, badly dressed, unattractive older couples who had every intention of being together till they died, and I began to find that simple loyalty overpoweringly moving. Heartbreak felt constantly hormonal, like persistent PMS. I was having trouble feeling sensible about the odds of finding somebody who would feel as natural and right at my side as my husband once had. But I needed to do something, even if it turned out just to be a phase on the way to being happy to live on my own.

A friend suggested internet dating. She'd plunged in and she had found someone lovely. Most people in the online pool were dull or odd or nuts, or love rats, she said (I assumed she was exaggerating), but it was a lot more fun than endless nights in with slippers and shiraz and Sudoku, and only a dog to talk to. Online dating! It wasn't for me. I wasn't an online dating type of person: that much I was sure of. I'd read the horror stories that circulate, and had heard some too, about cattle markets, players and lotharios, married men and psychos and scams. But it seemed daft not to look, so I hovered around the sites for a week or so. (It was 'free to join!'– though not to reply to messages, it turned out, when

I'd taken this promise at face value.) I spent time dipping in as a lurker and observer, equal parts horrified and tantalised. Being tantalised was surprising. There were male profiles that intrigued me: kind-faced, rumpled, witty men who'd managed to hurdle over the dignity issue involved in self-advertising, and had signed up. Once I'd done the same, I had a powerful sense of being part of something. It was strangely poignant, this feeling, as if I were part of a great river of people who had been bashed by life and were brave. They were bold enough to embark on the search for love in this new-fangled digital way, each risking humiliation, failure and ridicule in their determination to swim upstream. I was aware of the distinct possibility of all three outcomes – humiliation, failure, ridicule – but I was lonely, and I don't just mean for male company. I was lonely in general; unhappiness is a solitary state and I couldn't keep talking about it and going round in circles in my head and feeling stuck. I needed to break out of the cycle, and be fresh, to have a fresh life. The bizarre process of choosing potential lovers and life-mates from what is essentially an online catalogue would bring a broadening-out into my narrowing life, at least, and I was badly in need of something radical. Distraction, at the least. Was a second love possible? Was a second love found via a website for singles remotely possible? It seemed unlikely. But what else was I going to do – sit here festering, eating snacks and watching *Miss Marple* reruns?

So I decided to have a go. What did I have to lose, after all? I signed up to the biggest of the no-fee sites, filled in the questionnaire, posted a photograph that hinted at hidden depth, and took two hours to write and polish my profile, distilling life experience and interests into nuggets that offered fascinating glimpses of my inner world (I thought).

Gratifyingly, half an hour later I had two messages. The first said: 'Hello sexy. You look very squeezable. First, can I ask – do you eat meat? I couldn't kiss someone who consumes the flesh of tortured animals.' The second said: 'Hi. I can see from your face that you have shadows in your heart. I think I can help.' I hit the reply button and asked how he was going to do that. 'I will shine a great light upon you,' he wrote. I logged off and sat for a while, staring at the screen. Then I logged on again, to see if anyone else had written yet. There was a message from someone called Freddie. All it said was 'Hi' followed by nine kisses. I had a look at Freddie's profile. It consisted of two sentences: 'Honest, caring, tactile man, looking for sensual woman. Please – no game players, gold diggers, liars or cheats.'

I reckoned that what I needed was more sites and more variety, so I signed up to every worthwhile-looking one I could find and afford, a total of nine. (As time went on I whittled this down to four, with occasional forays into a fifth and sixth; and then, in the second phase, somewhat desperately, I added another eight.) It was quite an expensive endeavour. Online dating is big business and it's easy to see why. Basically it's money for old rope. If you build it, they will come: create a search engine and a messaging system, then stand back and let people find one another. It's a great big dance hall, though without the dancing, or the band. Or the hall. Generally what you're paying for is access to their database, though some sites claim to work hard on your behalf by matching people 'scientifically' via hundreds of questions (this didn't work for me, as you will see).

I decided that I was going to have to be pro-active and start some conversations, rather than sitting waiting for men to come to me. In general, men were not coming to me. I'd launched myself into the scene expecting to make some kind of an impression, but made very little impact. It was like bursting into a party dressed to the nines, ready armed with funny stories, and saying, 'TA DAAA!' and having almost everybody ignore you (other than the people asking everybody for naked pictures and hook-ups. I didn't count them in my success rate). Something had to be done to kick-start the process, so I began to take the initiative. I started with men in my own city, of about the same age, education and outlook. This didn't go well. The last thing most divorced men appeared to be looking for was women of the same age, education and outlook. You may protest that this is a wild generalisation and is unfair. I can only tell you of my own experience, which is that they have high expecta-tions, a situation exacerbated by being heavily outnumbered by women. But I didn't know this then. I was like a Labrador let off its lead at the park, bounding up to people expecting to make friends. A chatty introduction email went off to a dozen candidates who lived within a five-mile radius. When there were no replies, I thought something must be wrong with the message system. Then I found that one of the non-repliers had removed the three items from his likes and dislikes list that I'd mentioned I also liked. *Withnail & I*, dark chocolate, rowing boats: all had been deleted. Another of the men had blocked me so I couldn't write to him again. This, I have to tell you, stung me deeply. It winded me. I hadn't realised online dating was like this.

After the initial sting, I had the first experience of certainty. I was sure that I'd found him, the man for me. Graham had a lovable face and an attractive sort of gravitas (he was a senior civil servant). He wrote well, and lived a mere five miles away. His profile echoed my own, in the things he said, believed, wanted. We were 100 per cent compatible. Being a novice, I was sure he would see me in the same way. I thought, This is it; I've done it; here he is. It was an obvious match! I wrote him a long message about myself, a letter, picking up points of similarity and initiating what I was confident would be lively conversation. I was almost debilitated by excitement. It was the beginning of something wonderful, of that I was sure. But I was wrong, completely wrong. It wasn't the beginning of anything. Graham didn't even reply. Not realising that ignoring compatible people who'd taken the trouble to write a letter of many paragraphs might even be an option (people did that?), I checked my inbox over and over for the following forty-eight hours. It seemed clear that the only possible reasons his enthusiastic response had been delayed were that he was a) away, or b) too crazy-busy to write his rapturous reply. But that wasn't it. Graham had read my message and dismissed it. I never heard from him, not a word – though he came and had a look at me. Twice. He looked at my profile page, at what I said about myself and at my picture, and then he looked again, and then he decided to ignore me. So this was the first thing I learned: *men I had an instant attraction to, and who sounded like thoroughly decent people, could actually be arseholes*. That was Lesson One.

Because I had more or less talked myself into being horribly smitten, and because I'd given so much of myself in my lengthy approach letter, Graham's decision not even to answer my email hit me hard. I'd been judged unworthy of a reply. It was a powerful first hint that in this context, essentially I might be thought to be a commodity, one not much in demand at that. I felt hurt. I had feelings. This unreal situation was prompting real emotions, ones I didn't want to have. One of the problems with online dating is that it facilitates those who want to dehumanise the process just as much as it facilitates the romantic and genuine. The system, like any other, is a hard cold thing. People can take refuge in that, in the machine, in the distancing and anonymising that's built in to protect them. But they can also exploit it. My own response to these initial hard knocks was that I began to expect a lot less. I wrote shorter approach messages, while still taking trouble to personalise them: 'Hello there, I just wanted to say that I really enjoyed reading your profile, and also to say, the book you say you never tire of is the book I never tire of too. Have you read the sequel?' The recipient didn't reply. Ever.

It wasn't only the way people behaved on dating sites that astounded me, but also the descriptions some gave of themselves there. Perhaps it's social media's fault that lots of men have embraced the power of the inspirational quote. Sometimes these are attached to names at every sign-off (Gary 'Love life and grasp and hold on to it every day xxx'). Some had profiles that I suspect were drafted by their 14-year-old sisters. 'My favourite things are the crinkle of the leaves under my shoes in autumn and birdsong after the rain.' 'I don't care about beauty,' another had written. 'As long as you have a beautiful soul I want to hear from you.' I was charmed. I wrote to tell him I was charmed. He didn't reply; perhaps what he wanted was inner beauty attached to a 30-year-old body. Another early correspondent was enraged about my preference for tall men. He wrote me a one-line message: 'Your insistence on dating men over 6 feet tall is heightist.'

I explained that I am taller than that in shoes. 'I'm a tall woman,' I said. 'I'm sorry if you have an equal-opportunities-oriented approach to sex, but I like to look up to a man when I kiss him. I continue to allow myself that preference. Apologies if that offends.'

'You know the average height of men in the UK is 5'10 don't you,' he replied. That happened to be his own height.

'Luckily I'm not interested in averages,' I wrote.

'You may as well ask for an albino who's a billionaire,' he countered.

It was hard to know how to reply to that, so I didn't. I always replied to a first approach, unless there was something vile about it, but didn't feel obliged to keep responding to people who replied to my reply, and especially not those I'd said no thank you to. Otherwise some pointless conversations would never have ended.

I paused at the smiling face of a man called Dave who lived in Kent. 'Hi I'm Dave, an ordinary bloke, 43 years old and ready for a serious relationship.' What caught my eye was that Dave was 52. The age updated automatically on the heading of the page, though he hadn't updated the personal statement that appeared beneath it. His description had been written a full nine years ago. 'Oh God,' I said aloud. 'Dave's been here for nine years!' Poor Dave. 'I hope you find someone soon, Dave,' I said to the screen. 'Unless you're a bad man, obviously, in which case womankind has made its judgement and you should probably take the hint.'

Most people's dating site profiles say little about them. Some real-world interesting people have no gift for self-description and fall back on the generic; some people are careful to be bland and unspecific; and others are actually as dull as their blurb suggests. It can be tricky to deduce which of the three you're dealing with, at first or even second glance. There are those who appear to say a lot, but actually give nothing away. Everybody loves holidays and music and films and food, and wants to travel the world. Everyone has a good sense of humour, works hard and likes country weekends; everybody loves a sofa, a DVD and a bottle of wine. Then there's the problem of integrity. Some things that are said might prove not to be true: marital status for example, or age, or location, or general intentions (or height). 'I'm looking for my soulmate,' doesn't always mean exactly that. Sometimes it decodes as *I'm not looking for my soulmate, but that's what chicks want to hear.* Inside the anonymity of the database, nothing can be relied on at face value. I'm not suggesting there are grounds for constant paranoia, but I learned to be on the alert. In the early days I had a conversation with a professor at a certain university, and checked the campus website and found that he wasn't. When I challenged him his dating profile disappeared and my emails weren't any longer answered. When I told a friend – who was also searching for someone – about this, she said, 'Sometimes I'm confident, and sometimes taking on a second-hand man is like going to the dog refuge and picking a stray, not knowing what its real history is or how it might react under pressure.'

Not that this is everyone's experience of online romance. I know of dating site marriages … well, I know of one. Admittedly the woman in question is a goddess. The goddesses, the willowy ones with the cheekbones and the swishy hair, are probably swamped with offers. As for me, all the dating site gods (tall, articulate, successful, well-travelled; they don't even have to be handsome) were swishing right past me.

I asked my friend Jack for a male appraisal of my dating site profile. He said it was lovely, like me. That was worrying. I needed clarification.

'Well,' he said. 'You expect a lot. You make it clear you only want clever, funny, high-achieving men.'

'I don't say high-achieving. I don't say that anywhere.'

'You say it without saying it. And it's clear that you're alpha. That puts men off. I'm just saying.'

'So what should I do? Claim to be a flight attendant with a love of seamed stockings?'

'That would get you a lot of attention. But then you'd need to follow through.'

'I'd have to study the British Airways routes and talk about layovers.'

'Every middle-aged man in the world dreams of layovers,' Jack said, looking wistful.

He helped rewrite the copy so that I sounded more fun, though not as fun as Jack wanted me to sound. There was an immediate response in the inbox. 'Reading between the lines, I think you're holding out for something unusual,' one said. 'I believe I'm atypical. For a start I don't have a television. When I had one I spent a lot of time shouting at it.' I replied that I couldn't bear to watch *Question Time* either. 'No, no,' he said. '*Countryfile*, for instance. *Countryfile*'s really annoying.' I asked him what he did in the evenings. He said he spent a lot of time with his lizards.

It was a grim Tuesday night, the rain lashing down. I went in search of someone friendlier. There were lots of men who claimed to be the life and soul of the party, but who looked like serial killers on Wanted posters. In general, using a bad passport photograph to illustrate your page isn't the best of all possible plans. I rummaged through the first five candidates the system had offered and had a look at what they had to say. 'Scientific facts are never true. If you know why scientific facts are never true, you might be the girl for me.' 'Still looking for the right one, a woman who won't expect me to be at her beck and call.' 'Second hand male, in fairly good condition despite last careless owner.' 'I am a complex person, too complex to explain here, a hundred different men in one. If you want a dull life you are wasting your time. Move along – nothing to see here.' 'Looking for intelligence, co-operation and a natural blonde.' (*Co-operation?*)

Perhaps, I thought, I should narrow the search, by ticking some of the boxes for interests. A search based on ticking 'Current Affairs' brought up a raft of virtue-signallers. 'I'm dedicated to the pursuit of justice for all and hate political unfairness.' 'The top three things I hate are liars, deceit and war.' (Whereas, presumably, the rest of us are assumed to approve of wars and lying.) Then I had a brief conversation with a man who said he loved world cinema. I messaged him asking what kind of films he liked. Back came the reply: 'Hi thanks for asking, my favourite movies are *Driller Killer*, *The Lair of the White Worm*, *Cannibal Holocaust*, *I Spit on Your Grave*, *Cabaret* and *The Blood-Spattered Bride*.'

The first dinner offer came from Trevor, an American expat in London. Trevor had been dumped and was only just passing out of denial and into acceptance, he said. He was doing the work (the therapeutic work on himself, he meant), but was finding it hard. Four thousand words of backstory followed this statement, and in return, I gave him mine. A few hours after this another great long email arrived, talking philosophically about life and quoting writers. It was charming, endearing; I reciprocated with my own thoughts, quoting other writers. We were all set. Then, the day before dinner, Trevor cancelled. The last line of his message said: 'To be honest, I'm not interested in a woman who's my intellectual equal.' (I know this sounds as if it might not be true, but I'm sorry to tell you that it is.) He added that he felt honesty was the best policy. I didn't like to tell him what my policy was, but right then and there it could easily have involved a plank, a pirate ship, a shark-infested sea and a long pointy stick.

The first real-world meeting was for a coffee in town in the afternoon with an HR manager, between his meetings: a short, sharp interview that I failed. I didn't mind too much. He was pursed-mouthed, unforthcoming, with dyed black hair and the demeanour of a vampire. Determined to exorcise the bad first date, I agreed to another, with an apparently jaunty tax specialist. Ahead of me in the queue, he bought only his own cappuccino and cake, leaving me to get mine, and then for twenty minutes I heard all about the many, many times he'd seen U2, told one concert at a time. By then my cup was empty. In all sorts of ways my cup seemed to be empty.

It wasn't just the bad dates that were ending badly. I had a good date that also ended badly: a success so tremendous – dinner that led into dancing, and after that a walk by the river, and then a glorious snog – that I couldn't sleep afterwards, but lay awake imagining our life together, a fantasy outcome put to an end by his cutting me dead. Sometimes people have one great date with someone and that's enough for them. A series of great first dates is all they're hoping for; that's all they need. I hadn't anticipated this, not anything like this. I came from a much more straightforward, more traditional dating culture in which people got together at discos and parties and via friends of friends, and stayed together for a long time. We were open with one another, back then, and love was fairly simple.

I decided that what I'd do was establish a real friendship with men, over email and text and sometimes even over the phone (I've never liked the phone), before agreeing to meet them. Talking people into being interested in you before meeting – that's where you might expect the internet to excel. That could be a process designed to work in a middle-aged woman's favour, circumventing the shock of her physical self when a man met her in person. Undeniably, I had been a shock to some men I'd met, and I wasn't the only one to have had that experience (look, I'm not particularly hideous). I'd been talking to other women of around my age who had found the very same. It was agreed that there were notable (noble) exceptions, but in general men had expectations that a woman who'd 'put herself out there' would dedicate time, effort and money to her appearance, so as to compete. Some men are of the opinion that the whole physical manifestation of a woman on the earth should amount to an A–Z of efforts to please, and that we're all madly in competition with one another. There are men who think that's all that lipstick means. There are tabloid newspapers that suggest that's all that clothes mean, and who divide women into goat and sheep camps, the frumpy and those who flaunt themselves. There have been men, in the course of this quest, who have been openly scandalised about my lack of commitment to looking younger. But then as Jack kept telling me, 'Men are visual creatures.' He was doubtful about the Scheherazade strategy, one involving telling stories and general email-based bewitchment. Nonetheless, I resolved to stick with plan A. I decided that I would be quirky, and bright, and a little bit alpha, and I was going to be my real age, for as long as it took. Initial disappointments wouldn't deter me. I was going to beat the system and find the man I'd want to be with for the rest of my life. I was just hoping it wouldn't take another 1001 nights.

Trying to Write the Right Profile

Here's my first attempt at a dating profile. The additions in bold in brackets are my reactions to reading it now.

ABOUT ME

Tall, dark, reasonably handsome woman, just turned 50, hoping for second love after the end of a long marriage. (**Is tall, dark and handsome a bit of a macho way to introduce yourself? I'm trying for witty, but I think I'm just coming off as annoying, to misquote Rex the dinosaur in** *Toy Story*.) Intelligent, lively, curious, bookish. Not a skinny person. I'm just saying. Not obese either, but if slender is your type, then I might literally be too much to handle. (**Christ, no, that's not even funny.**)

WHAT I'M LOOKING FOR

A tall, clever, funny, loyal, lovely man. (**Not much to ask, is it?**) Ideally, someone to grow old with. Someone bookish, good-humoured, sociable, kind. (**You should probably have written: 'Happiness; not interested in flings'. That's probably enough.**) I have a bit of a thing for big sturdy academics who rock a linen jacket. (**Oh no.**)

MUSIC

My music likes are catholic, as in wide-ranging and not as in Vatican City. (**You've just offended somebody.**) Jimi Hendrix, Kathleen Ferrier, Pat Metheny, Philip Glass, Rolling Stones, Talking Heads and all the usual classical. Not really an opera person. Fond of seventies and eighties tracks that remind me of being a student. Neil Young, Joni Mitchell, Glen Campbell, Velvet Underground, John Martyn, Blue Nile, Marvin Gaye, Blondie, Pretenders, The Cure, David Bowie. Very fond of wordless film scores and ambient. Favourite guilty secret: Fleetwood Mac. (**Accurate enough, though you've completely omitted the jazz you listen to all day. And I'm not really sure why you've written all this.**)

BOOKS

Usually have a book stuck to my face. British and American nineteenth and twentieth centuries, and the usual retinue of greatness: Dickens, Austen, Brontë, Wharton, James. Oh, and those Russian chaps, and those French chaps (**that you don't read much. Plus, your cuteness is already annoying**). Currently on the bedside: Michel Faber, Richard Ford, Kazuo Ishiguro, Fitzgerald, Franzen, Forster, Iris Murdoch. Larkin and Eliot. Art books. A.N. Wilson's *The Victorians*. (**This is true but you might be trying too hard. Perfectly nice men who read only 99p Kindle thrillers will be deterred. It doesn't matter what you read or what other people read.**)

FILMS

Twelve random Desert Island films: *Local Hero, Some Like It Hot, Philadelphia Story, Annie Hall, Hero, Blazing Saddles, Two Days in Paris, Stranger than Fiction, Rocky Horror, Monsieur Hulot's Holiday, A Night at the Opera, All About My Mother, Blade Runner.* (**Except that's thirteen.**) I'm a big fan of world cinema of all sorts. Guilty pleasures: The *Bourne* franchise, popcorn thrillers.

FOOD

Basically Nigella. (**You are embarrassing.**) Very greedy and eat almost anything (**you're saying you're fat**). Cooking and eating are important, as you will see immediately you meet me. (**You keep telling the boys that you're fat, you know.**) World food rather than just traditional British, though in reality there's a lot of chicken. In summer, fish and chips out of the paper while sitting on a sea wall. Restaurant pick for a blowout dinner – mussels to start, venison or duck, lots of cheese, a clever chocolate pudding. And wine. Lots of wine. Garlic with everything except custard. Death Row meal: steak and sweet potato fries. (**Really not clear why you've written down any of this.**)

ART

I'm an art nut and go to galleries a lot. I have trouble with some of the conceptual stuff but am not completely ungroovy. (**Oh God.**) I've even admired the occasional video installation. I like primitive art, Renaissance art, nineteenth-century art, early/mid twentieth-century modernism. I like abstraction, colour, some expressive work. Howard

Hodgkin. (**At this point you've probably deterred people who think this is a spec, rather than just your own ramblings.**)

HOME

Home means a lot, physically and as an idea. I like to decorate, in different senses of the word. (**No, me neither.**) Having said that, heading off with a rucksack and being forced to be a world citizen would probably be good for me. At home I feel the pull between sleek functionality and a more cluttered, wildly coloured nineteenth-century approach with some Moroccan-boho touches. (**A chap might wonder if you're asking to be housed and to be given a furnishing budget, at this point.**)

TV AND RADIO

Radio 3 and 4. Not a live-TV watcher, in general. Low tolerance for commercials. No tolerance for reality television, of any sort. I like thrillers, crime, suspense, psychological. Quite partial to the occasional bonnet drama (I don't mean cars). Culture and science docs. (**You sound like a media snob. But that is accurate enough.**)

PLACES

I haven't been to enough places. I know bits of Europe well and tend to return to them. Ideal holiday: a place with swimming plus exploring opportunities, interleaving history/travel days with relaxing days. Wild swimming fan: lakes and rivers often preferred to beaches. No interest in the Caribbean or tanning. I want to see more of the world. (**Add** that trekking in Nepal and Machu Picchu are not on the list.) I want to see 'Arabia' as the nineteenth-century explorers saw it. (Do not say this – people will delight in misunderstanding it.)

POLITICS

Sensible-compassionate left-middle. (Don't use the word compassionate about yourself. Or charismatic, come to that.)

SPORT

No. Unless you count walking the dog. Or watching Wimbledon and Six Nations rugby. On the television. On the couch. (This is brave, perhaps, but necessary. Too many midlife men are gym-oriented.) I cycle, but rarely uphill.

WEEKENDS

An ideal weekend: eating, reading, going out for a mooch and a coffee, dipping into a museum, going to the cinema, making dinner and drinking wine. Or: off to a wild green place for walking and the pub. Or: gardens and NT houses with tearooms. Weekends away in B&Bs. Walks on the beach in winter. (Beaches in winter are a total dating cliché.)

What I think when I read this over now is: I wonder how many people thought they wouldn't fit the bill, because they watched, read or did the wrong things, and because they interpreted a detailed account of myself as an equally

detailed wish list. In a way this can't be helped: the whole
point is to give an idea of what you're like and how you tick.
It's very difficult to get it right. Some of the reactions I had
to this first attempt were, 'Well, you're not expecting a lot,
are you?' (sarcasm) and, 'You come over as a smug middle-
class bitch.' But, you see, I wasn't interested in the sort of
men who would write to women to tell them that. So,
perhaps, although some of the above is cringe-worthy, it's on
the right tack, in being personal, at least. Smugly middle
class and with high expectations, maybe – but personal, at
least.

First Bites
and Backbites

SPRING, YEAR ONE

So, the plan was to make a man fall a little bit in love with me by email before we met. The idea was that this would make me feel less nervous about meeting a stranger.

The project didn't start well. The first attempt was utterly doomed, because the man in question wasn't a communicator. To Ralph, texting was for making social arrangements, and emailing was for making more long-winded social arrangements, and he didn't grasp that both could be used as a form of foreplay. I'm not saying this was a bad thing, *per se*. Each to their own. But yes, Ralph and I were a mismatch, in this and in other ways. I persisted, though, for five weeks and seven dates, because he was an incredible kisser. We're talking world-class osculation. It was the kind of kissing that could turn a person's head and make them conclude, totally wrongly, that a lifetime of bliss lay ahead. Sex (sixth and seventh dates) was a complete disaster, though. I don't mean that the mechanics of it were a failure, despite the fact that I was undoubtedly a nervous wreck. It was just unsexy: weirdly, profoundly unsexy for both of us. It was odd. The kissing was our sex. The kissing was as erotic as hell. The sex, however, was more like shaking hands with your bottom.

I did wonder if Ralph had an aversion to body hair. There were men, in this story, who were enthusiastic about 'a seventies vibe' and there were men who had to stifle a shriek. There was a man who asked, flat out (via the messaging system) if I shaved, and who was angered by my response; my having pubic hair of any kind was rude to him, he thought, like being unshowered. The best sort of men are those who don't give a shit how much hair you have, or where. (Listen, chaps – try having your pubes ripped out with hot wax, on a regular 'maintenance' basis, before declaring a preference.)

So, things didn't work out with Ralph. For him, perhaps it was that I didn't have the pudendum of a 10-year-old girl. For me, it was his lack of interest in talking when we were apart that killed the urge to keep trying. He was perfectly friendly when we were face to face, but terse or silent between dates. A goldfish, in online dating terms. Often he ignored texts and emails, and if he replied at all it was usually three words, using his catchphrase: 'Catch you later!' I sent him an email one night telling him about a bad day, and his reply was: 'Looking forward to catching you soon!' I'm sorry if this sounds needy, but I needed more. Six words seemed like they might indicate a lack of interest.

Not that I could make claims to be the norm from which Ralph was deviating. Ralph had no way of knowing that I was emotionally rather catlike in needing frequent small meals of love. He had unwittingly stepped into a game in which he wasn't really aware of the rules. I texted him after date number six, asking if we were still on for Friday. 'Yes! Looking forward to catching up with you!' the reply said. He'd signed it with his full name, including his surname. Who writes their surname on a text? Did he think I'd need to distinguish him from all the other Ralphs I was seeing?

So, date number seven came, and we had our romantic dinner, in candlelight, and talked about work. It was a dull evening – to be honest they had all been dull – but I was determined not to give up. There was the kissing to consider. There was the whole 'having a boyfriend at last' thing to consider, too. I'm not by nature a quitter. 'Look,' I said, 'do you think … could we talk a bit more, between dates, so that we're a bit more in touch with the day-to-day, what's happening and what we're thinking? I'd enjoy that.'

'Sure,' he said, scrutinising the wine list.

We had weird unsexy sex, and later on, back at home, having soaked in the bath, naked in fresh crisp sheets, I texted him saying that I was warm and naked in bed, just bathed, feeling restless and thinking of him. He didn't reply. The following night, having turned out my light, I texted that I was thinking of him. That was all I said: 'Thinking of you.' The response was: 'You take care!' (Seriously. Really.)

It occurred to me that I frightened Ralph. Ralph was scared. It began to look, at the very least, like an unusually short attention span. Whatever the actual diagnosis, I knew it wasn't going to last even a week longer. I needed romance, of some sort, some sense of a progression, some inkling of a relationship. I needed more than a fuck-buddy who didn't want a friend. And that's why I went quiet. I stopped texting and emailing, leaving a vacuum, to see what Ralph would fill it with. Ralph didn't fill it with anything. It was easy come easy go, and it came and it went. Nothing was put to an end because essentially nothing had begun. He wasn't in touch again, and that was that. It was as if the whole thing had been a hallucination.

I did start to wonder, at that early point, if a middle-aged woman on a dating site might be considered as really only useful as a fuck-buddy. I did wonder if men assumed I would know that, and that I'd take what I could get. I didn't get a lot of messages unless I'd written first, and those I did receive tended to be only a notch beyond grunting. 'How About It Darlin, You and Me? Xxxxxxxx' There are plenty of men online who think a woman over 45 will react to the offer of a shag in an alley with tears of gratitude.

Men online use kisses, all the time; perhaps they picked up the habit on social media, where women who don't know each other and will never meet have developed intricate hierarchies of kissing. This is a cultural shift. I'm sure men never used to scatter kisses so freely. Plus, a new function enabling people to send mass mail-outs had been introduced on one of the sites, which some men took to eagerly. It meant that they could write one message and press EMAIL ALL and have it sent to every woman they'd ticked. One such that I received acknowledged that it was a mass communication, as if that wouldn't put us all off him, at all. 'Hello ladies, this is Pete, I'm an average guy, like a laugh, like sofa and the telly, like my footie, like to make a lady happy, so let me know if any of you would like to take a chance on a 45 year old man: one careful owner, reasonable bodywork for age, full service history.' Another had used the mail-out facility to get a lively competitive vibe going. He'd set us all an essay question. He wanted submissions in reply to the following: 'Do what thou wilt shall be the whole of the law.' It wasn't clear what the prize was.

Other messages were misdelivered. An email arrived from a man in South Wales. 'Jessica,' it said, 'I knew the minute I saw your face that it was meant to be. Do you believe in love at first sight? I'm visited by intuition that I am the man for you. Send me a long message telling me all about yourself, and I'll reply by tonight, and we can get this thing started.'

'You've sent this to the wrong person,' I replied. 'I'm not Jessica. I'm afraid this is the hazard of using cut-and-paste.'

'You're the right person,' he insisted, styling it out. 'I'm just not very good with names.'

After this I had daily on-screen dating site conversations with a man called Alexander. He was Dutch in origin, six foot four and the kind of blond that takes grey well, and looked good in his photograph, in dark jeans and jacket and a white shirt, with a big brown satchel hooked across his body, and a floral scarf. He was unmistakably *not from around here*. We met first on a Sunday. Well, we didn't really meet. All we had to go on were photographs and the usual clues: carefully veiled descriptions of who we are and where we work; our likes and dislikes; our favourite films, books, music, food, places in the world; what we're looking for and our ideas about the future. We didn't reveal our real identities or email addresses. We didn't speak on the phone, or see each other talking on Skype. It was a connection built – and then dismantled – entirely by typing.

After a few days, Alexander wrote a very long message in the middle of the night, listing all the women he'd ever loved and how they'd let him down. Dates were supplied and first names, and vivid descriptions. He was 55, and his second marriage had come to an end in the spring. It failed, he said, because the children were too much; he'd realised he couldn't handle living with young children. He'd moved out and left his wife to handle them alone, other than for a weekend a month, when he took them to the zoo, like an uncle. He wrote that he was looking for someone who would make him feel more rewarded by life than his wife had. As time went on, that sentence bothered me more and more.

There are men who will take on the role of therapist and draw you out, who'll draw it all out of you like knotted silk handkerchiefs from a magician's pocket. This feels wonderful at the time. It's only afterwards that you might look back and shudder. There are people who get a kick out of owning other people; some people own others by knowing their secrets. Some men want to engage in the dance, and some men only want you to dance, while they watch you. 'Tell me all about your past relationships and what went wrong,' he wrote, at the end of his own exhaustive list, and, feeling pent up, feeling the thrill of letting loose and being listened to, I did. Alexander, a man I had known for less than a week, disagreed with my analysis. 'It's obvious to me that your ex never loved you,' he wrote. 'I'm beginning to see that lots of people end up married to people they don't love, though it can take them a long time to admit to it. Adultery is often the beginning of a search for something more real, and the sex is just a smokescreen. I realise that's been my own pattern.'

When I tried to bring the conversation to an end, Alexander became even more assertive. He said he'd taken the red pill. Dating sites are awash with men talking about the blue pill and the red pill. It's a frame of reference taken from *The Matrix*: if you've 'taken the blue pill' you're someone who doesn't want to face reality, happy to live in your illusions, while if you've 'taken the red pill' you see the world as it really is. (You think.) Among those who claim to have 'taken the red pill' are men who've gone through a bad divorce and know all about women, how we think and why, how men behave and why: it's all become clear to them. I told Alexander that he didn't really know me. He disagreed. He'd come across my situation a hundred times. It was the way of things, he said. I had my first serious case of dating site revulsion. Why had I said any of what I'd said to him, and told him my history, this arrogant stranger? Though I didn't write that. I wrote that it had been nice talking to him, and that I wished him luck. His reply said: 'I could say that I'd be back to talk to you at a later date, like all the other arseholes, but as you've already gathered, I won't be contacting you again because it's already clear you can't give me what I need. This isn't what I need at this stage of my life.' Everywhere I looked there were people who'd hit middle age and were talking about stages in their lives.

A message arrived shortly afterwards, from a man in Shetland, that took the form of a one-line quotation: 'But risk we must, because the greatest hazard in life is to risk nothing. Anon.'

'Nice quote,' I wrote back.

'Thanks,' he replied. 'Most of the shadows in your life are caused by standing in your own sunshine.'

'Corny, but possibly true,' I wrote.

And that was that. I think I lost him at corny.

After this I went for coffee with a man called Sean. We didn't have any kind of a lead-up. His request came out of the blue, and something about the plainness of that, the low expectations, made it easy to agree. It wasn't a date, we said. It was just coffee, we said. (It wasn't just coffee, of course. It was an audition.) I wasn't hopeful, but you never know until you meet people. Plus, I was badly in need of something cheeringly ordinary. Over the previous week there had been a string of approaches from those that – kindly – we must refer to as oddballs. 'I love women. Thin ones, fat ones, young ones, droopy ones, smooth ones, hairy ones – but especially the hairy ones.' (Well, that was something, at least.) Closely followed by another message, one that was a lot less practical: 'This fading world is a mirror of myself dying; I'll be more alive a thousand years from now than at this moment. Discuss.' And then: 'I am interested in the

occult, Satanism and Celtic mythology, which will be obvious from looking at my paintings, some jpgs of which are
attached.'

Also, there had been a humiliating glass of wine with a
man in a city pub. David. David was worryingly good-looking (I'd already lost all faith in my power to attract a handsome man) and he'd only seen strategic photos of my head
and shoulders. His face literally fell when he saw me coming
towards him in the bar. He spent most of our date acting out
a fervent need to listen closely to the live band, and more or
less shushing me when I spoke. At the end, out on the pavement, he said, 'I don't think so, do you?' and strode away,
smiling. I hate to think about being one of the stories these
men tell each other in the locker room. I break out in a cold
sweat thinking about my friend Jane, who had text sex with
an online suitor, after he sent her links to cottages in Italy he
thought they should buy. When finally they met, he went to
the bar to get drinks and was never seen again.

Essentially the meeting with Sean was a blind date,
though we'd seen each other's pictures. His showed him: 1)
on a boat, manning the helm; 2) with ice in his beard, on
Mont Blanc; and 3) in sunglasses, in Spain with a beer. For
online males this amounts to a fairly typical spread. My
photographs were typical too: one serious face, one smiling
one, and three flattering, semi-misleading holiday pictures
(tanned and in wrinkle-obliterating light). After a while I'd
added a frank head-to-toe one, too. Coincidentally, a certain
Jeff wrote demanding properly full-length photographs.
'Often the women here prove to have fat ankles,' he said.
(We didn't talk further.) There's a huge amount of dating
site commentary by men reporting that women prove to be
'fat', though to some people that merely means 'eats properly' or 'her knees aren't the biggest part of her leg'.

It's easy to get in a tizz about your pictures on dating sites. They say the camera doesn't lie, but that's a lie. Sometimes it does. It lies because it's been digitally manipulated, or because its truth is a decade out of date, or because it's one of those freakish rare shots that glamorise. We all have at least one photograph in which we look like someone else, someone better looking; in my case I'd been told I looked a bit like Elizabeth Taylor (I don't). It's tempting to use that freakishly good one on your profile, not only for the obvious vain reasons but because the lucky angle with the filter applied offers a little bit of useful anonymity. None of us wants to be accosted in the street by someone exclaiming, 'Oh my God – aren't you Bunnykins27, who has a thing about men in linen jackets?' (I'm not, by the way. And I might, but not more than the average woman.)

So, when I got to the café I found that Sean didn't look much like his pictures, and nor was he 'lanky' either. His photos, he admitted, were fifteen years old. There's nothing wrong with going bald and acquiring a post-divorce paunch and having teeth like tombstones, but it wasn't what I was expecting, and so when he approached the café table I didn't recognise him and told him I was waiting for some-one. He was amused: the teeth were unveiled in a faintly alarming smile reminiscent of Alec Guinness in *The Ladykillers*. But he was nice. He was very nice and I was nice back, and we had a civilised cup of coffee. Afterwards, I said, 'It was good to meet you,' and he patted my arm and said, 'Very best of luck with it.' We exchanged a smile of mutual understanding and parted.

For a while, my personal statement said that the end of my relationship wasn't my idea. I thought people would find it reassuring that I wasn't a dumper but a *dumpee*. Most men didn't find it reassuring at all. They preferred women who'd ditched men and were now about to choose them in preference. The spectacle of a dumped woman seemed to trigger something, curiosity and then a rush to judgement, disguised inside a series of questions. There was worry about taking on a woman another man had discarded. 'What did you do to get dumped? Are you a bitch?' I mentioned this in an on-screen chat one evening with a man called Neville, and asked what he thought.

'You may as well give up now,' he wrote, 'and withdraw from here and save your money.' I asked him what he meant. 'It's porn that's your problem,' he told me. 'Now that porn is normal, now that it's normal to look at porn online, that's the downfall of the middle-aged woman. Men are convinced that if they become bachelors again, that's the kind of sex life they'll get. Young women, big tits, flat stomachs, a tight fit where it matters. There are loads of gorgeous young things here who'd be happy with a 50-year-old sugar daddy. You can't compete with that.'

The question of competition kept coming up. I'd spent most of my life not fretting too much about whether men approved of me, but now I was having to resist scrutinising myself as if through their imagined eyes. I had flashes of self-disgust about the fact that I was so tall, and so big-boned and well-upholstered, and had such big feet. My waist had thickened and *How was I going to compete?* It was deeply disconcerting. I hadn't ever seen myself like that, as someone not physically good enough to be loved.

Not having seen profiles written by other women (only women seeking a female partner see them), it was hard to know what the norm was, and how far I deviated from the average. I mentioned this to my friend Jack. Together we went in to my page and blitzed every one of the errors he identified: being whiney, being needy, being pompous and self-aggrandising (that hurt), overly conventional (Radio 4 was tussled over; I won) and too bookish. The argument that it was best to be myself cut little ice. Despite his efforts, despite adding baking, Sundays in London parks, gigs and beer to the list of things I like, I was still, Jack complained, all too evidently an alpha control freak and raging intellectual snob. That was limiting the response types. It was putting people off. It's important online not to be seen to take yourself too seriously. Men engaged in online dating constantly say how unseriously they take life, as if that's a good thing. I find it a complete turn-off, but then it's evident that I have way too many opinions. Having considered the matter, I decided to persist with the accurate, off-putting version of myself. What's likely to happen if you pretend to be someone else, and attract someone attracted to that imaginary woman? Exactly. It's not going to end in bliss, is it? The best that could come out of it, it seems to me, is that it would end in a farce that was hilarious to tell other people about, but only ten years later when it ceased to be mortifying.

Jack set up his own dummy page on one of the sites, as an experiment and in the interests of data-collection, and reported back. He advised me not to look at the profiles of my competitors. Too many of them were pert, yoga-doing women with doctorates and waists. 'There are, like, fifteen of them just in your postcode,' he said. I decided to make a fake male profile and go and have a look for myself. Jack counselled against. 'I wouldn't go there. You'll delete your page and join a monastery.'

'A nunnery, you mean.'

'A nunnery. Though a monastery would be more fun. In any case, how many women have ever looked at your profile, checking out the competition?'

'None. Women don't do that. Well, I thought there was one, but she turned out to be a transvestite. Women can't see other women unless they do a same-sex search.'

'Exactly. People would think you were secretly a lesbian. If they were secret lesbians too it could become a bit awkward all round.'

Jack had saved some of the profile pages written by skinny middle-aged Pilates-babes in my neighbourhood. The ones he judged successful had a winning combination of softness and steel. They showed a modest sense of achievement and ambition, but not too much. They referenced cultural phenomena that men can relate to (*The Fast Show*, *Blackadder*, *Shawshank Redemption*), and hinted that they had a ditsy side ('I'm a modern girl, but I admit not great with fuseboxes!!'). They reassured men that they liked sex by using the dating site code-word *cuddle* ('cuddles are my favourite thing, and I will look after you'), and they listed outdoor stuff – a passion for hills, skiing, scuba – under Hobbies and Interests. Being outdoorsy is important to lots of middle-aged men. 'I don't like to sit still too long,' the men on dating sites said, over and over. 'Life is for living and I'm looking for a woman to share the adventure with. No couch potatoes please.' Perhaps it's to do with being middle-aged, this insatiable quest for fitness: a sign that a man is resisting time as much as he can, and that he expects a future partner to have the same King Canute-like determination. It helped explain why some of the dismissal of a well-upholstered woman was so sharp and sneery.

A message arrived from Morocco.

'I see you here tonight and I think you are very beautiful and clever,' the message began. The sender was sturdy, bald and had a lovely smile. 'I have a bold idea I would like to put you. I think we are ideal for match and I propose that I send

you a ticket to coming to Tangier for a weekend to stay in my
house and to have food with me.' Another message arrived
before I could reply. 'I hope you do not think I am not genuine. I am very genuine.' He sent references, scans of his
diplomas, photographs of him with his children – they did
all look very happy – and of his houses (a city one, and a
country one with a pool). Half an hour later another message
came, telling me more about his life, how I shouldn't be put
off by his being Muslim, how modern he was in his outlook
and how international. He said he was aware that his English
wasn't the best, but that I should consider his many educa-
tional attainments. He was actually a great catch.

I sent a copy of his second email to Jack. 'What's the
delay?' was Jack's only comment.

'Casual dates not possible when they involve journeys to
Tangier,' I told him, stating the obvious.

'It's not because he's five foot six and a bit plain, then.'

'Height I admit is a factor.'

Height was a factor, but I wasn't fixated on handsome-
ness. I like the idea of plainness, in fact; plainness is comforting when it's a plain face that you love. And sometimes,
people can become handsome in front of your eyes. Fall in
love with someone's mind and find it beautiful and their
face might follow. It happens. I had a photograph of a snag-
gle-toothed ex-boyfriend on the laptop to remind me of this.
What you don't see in the picture is the power of his eyes,
his magnetism, nor how interesting he was in conversation:
how he could start to talk and hold a whole room spell-
bound. In person he was irresistible, but none of that was
apparent in the photograph.

Another message arrived from Morocco. I could stay with
his sister, my suitor said. She wanted to send me a note
assuring me of her brother's decency. I had to come to a

decision and it came down to this: despite all enticements, was I really going to travel to Tangier for this date? No. I replied saying so, with regret, and my correspondent didn't write again. This annoyed Jack. 'You could at least have got a free holiday out of it,' he said. 'You reject people way too soon. You might have fallen for him. It would all have been a great adventure. You said you wanted an adventure. You could have had a nice life in Tangier.'

'You're being ridiculous,' I told him. 'You wouldn't have done it.'

'Yes, I would,' Jack said. 'Like a bloody shot. But nobody ever asks.'

Simultaneously there was the question of Phil. I'd been trying out my policy of wooing by written word on someone I sort of knew. I hadn't ever met him, but we were friends of friends, and so the meeting on the internet dating site might have been a bit embarrassing. He didn't think it was, not at all, he said – or, rather, he wrote, because I never spoke to him or met him. Phil and I illustrated, at an early stage of the quest, the enormous danger of too much emailing. We started out in a pally way, comparing notes on our dating experience. By the second weekend, the messages from him had begun to emit a faint erotic charge. He thought we should meet, he said, but he was *so* busy. I was enjoying the frisson of email adoration too much to ask why we didn't fix a date. He resisted making a date. He was up to his eyes in work (he was a lecturer). Instead, he kept writing, and I kept replying. When you live two miles from one another and could put down the laptop and put on your shoes and go and meet for lunch, but instead you confine yourselves to emailing, that's actually a bit weird. The truth was that we treated each other as substitute people for those we had lost and couldn't yet find; we had a synthetic kind of intimacy that made us both temporarily less sad. We didn't admit to that, however. Phil just continued to be busy. And then he said he was muting himself on the dating site, for now, because he really was just *too madly busy* to have time for it, which was a clean way of ditching me, and I understood, and that was that. This was another lesson learned from internet dating: Lesson Two is that *email relationships aren't relationships*. I wish I'd learned that one sooner. Or at all.

I decided not to send any more messages to academics. I suspected that many of them – despite talking the talk about equality, and how a certain age in women is tremendously sexy – nurtured a secret desire for a winsome 35-year-old and a second batch of children. There had also been, pre-Phil, a doomed dating site encounter with a man who lived so much in his head that he was barely sexual at all. He had that bloodless elongated look of a plant grown in the dark, someone who spent all their time indoors. He was looking for someone to talk to about Wagner, and was straightforward about being low-sexed. The highly educated male on the dating circuit is often a creature in need of elaborate mating rituals. Sometimes they are too diffident to suggest that an actual meeting takes place. Sometimes they give the impression of being too sensitive to have an erection. Perhaps, for some, continuous verbal sparring with someone of like mind is enough to achieve orgasm, though it might only express itself as a kind of juddering in the temporal lobes. I felt I needed someone a little more vital, someone who lived in their body more. Not Mellors of *Lady Chatterley's Lover* fame, maybe – but someone with appetite.

Sex and Sensibility

SUMMER, YEAR ONE

One evening, walking the halls of a dating site, looking in doorways and finding other doors firmly closed to me, I began talking to a man called Oliver, who – if that really was him in the photograph – was six foot three and darkly handsome. He was also twenty years younger than me. Prior to his first message he'd looked at my profile almost every day for weeks, unaware or else unbothered that the site notches up each viewing. It got to the point that he'd visited twenty-three times. What's he thinking? I asked myself each time he came back and looked at my page; what's he deciding? Is it the picture? Is it my age? The alpha-control-freak intellectual-snob thing? Eventually there was a message.

It said: 'Hello, how are you?'

This is lazy, as opening gambits go. It gives away nothing while asking for a lot, and is fundamentally unanswerable. What was he asking for – the news that my glands were up, that my bank balance was precarious, that I couldn't find a novel I wanted to read next, and that I'd put on a swimsuit earlier that day and said, *Oh God in heaven, no*? I think what he really hoped for was: 'Feeling horny, shall we meet at a Holiday Inn and screw?' The best reply to the 'How are you?' query is equally bland and meaningless: 'Fine thanks. You?' That way, the ball goes back into his court. He was the one who initiated contact, after all. A dating site shouldn't be a machine that men feed a pound coin into and that delivers entertainment down a chute.

What I did instead, because I was bored, was tell him exactly how I was. It took five paragraphs and a lot of rewrites. At the end of my answer I asked how he was. He didn't reply. I couldn't believe it. I'd done it again.

So the next evening when he asked how I was tonight, instead of saying, 'Fine thanks, you?' I sent him an even longer answer, with reference to meals eaten, energy levels, lengths swum, the working day and the outrageous cost of a Fry's chocolate cream at the corner shop: 80p! That's 16 shillings! (He took my quaint shilling talk in his stride, perhaps aware that it was intended to emphasise our age difference.) I asked him how his day had gone. There was no response.

The next day there he was again. 'How are you today?'

'I could tell you,' I wrote, 'but what's the point? You never talk back.'

'You're very attractive, do you want to meet for dinner?' he answered. 'Tonight?'

I said I couldn't, sorry. And besides I'd already eaten. (I hadn't. It was a lie.)

'So what are you doing now?' he typed.

'Sprawled on the sofa with a book,' I wrote, unguardedly.

'Mmm. I like the idea of you *sprawled*.'

'Ha,' I typed back, completely unnerved. 'But you are way too young for me.'

'Girls bore me,' he wrote. 'I'm more interested in women, real women like you. Looking forward to our first date. Saturday?'

'I can't this week,' I replied. I was sure that Oliver would take one look at me and run, which was a pity, because in many respects he was absolutely what the doctor would have ordered, if the doctor was a middle-aged woman who hadn't had sex for quite a while. 'Tell me more about yourself,' I said. It wasn't even that I was interested in him. But I was determined to win this one. Online dating can be gladiatorial and I was determined not to be one of the Christians, munched up by a suave and smarmy lion.

'You can find out all about me over dinner,' he wrote.

The next day, there he was again. 'How are you tonight?' he asked.

Fine, thanks, I said. I left it at that.

He responded in real time, in twenty seconds – we were now having a real-time conversation on the screen. He wrote: 'When we go to dinner, will you be wearing a skirt?'

'Probably, or a dress. Why?'

'Will it be short?'

'Unlikely.'

'Will you wear stockings, so I can put my hand under your skirt as we're having a drink?'

'That's forward.'

'I bet you have gorgeous long legs. Are they long?'

'Not really,' I lied. I am way out of my depth here, I thought.

'And will you wear heels?'

'Probably not. I might wear heeled boots.'

'Wear heels, a short skirt and stockings, just for me.'

'Oliver, I'm not really a heels and stockings kind of a woman,' I wrote. 'To be honest, I get kind of sick of all these clichés of femininity.' I knew this reply broke one of the iron laws of online dating – pomposity! – but I *was* sick of them.

'I have total respect for that,' Oliver wrote. 'It's a good point.'

A thirty-second silence fell, while I contemplated his response, and he contemplated it also. I broke the silence. 'Why aren't you taking a woman your own age out to dinner?'

'Women my own age want marriage and babies. I don't want marriage and babies.'

'Ah.'

'Meet me.'

'Not now. But some time. Maybe.'

'You like to play hard to get, then.'

'Hard to get? We've barely said hello. Tell me more about yourself. Something. Anything.'

He didn't reply, but for ages afterwards there were near-daily messages wanting to know how I was. I stopped responding, other than to ask him, twice, why he kept doing it: what was in it for him? He didn't say. It was mystifying.

I had a chat with two friends who were also 'listed'. (This was the shorthand we'd developed for discussing online dating. 'Is X listed?' 'Yes, she's been listed for over a year.') One of them couldn't help but be amused about my discussing 'the search for the One'. 'You don't really think men are looking for the One, do you?' she asked me. (She had become cynical by then.) 'For most of them, sex with a lot of people and avoiding being in a couple is precisely the point of the exercise.' According to her, men were treating these sites like a giant sweet shop, and were picking bagfuls of sweets. Some of them were tasting in order to whittle the choice to one, she conceded, but others had begun a bachelor life of new sweets every weekend, and had no intention of stopping for anyone. 'Men see the sea of faces on dating sites and think, All these women are basically saying, "You can have sex with me if you want," but I don't think that's what most of us are saying.' The woman in the group who'd been dating the longest said she understood the male perspective. It wasn't just men who were behaving that way. She was too. 'I find I'm the same these days. I find someone nice but then I get drawn back in. There is always the possibility of someone better. It's difficult to draw a line.'

Sometimes a Sunday was spent at home, trawling the listings in my pyjamas, sitting cross-legged and eating leftover Chinese takeaway (and every other food not nailed down in the fridge). It's easy to become obsessive about the online dating search. It's like the kind of feverishness that can grab you when you've sold one house and can't find another. The process becomes compulsive, until eventually, inevitably, you begin to reconsider places that you put in the No pile. Hours could pass unnoticed in the time spent 'just popping in' to a dating site. I found myself scrolling through the hundreds of faces on screen, all of them saying (at least theoretically), 'Talk to me; I'm here, I'm free, I'm looking for someone to love, and it might be you.'

But maybe not this one: 'I like my independence but I'd also like a certain kind of female company on my days off.' Or this one: 'Living the dream working in a call centre, and need something to come home to other than existential despair.' Though he received a comradely pat on the shoulder.

In online dating there is such a thing as a kind lie. It's sent in response to an unwanted approach, as a sort of kindly meant shorthand. It's a brush-off that's politely worded, designed to avoid hurt. It avoids listing the nine reasons why you don't want to have coffee. Usually I'd say something like, 'I've just begun seeing someone and am only here checking my messages, but thank you, I was flattered, and good luck.' In online dating, the kind lie is vital. I wish the men who use the sites understood this. I'd much rather be sent the kind lie than be ignored. Being ignored doesn't say, 'Sorry, not interested,' so much as 'You are beneath my notice.' It says, 'You're not worth fifteen seconds of my life.' It might also say, 'At your age and non-thin, you need to lower your sights somewhat; please take my non-reply as a hint.' These are not good thoughts to be sent swirling into the 3 a.m. insomnia of a person with flat-lining morale.

Ignoring is just bloody rude. None of the men who didn't reply would blank me if I said hello to them at a party: why should the internet be different? At a party you'd be polite in a style that indicated, in a grown-up way, that you weren't romantically interested. You'd say you must mingle, and you'd move on. You'd give the impression of being already attached. These are kind lies we all use in life. But perhaps when they're online, some people behave in a way that they would all the time if they could get away with it. Perhaps there's a gloriously liberating quality to being able to behave badly, particularly after a long marriage, and decades of behaving well.

I began using the kind lie quite a bit. It was a way of dealing with being pestered – not for dates, you understand, but for sex. The lie about having just got involved with someone is effective with the sex-pests. It reads, to them, as, 'You were just too late at the sweet shop, sunshine; sorry.' The sex-pests are generally attuned to the Man Code (one item of which reads: 'You don't shag another man's woman in an alley').

I also used the kind lie on the man who had a very particular vision of what his woman would look like (despite closely resembling a fruitbat himself). He went into detail so specific that it even considered her fingernails (short, but shaped, and painted with clear gloss). He wanted to know if I'd consider dyeing my hair red, and whether I was even-tempered. 'The woman I'm looking for will make me smile continually when we're together and will ensure that I miss her when we're apart,' he wrote. I told him I was in the early stages of talking to someone, and wished him luck. Ordinarily I wished people luck, though I didn't to the bloke who wrote to assure me that being the bit on the side to a sexless union (his) would prove glorious and liberating. I got his picture back up and stabbed him in the heart with a chopstick.

I've had the kind lie used on me, by men who considered themselves out of my league. In one case I knew it was 'the kind lie' because I saw the person in question's online light lit night and day for the next six weeks, as he scoured the listings restlessly for someone better. On one occasion I was caught out doing that myself, by a man I'd delivered the lie to. He called me on it. He'd seen my green light lit for days on end, after I'd said I was only there checking my messages. I felt bad about this. I had to apologise. I had to admit that it was just a useful shorthand. 'It's because you're almost 70,' I confessed. 'And you live on the Isle of Wight. It wouldn't be worth making huge journeys to see one another, because it wouldn't work: as you say yourself, you don't read, and you don't like music and you're allergic to dogs, and that makes us incompatible. You see, it isn't better if I give you the real reasons, is it? I'm sorry. Don't take it personally. There's someone for everyone. Perhaps start with people who live on the same island as you.'

'Don't be so fucking patronising,' he responded.

I went through a period of getting a whole series of approach emails from men over 60, men approaching 70 who were aware that they were fighting the odds. They arrived in such a cluster that I wondered if one of the sites had put me onto a Seniors Site of some sort somewhere (and yes, this does happen – sign up to one outfit and you can find yourself repackaged elsewhere without permission being asked of you). I felt sorry for the men of 69, pretending to be 59, pictured looking caved-in and dejected, in an ill-fitting suit at a wedding, the ex-wife cropped out of the frame. Their way of approaching me was faultless and unappealing. They assured me they were gentlemen, that they were solvent *LOL*, that they had their own teeth *haha*, that they loved to travel and wanted a partner to spend their twilight years with. They were unanimously in search of a Lovely Lady. The trouble they were having in looking after themselves was sometimes mentioned, since being widowed, and it was clear that the lady being sought would be kept busy in the kitchen and at the ironing board. Though not all the seniors were merely in search of apple pie. There were plenty who were determined to get laid. I wasn't charmed when a 75-year-old man told me he wanted to lick me all over. My response to an invitation from a 68-year-old, one written in textspeak – 'how r u, u luk gr8 to me' – was, frankly, openly snotty.

'Was that message even in English?'

'Love it, love a bitch,' he wrote. His profile was headed: *Looking for a quiet trustworthy woman – does she exist?* He went on to say: 'I should state right away that trousers, jewellery, high heels and makeup do nothing for me.'

I was tempted to tell him that I didn't think they'd suit him, either.

Sometimes there's a revealing little nugget hidden in an otherwise bland self-descriptive passage. 'I have no objection to helping in the kitchen at weekends, but detest dinner parties and draw the line at home-baking.' (Okey-doke. Well, have fun, won't you, drawing your line and being single for ever.) 'I'm widely and well-read, and can be relied on not to make embarrassing remarks in art galleries.' In a way he was saying the right thing, but it was the way he said it. It wasn't even that – it was the way I read it. The trouble with the written word is that it has no tone, or humour; there's no corresponding facial expression. Both statements could have been meant jokingly. Among the sea of Man Vanilla, some-times a person of strong individual flavour leaps out from the page. Sometimes a statement patently isn't meant to be funny. 'I'm looking for someone who has slept with fewer than six men,' one man declared. 'Apologies if this seems harsh, but I need someone I can feel morally confident about.'

Sometimes, it's okay to ignore people.

When I joined a new site, a fairly new site that didn't charge (yet) to list yourself like an old painting at an auction, I thought I'd hit gold. Zowie! There he was, on page one: Peter, an interesting-looking man, not handsome but inter-esting-looking, 56, and tall and sturdy in a cricket-playing sort of a way. He worked in education (despite my intended avoidance of men in education, I kept coming back to them, a moth to a flame). He had kind eyes and a nice mouth, a broad face and a big brain and a silvery patina; he had deep smile lines, and an expression of complete and benign friendliness, like a cow that comes to a fence. He was slightly bedraggled, unmaterialistic, disorganised, clever: that was my reading of him, in the lines and between them. I had an immediate feeling, an intuition. I looked at other pictures he'd uploaded: in one of them he had an attractively scepti-cal expression, and in another an expectant, amused look, like he'd said something mildly outrageous and was hoping I'd find it funny. His profile made me laugh because it was so guileless and rubbish and uncrafted, and he was four inches taller than me. I wrote admiring his writing style and didn't expect to hear from him.

I got a reply the following morning. 'Hello to you too,' he wrote. 'You look very interesting. I see we have things in common. We probably have mutual friends. What a pity we're 100 miles apart. But let's talk some more. As it happens I'm going to be in your neck of the woods in two weeks. Lunch?'

This gave me a thrilling idea. He wasn't really going to be in my neighbourhood. He made that bit up, because he'd had the same intuition.

At Exciting Date Minus a Week it was proving difficult to think about anything else. I kept looking at Peter's dating profile, saved onto the laptop, and rereading his emails, as if I'd notice something new, some small detail that would feed my expectation, or undermine it. I needed to know everything. We swapped real-world email addresses, and the letters kept coming, short but regular ones, at coffee pauses in the day and longer in the evening. I Googled him, reassured to see his identity confirmed, and saw him pictured in various online contexts: a slightly creased, almost-handsome, linen-suited academic. He had a bit of a food-loving, France-loving midlife belly, and eyes full of irony and warmth, eyes that hinted at arcane knowledge and originality. *Irony, warmth? Arcane knowledge, originality?* I was making huge assumptions about him, I was well aware, but couldn't seem to put a stop to it. He might hate France; he might be well educated and stupid; he might be a wife-beater. I'd taken scant facts and joined the dots. I'd developed my own idea of Peter from the little fragments he'd given and that I'd collated from elsewhere, building up a picture, and Peter, no doubt, was forming his own idea of me. Until we could meet, nothing could really be done about that. It's what happens. The mind rushes on.

I Googled myself to see what he'd see if he were to search for me. There wasn't much, certainly nothing controversial, and there weren't recent photographs, because I'd been hiding from cameras for five years. I was a good deal less slender than I was at 45, but shrank from mentioning this; I mean, why draw people's attention to something they might not even notice? 'Oh, PS, just so you know and aren't surprised, I'm fat and probably sexually undesirable; I'm one of those overreaching overweight midlife women the name-less vampires of the bloke-internet enjoy disdaining. Just so you're aware.' So I didn't mention the weight issue. It would be fine, I decided. I just wouldn't eat any bread between now and then, and I'd wear a black dress with cunning fat-clamping panels. It would be fine.

Peter said that meeting would be great; meeting would be *a hoot*. 'Hoot' might be a word that signals fundamental unavailability. It might also be a word that brings its own lightness, its lack of expectation: it might be to do with fear of rejection. If events were only a hoot then there wasn't much to lose. But that was fine. I was also badly in need of a hoot. Hot on the heels of the hoot email, a longer one arrived, one more frank about hope and heartbreak. It turned out that Peter had been married and divorced twice. This gave me pause.

'So let's get the nitty gritty over with,' I wrote. 'One para-graph on how your marriages came to an end, and then I'll reciprocate. We'll indulge ourselves just once in self-pity and then never speak of it again. You first. What did you do, to go and get yourself dumped?'

It turned out that he was the dumper, both times. The reasons were plausible enough: they'd been too young, the first time, and they'd grown apart the second time, and relations with the exes were said to be good. That's how Peter passed the Dump Test.* (*If a man in consideration was a dumper and not a dumpee, my ears pricked up. If a man was a serial dumper, if he kept getting bored, like a restless kid with too many toys, or if he'd found a string of women sexually dull, there was often a loud buzzing in my ears. If he'd left a woman because she had *let herself go*, the conversation was probably over.)

This was the beginning of a bout of constant messaging, in which we swapped our sad stories, though we told them to each other in a Woody Allen-style voiceover, competing to see who could be funnier. 'How are relations with the ex now – amicable enough?' he wanted to know. Men kept asking me this. Men are somewhat obsessive on the question. Women don't envisage punch-ups in suburban driveways with jealous ex-wives, but it seems that men do have visions of the reverse case. And of course none of us wants to be with someone with a lot of *baggage*, that horrible term for *stuff about the past that still niggles me*. The truth is that we all have stuff in the past that still niggles us. We all need to be with someone who can put their baggage aside, into storage. It can't be eradicated but it can be left to gather dust.

Peter and I seemed to have equivalent baggage levels, ones that were minimal and undramatic. We both had a residual sadness, one we were confident could be assuaged by another love, by hope. Old sadness had become a new thirst. We agreed that in midlife there is always sadness, and it's not all about lost relationships. At this point we're likely to have suffered all sorts of losses – of family and friends, of hopes and dreams, ambitions and plans, of wild ideas and time. A lot of time had gone, never to be recovered. We agreed on all this and then we agreed not to talk about past relationships again, not until we knew each other a lot better. Each of us wanted to draw a line and reinvent life: that's how we talked to each other, on the fourth day of emailing.

On day four Peter asked if he could have my mobile number. He had something important to ask me, he said. I handed over the number in some trepidation (please, not more deadly, unerotic stockings and heels talk) but there was no need to fear. The question was this: 'Cryptic cross-words, yes or no?' I answered – yes! – and asked him in a second text: 'IKEA, yes or no?' to which the answer, quite rightly, was, 'Addicted to the meatballs.' After this we were off, texting random questions to one another. By day five, dozens of whimsical queries had been sent. Whimsy was the key element. It provided safe and solid foundations. We were developing banter and were going to be friends, even if we weren't going to be lovers.

Simultaneously via email we began to exchange Top Tens – our top ten films, songs, books, meals, cities, heroes, places, dates to return to in a time machine … you name it, we were Top-Tenning it. I barely had time to work, so intent was I on watching my phone and waiting for its little light to flash.

At the same time a small patch of unacknowledged anxiety had developed a pulse. It wasn't just my physical self that was being misrepresented in this lead-up, by the sending of out-of-date photographs. In my communications with Peter I wasn't really me, either, because I'd reframed myself so as to be more attractive to a man who seemed tremendously self-aware and self-possessed, and needed me to be the same. I camouflaged myself so as to attract him. I became, in the letters, the kind of person who could handle most things:

charming, cheerful, non-melancholy and staunchly un-neurotic, whose response to the ups and downs was (almost relentlessly) philosophical. I wish I really was her, I thought – that woman Peter's writing to. Of course it was perfectly possible that he was doing the same ventriloquism, covering up weakness and fear with comedy and wit, so as to impress women with his tremendous psychological health. It could have been a mutual confidence trick; there was no way of knowing. We had no inkling of each other's complexities. As yet, we hadn't even spoken on the phone.

One afternoon, his messages began to venture beyond friendship. He texted that he was drinking coffee and about to go into a dull meeting, but was feeling happy because he had me in his life. The die was now cast. Once you go into this territory, and begin to talk ahead of your current reality, there's no going back. It's genuinely very hard to resist: it may not seem like it, sitting where you're sitting (I wouldn't have believed it either) but it is. Romance, real romance, being courted and wooed, is a thing difficult to say no to. It's especially difficult when you're sad. You're sad, and not very hopeful, and suddenly there's this wonderful man, clever and witty and kind, telling you that his day has been made better and brighter because he has you in his life. You might find yourself swept up in it, and responding in kind. It's easy. 'I'm so glad I have you in my life, too; I have a spring in my step that wasn't there a week ago, and that's down to you, Peter.' When you respond in kind, it's *game on*. The trouble is that in many cases game on leads swiftly to game over.

'I can't wait to meet you; I can hardly wait,' he wrote. 'I'm enjoying this, but I want more. I want a lot more.' It was clear that it was time to come clean, so I sent him an email confessing to looking my age. His reply was titled SNAP; he said he'd put on a good stone and was considerably greyer than in the site photograph. He didn't care a jot, not an infinitesimal part of a jot, about my weight, he said. I wrote all this in my dating diary. And I wrote this: 'I may be in love with him already.'

Because we'd already stepped over the line – not only into the possibility of love but the expectation of it – in the days before meeting we continued to rush things in a way that isn't wise. We sped ahead far too fast; we were both accelerators, and it got seriously out of hand. Not sexually: we didn't talk about sex but we were both madly romantic and sure. Some days I got twenty messages, many of them beginning, 'Hey beautiful'. This bothered me because I'm not beautiful. If he'd decided I was a beauty, I knew that we could both be in a lot of trouble. The communications ratcheted up. I'd get a text saying, 'I've been thinking about you all day,' and could reply that I'd been the same, because it was true: thinking about him, and composing emails and questions, and answers to questions. And yet, so far we hadn't even spoken.

Two days before the date he texted that he wanted to hear my voice. I'd avoided the phone, feeling that it was an extra audition that I might fail, and was nervous all day, watching the clock, but needn't have been. We talked for over two hours, and afterwards he texted that he seemed to be falling in love, though how was that possible? It couldn't be real, this attachment, he said, but it felt real, and this was all new territory and he didn't quite know how to navigate it. I confessed that I felt just the same. When he didn't reply to a text one afternoon, and then didn't react to a follow-up one asking if all was well, I messaged saying, 'It's been four hours since I heard from you and I'm getting withdrawal symptoms. Is that weird?' Of course it was weird; it was downright dysfunctional. I'd sit at the computer, trying to work, and really I'd be waiting. I'd smile at the mobile when another of the questions arrived that we continued to ask one another. 'Do you like Victorian novels?' 'Do you ever make bread?' 'Do you have any phobias?'

In two short weeks, my life had become Peter-oriented. All the usual procedural stuff – house chores, phone calls, admin, arrangements, seeing friends, the ordinary obligations, and yes, doing the work I was contracted to do – began to feel difficult, even unimportant. I put things off. Others were put on hold. A period of romantic mania gripped me. I was in an altered state, one that was all-consuming. I was constantly, tiresomely upbeat and full of energy. I was of Doris Day-like chirpiness. I laughed easily. I sang as I cleaned the bathroom. I smiled all the way round the supermarket, and made slightly manic chat with checkout operatives. I had become someone who talked to people in the street, if the opportunity arose. I was Pollyanna, relentlessly playing the glad game. This is it, I thought: this is all it takes to be happy – a constant flow of love and attention, given and received. I told myself it didn't have to come to an end, this flow. I found myself wondering if we'd always text each other these little endearments, even when we lived together. I was genuinely thinking in these terms, but this was somebody I hadn't even met yet. I was infatuated by the state we had talked ourselves into; each email, each text provided another rush of love sugar. Ego, insecurity, narcissism, fear: they were tangled together like the jewellery I never wore any more.

So, the day of the date arrived.

I was nervous, not least because, owing to the distance, he was staying for the whole weekend. He'd booked a hotel not far from my flat. Our first date was to be a weekend together. This was fine, though, because we were already in love, or so we imagined. I joined him after his meeting, outside a bistro, and our eyes met as I was threading my way through other pedestrians. I'd gone to a lot of effort: a mid-calf black dress with fat-clamping panels had been purchased, and new black boots, and I'd had my hair done. Despite this, Peter's face registered disappointment that he struggled to hide. His appearance surprised me too. He was broader, greyer and looked older than I was expecting, and he had a weary and anxious air. I don't know why, but I'd assumed there would be a romantic first contact, a kiss that would set the tone for the day – it felt like we'd already had a lengthy build-up to that – but the hug he offered was a formal one. I stepped back, and looked into his eyes, and his cool blue eyes looked back. I looped an arm around his neck and kissed him on the mouth, a closed-lip kiss, perhaps, though not a great-aunt-at-Christmas dry peck of a kiss. He seemed surprised; he pulled away. We were five minutes into an itinerary involving lunch, strolling, drinks, theatre and dinner, a night and then another day – and it already felt like a disaster. It was a disaster. Things were going to get worse.

Despite the big preamble, our big lead-up, everything we'd shared, the intimacy we'd achieved, Peter and I were strangers. There was no natural resumption of where we'd left off, like old friends who meet after a long time. It was awkward, because we were strangers. We hadn't expected one another. I had thought I knew him – that had been the illusion we'd both created – but he wasn't what I'd anticipated at all. I don't mean in terms of his appearance, but in every other way, in his body language, his natural scent, his demeanour, what he said, the way he spoke, and the look in his eyes when he did so: his whole vibe. He was alien and so was I. I was a woman he hadn't expected, either, one he knew already that he wouldn't ever fancy, perhaps, but there wasn't any easy ducking out. The detail of the day had been gone over and over, and I had theatre tickets in my wallet.

We began with lunch, where, once we'd ordered the food, the conversation immediately flagged. Peter, staring off towards the windows, looked like a boy who'd been kicked hard in the shin, or like a man pleading with the universe to send someone to rescue him. I began to play the straight man, feeding him lines from emails of his that I knew would prompt long anecdotes. He'd worked for a time in the USA, and I asked eager questions about places he'd been, places where he'd felt at home and not felt at home. I was smiling so much that my cheek muscles hurt. Once he felt that I admired him and that he could make me laugh, he began to like me better.

After lunch we had a walk around the city together. We had a perfectly nice, if awkward day, wandering and visiting a museum, and stopping off at coffee shops. Over the third coffee I think he began to sense that I was disappointed; I think he saw that his own disappointment was obvious, and that he hadn't taken care to disguise it, which was rude, and so he raised his game. Perhaps it had occurred to him that he wouldn't ever have to see me again, and he was right, of course; he didn't. Despite its preposterous origins it was, after all, just a date. So he did this mad veering in the other emotional direction. He acted like a man in love. He became almost giddy, when we came out of the café, and wanted to buy me a dress (an offer politely declined). We looked inside churches, like tourists, and he began to walk with his arm hooked around my shoulder. He asked me repeatedly if I was happy, and said repeatedly that he was. It was all becoming quite baffling.

At about five o'clock he said he needed a shower and would return to his hotel, and did I want to come. I said,

'Sure, why not,' and went with him, with a man I didn't really know, on a first date, into his hotel room, because I felt safe, like most murder victims probably do. He made me a coffee and we sat together. It was a fairly lavish affair, his room, with a sofa at the end of the bed. It was possible that he'd picked it in anticipation of a seduction he no longer wanted to go through with. He was keeping his distance, so I had to sidle up to him. There were, at my instigation, short periods of kissing, but they didn't go anywhere further and it was Peter who broke them off. He made a bumbling speech about liking to take things slowly. He began to have the body language and tone of someone trying to make light of an unsolicited seduction attempt. Perhaps he'd been deter-mined that there would be no physical intimacy, and maybe there were good reasons for that, but I had come to meet him absolutely sure there would be, and each of us surprised the other with our assumptions. I tried to make a joke of it and he made fun of me. It was clear that my assumptions were inappropriate. He said he really must have a shower, and I sat pretending to read yesterday's paper, while he showered and changed somewhere out of sight. He'd already been there one night, and there was a Jack Reacher novel on the table, and I was surprised because the author hadn't appeared in his top ten novelists. They'd all been deter-minedly highbrow. The minute he reappeared he said, 'Right, let's be off,' and we trooped out.

I was deeply confused, at this point. The massive build-up had felt like a series of dates and (this does seem strange, looking back) I'd been sure that we'd be desperate to get our hands on one another. I'd imagined that we might even spend the next morning in bed, enjoying sleepy pillow-talk, face to face. I wanted to get first sex over with, so that it would be the official beginning of us as a couple and we could both stop being nervous, but the signs were that none of what I'd anticipated was going to happen. The signs were that the whole thing was already a failure, and my heart was heavy as we walked along the road together. He said nothing and his face had closed to me.

I was already dreading the evening, but in the end it was survivable. He downed three gin and tonics before we went to the show, and talked about his work, and in the theatre he startled me by reaching for my hand as we sat together in the darkness. Afterwards, over dinner, we talked about Shakespeare we'd seen and favourite box sets, and it was fine, though I had to pedal hard to keep the conversation going. Then, out on the street, he hugged me one-arm style and kissed my hair and said he was tired, and went off to bed. But not before a second attempt on my part. I felt the need to make things worse, which has been a habit of mine, at various times in my life: if things are bad, sometimes I just can't resist making them a whole lot worse. In this case, my self-esteem had crashed, even faster than the relationship had. I tried to get him to sleep with me, once more. When he was hesitant I said, 'I'm not going to talk you into this, Peter, obviously.' (Looking back at this makes me sad.)

His train wasn't until lunchtime, and we were supposed to be spending the morning together. He texted saying that unfortunately he had to work, so there would only be time for a quick coffee. I met him at a station café. He stood as I approached, but there was no kiss hello. He asked me how I was and said it had all been lovely and we must do it again soon, mustn't we? I walked with him to the platform, where he said, 'Bye, love,' as he got into his carriage, kissing my cheek and not looking back. I went home feeling like a dam that would burst its banks, and had a good cry, because mysteriously the wonderful thing had been all wrong. I told myself that there had been too much for the day to live up to. I'd already had a text from him that said, 'Well THAT was fun,' with a smiley attached. The useful thing about emoticons is that they preclude the need for kisses. When the email I expected arrived, it said that he'd been thinking a lot about how difficult it would be to sustain a distance relationship, and how booked up most of his weekends were for the next two months, what with one thing and another.

I'd invested such a lot in this and I wasn't prepared to let it go, not like that. But when I replied, suggesting we keep in touch, I got a long-winded response explaining that he was too busy to reply. The signs could not have been clearer – the man was virtually wearing a T-shirt with *I DO NOT WANT YOU* written on it; the man was virtually digging an escape tunnel – but I couldn't let the episode go, partly because of a profound sense of failure. There were things that had to be said, and I said them, in eloquent letters that were deleted unsent. There wasn't any point bringing something to a definitive end that might not be absolutely over. Perhaps it was just a blip. There are blips in marriages, after all, so why don't we allow for the ups and downs, the shadows and light, in emergent relationships too? Why are we so quick to call it a day if things take a chilly turn? People are complicated and their lives have hidden complications, if you don't know them very well (or indeed at all). I had been the one who'd rushed things on; I'd expected snogging, at the least, and he had resisted me. I think it was his absolute determination not even to kiss me that made me need to humiliate myself. He'd been really, really clear, in some ways, but then he hadn't been able to stop himself transmitting mixed messages, perhaps out of kindness. And so there was leeway for more self-delusion to take hold. It might not be the end of the relationship, I reasoned; it might just be a rocky beginning. I gave myself this talk and was partly persuaded.

I decided to have another go at resurrecting the situation. I texted Peter the next afternoon and told him I'd eaten too much lunch, a plate of spinach pasta dressed with oil and parmesan shavings, and had fallen asleep on the couch afterwards.

'You should have anticipated that I was going to do that,' I wrote jauntily, 'and stepped in and stopped me.'

'You need to take responsibility for your own life,' came the reply. (What the hell? I was just attempting banter with you, Peter. You were supposed to reply in kind. It was silliness. Are men so unused to bantering with women that they think everything they utter is only ever literal?)

Stressed by a peculiar sense of injustice, I went to stay with my mother. Bored on the long train journey, I decided to initiate a text Q and A. Two weeks ago Peter had been mad for a bit of whimsical Q and A. I began with, 'So when did you last eat cheese?' I admit I felt a little unwell, a little neurologically unusual. I was exhibiting signs of being just the kind of woman men on dating sites are talking about, when they say, 'No stalkers or bunny boilers.' Peter didn't reply, so I texted again, saying I was on a train and bored, and off to see my mum.

His response was, 'Have a great trip.'

I texted straight back. 'Are you okay, is everything okay?'

The phone buzzed a minute later. 'Lot of work to do, and things on my mind. Talk to you when you get back.'

I couldn't leave it that long, the not knowing. We had to have a straightforward conversation. But I couldn't ask the question I wanted to – namely, 'Is it over, our thing?' Instead I texted again. 'Do you like trains and long train journeys?' He didn't answer. Forty minutes later, a long, long email about his work travails and tiredness and low mood arrived instead. 'I'm sorry,' he said at the end. So that seemed to be that. I felt a kind of relief. It was over, whatever it was. It wasn't going to drag and dribble on, at least, and there's a lot to be said for that. But – and I couldn't help obsessing over this – what was the reason it had failed? We'd had a connection and something had happened to it. It had died. Was it my fault? I wasn't going to take responsibility for the madness, the twenty million emails, each growing more intimate and rhapsodic, that had preceded the date, because that was absolutely mutual behaviour. But I had the unsettling feeling that somehow or other I was blamed, for bewitching him and then letting him down. For not being pretty, perhaps, or slender, or charming enough, or young for my age, or fascinating. Since meeting me in person, his sense of let-down had been almost palpable.

My poor mother suffered three days of dealing with a lunatic oriented completely towards her phone. I said I seemed to have developed an addictive personality and alarmed her. 'Not drugs, surely not drugs,' she said. 'Please tell me it isn't drugs.'

'It isn't drugs,' I soothed. 'I have no interest in drugs, honestly, other than cabernet sauvignon.'

Cabernet sauvignon, or at least the second bottle, was a really bad idea, the kind that seems inspired and brilliant at the time, and makes everything wonderfully clear. Late that night, cabbed up, I wrote a heartfelt email, full of reckless honesty, and went to sleep happy, and woke up shrieking. My mother rushed in, because I was shouting, 'No, no, no, dear God, please no!' And yes, the email I had sent him was as bad as I feared, not only needy but borderline unhinged. In general I'd become borderline unhinged. So I sent a second email, which said: 'Please digitally tear up last night's drunken ramblings. Like you, I seem to be at a low ebb. It will pass. It'd be nice to see you again, if you're ever back here. Meanwhile, I wish you all good things.'

A reply came shortly afterwards, saying he'd been tired and overwhelmed with work, and that's why he'd been so humourless, and that he was sorry. Immediately following this, the phone rang and we talked for a while, about anything and everything, but not about recent weirdness. Afterwards he sent me a text message that said: 'When we said goodbye just now, I felt like I'd been ripped from your side.' This, of course, made everything all right. 'Yes, yes,' I said to myself. 'You see, you see!' It was worth persevering; sometimes good things start badly and this was going to be a prime example. I spent twenty-four hours thinking this, but then received an email from Peter saying that a) I was wonderful and also b) that he didn't want to see me again.

Once it was properly finished, I looked back on our communication cycle with disbelief. I read it over again and didn't recognise myself. It looked like an altered state. It was a hard transition, when the love-bombing came to an end, through Adoration Cold Turkey, desperate as a junkie and utterly miserable. But, in the case of imaginary relationships that have their origins online, maybe it was a typical pattern. My guess is that Peter saw immediately we met that the whole thing had been illusory, and if he decided that unfairly early, there isn't any arguing with it. Intuition and chemistry – they both count for much more than internet dating would have you believe. Setting out to find a compatible person who thinks, talks and lives like you do is all very well, but box-ticking counts for little in the end.

Next, a nice-looking man called Henry wrote to ask if I was ever in Cumbria, because he'd love to invite me to lunch.

Henry was 60, and I had to ask myself how I felt about 60, and specifically about being naked with 60. (You may already be saying that this is ageist. I'm just telling you honestly what I thought.) In any case, it wasn't a qualm that lasted long. Most of us are going to get there, after all, to 60, and we'll hope to be loved then, whether we have a wrinkly bum or not. I reminded myself that Harrison Ford was now in his seventies; would I say no to Harrison? Reader, I would not. An ex-policeman, Henry was tall and upright, broad-shouldered, and had a knowing look around the eyes, as if he'd been dented by life and had survived and wasn't going to be a pushover. He was also near-bald, but a middle-aged woman who has issues with hair-loss had better go and buy a stack of jigsaws in readiness for the long nights alone.

He sent a head and shoulders shot that he'd just taken in his kitchen, showing a smiling attractive man in a frayed blue shirt. He was standing in a tiny cottage in the wilds, where he was attempting to live self-sufficiently. His dating site profile was skimpy; when I asked him why it didn't give much away, he told me that words are meaningless and meetings are everything. After the Peter fiasco it was a view I'd come to have some sympathy for. On the other hand, a woman needs some clues and pointers if she's going to travel right across England for lunch. He'd volunteered his surname and village, but I couldn't find him anywhere via Google. I realise this is new-fashioned, but not being able to find someone on the web, not a trace, is a cause of anxiety to me. I'm simultaneously repelled and reassured by people who are bedded in to social media, who can be observed being droll on Twitter, who have many friends on Facebook and are demonstrably non-psychotic there. Henry seemed like a loner. He confessed that he didn't like the internet; in fact, he loathed the internet and all its workings, he said. He thought it was responsible for a decline in our human culture. It's an interesting debate but Henry didn't seem interested in arguing the point. Some things are black and white, he said, and the internet has been bad news for the world, and that's that. Well, not politically, I don't think, I ventured; it's brought people together, in terms of political cohesion, don't you think? I mean, I think it's hard to argue that it hasn't become a voice of the voiceless; at its best it can sidestep news blackouts and bring worthwhile stories forward; it's been known to threaten tyrannies, and help right wrongs. Henry wasn't having it. He was, he said, a happy Luddite, and was convinced that humankind would be happier if it followed his lead.

'I have paper books, and vinyl records,' Henry wrote. He was confident that this was a superior culture to all others. 'Come and see me. Come and visit. I'll sacrifice a chicken.'

'We could meet at a restaurant,' I replied. 'I wouldn't feel comfortable coming to your house.'

'It'll be fun to meet someone younger,' he said. 'You seem young to me. The last woman I dated was 66.'

'Can I ask you something? Are women of 66 looking only for companionship?'

'God no; they're all gagging for it,' he wrote. Then another message arrived. 'Why are you on this dating site? The truth now. No fibbing.' It was hard to know what he meant. 'You're not coming to see me, are you?' he wrote before I could reply. 'You wouldn't like me anyway. I have dirt under my fingernails. I don't have any money. I watch a lot of sport on TV.' His Luddite sensibility, I noted, didn't extend to banning television.

While I was pondering, I received a surprise invitation to dinner. I emailed Henry and said that I thought it best to tell him that on Saturday I was going out to dinner with a man

I vaguely knew. He didn't reply, and when I went back on the site I discovered that he'd blocked me, so that I couldn't message him again. The man who was going to take me out to dinner realised on Thursday afternoon that he was still in love with his ex-wife, and cancelled.

The turn of summer into autumn brought Finn, a man with thick, layered short hair, reddish brown, and smiley eyes and a beard and an interesting job in the arts.

Finn had a lot of charm, and a diverse life and plenty to say for himself. He had a creative job and a wide social network, and I was chuffed when all this light was shone in my direction. We emailed a little bit and then he wanted to go over to Skype. There are online daters who like Skype, and I can see why: quite apart from the potential for naked-ness between strangers, it can be used for pre-screening. It's almost like meeting. There are people who regard an hour spent on Skype with someone as a date. I've heard it described as *a clean date*: you get to 'meet' without having to risk a coffee shop or wine bar failure, without having to climb out of a bistro bathroom window. But I didn't like Skype. I found Skype nerve-racking. I'd chatted to a man on Skype once before. I passed the first-round interview – which is how I thought of it – and was asked out, but then the date's face fell when we met in person and he saw the body that was attached to the head. I was made to feel that I'd been guilty of some sort of confidence trick (what had I been expected to do – parade round my sitting room in a swim-suit?). So I wasn't that keen on Skype. However, Finn was insistent that we should break the ice before meeting. He was more of a visual person than a verbal one, he said; he was dyslexic and typing took him a while. I felt bad, hearing this, about my knee-jerk reaction to men who can't spell or punctuate properly. It had been a blanket kind of rejection thus far. I'd had a policy that associated those who couldn't spell with those who didn't read. (There's a correlation, for sure, but no, it isn't reliable.) I'd written, earlier in the dating diary: 'I'm sorry, but if he can't punctuate I don't want to go near his pants.' And now I felt bad about that.

Anyway, the upshot was that I said yes to Skype and answered nervously when the laptop screen began to ring.

So there he was – the cherubic and yet grave face of Finn the bearded. 'Hey,' he said, his eyes amused. 'How are you?'

I've never found that an easy question to answer; I mean, what is it really asking? I told him I was all right. I didn't have any comedy lines prepared. I was too nervous to be anything but robotic. 'And how are you?' I asked. 'What have you been doing today?'

He didn't answer the question. Instead he wanted to know what sort of sex I liked. I was vague and embarrassed. What's wrong? he asked me. I said I was just nervous.

'There's no need for that, my little peach,' he said. 'Look, let's ring off now, but let's do it again tomorrow.'

I agreed, even though I didn't want to. I had a general sense of having been cornered. Sometimes, though, we conspire against and corner ourselves.

'Would you show me your tits?' he asked, half an hour into our second Skype call. Strangely, for someone who detests this kind of behaviour, my reaction was helpless laughter. I got the giggles, and didn't go into immediate emergency laptop shutdown mode. I'd drunk a whole bottle of wine – cabbed up – so as to feel less ill at ease, but it also dealt with the inhibitions.

I was lying on my side, and did as I was told and unbuttoned my shirt. I've always been a people-pleaser, keen to impress, keen to be liked, and sometimes this overrides my own inner voice, and caution, and basic good sense. 'Oh my God,' he said. 'Look at your tits in that bra, oh my God you're incredible.' I slid the straps off my shoulders and he groaned. He was standing at the webcam wanking by then. 'Christ, we have to meet, we have to meet soon and do this in person,' he said.

I wanted to have a good cry. I said I had to go and ended the call.

The next morning when I woke, I had a hangover and was ashamed. But I didn't cancel the date. I was miserable about the prospect of meeting him but I was overriding this with pep talks to myself, of the people-pleasing kind. I told myself not to be so uptight. Why was I so uptight about something so harmless as Skype sex? Why was I such a *square*? Why couldn't I do as other women suggested and just have a good time, sleep around, enjoy being single, sow some wild oats, be adventurous with technology, without over-thinking it all? (Because I couldn't. Because it wasn't what I wanted.) In any case those weren't the questions I should have asked. What I should have been asking was, why did you agree to that when you didn't want to? Why did you pretend to think it was fun when you found it degrading? Why have you arranged to meet this man for a drink?

The following evening, Finn bombarded me with requests for another Skype call. I found myself having to be defensive. I had to be too busy. Were we in a Skype relationship now? Were there going to be expectations? I was the one who was going to look like a player if I backed out now; using a man for one cybersex episode and then dropping him like a brick; that wasn't something I felt good about. On the other hand, I just didn't want to do it again.

When we met in a large, dimly lit, vaguely trendy wine bar, I was already sure it was a mistake. I don't know why I went. I had it vaguely in mind that it would be one drink and then I could send the liaison-ender, the text that explained that I didn't want to meet again. How could I cancel a drink with a man I'd had sort-of Skype sex with? That would be horrifically shallow, wouldn't it? (Wrong question, again.)

I got to the bar first and ordered a bottle of wine and two glasses, and drank a glass down. I felt quite sick with nerves. When Finn arrived, the first thing I noticed about him was that he had short legs, and was altogether not the five foot eleven advertised. He was Tom Cruise-sized, but had a megawatt smile, also à la Tom, and sat down heavily with a sigh saying he'd had a beast of a day and thank God for alcohol. I had a whole story prepared about a funny thing that'd happened to me that morning, and he listened, stroking his beard, laughing along. I noticed that he had really small hands, with short fingers, his nails bitten to the quick.

The hour that followed was pleasant enough, though it was devoted to the kind of biographical chat that you know is going to run out eventually. When we'd both tired of filling in the other person on what we'd done and places we'd been, the chat really did run completely dry, and the atmosphere grew strained. We both filled the gap by looking at our phones to see if there were urgent messages. There weren't, not on my side anyway. He spent five or six minutes tapping away answering a work email while I gazed around at all the people who were a lot more relaxed than we were. When Finn had put his phone away he said, 'Right – shall we go?' We went out into the street, where people were standing smoking and groups of Friday night revellers were going by. Finn took hold of my lapels and drew me closer – I was in heels and he was quite a bit shorter than me – and said, 'I know you're unsure, but I have an idea of something that will make you a lot happier than you are right now.'

'Oh yes,' I said, 'what's that?'

He kissed me softly on the mouth and looked into my eyes, and kissed me again. He said that as it happened he was staying just over the road, at a friend's flat, and did I want to come up for another glass of wine? I followed him across the street, and up narrow stairs to the second floor. I can't tell you, convincingly, why it was that I agreed to this. It goes against every safety code, and I didn't want to, but mysteriously I agreed nonetheless. I most certainly wasn't going to have sex with him. I'd stick to one glass, and make my excuses and leave. I'd do that, and then later I'd send the text about not wanting to meet again. I'd use a kind lie of some sort. As soon as we'd had that drink.

The flat was small, a one-room studio, and it turned out that the friend wasn't there; he'd given Finn the key. We were alone and it occurred to me that I might be in danger. I said I was just going to let a friend know where I was, because I hadn't expected to be late, and then I went into the tiny bathroom and texted the address. When I came out he was sitting at the pull-out table by the bed – it was a studio so the bed was unavoidable – with soft music playing, the blinds down, the lighting dimmed. We had a drink and talked about jazz and then I said I ought to go, and he kissed me again. I didn't want to kiss him, and the nylony strands of the moustache and beard didn't add to the fun.

He began to remove my clothes, though for the first few moments I held on tight to the shirt that was being unbuttoned, because I didn't want to have sex with him. Finn kissed me again and said, 'Come on, let's just have pleasure, and not worry about anything,' and, more out of social embarrassment than anything, not wanting to be a square and no fun and a drag, I let him remove my clothes, and watched as rapidly he shed his own. I didn't want to have sex with him, and yet I did. I already felt bad about it, and yet I let him continue. It had got to the point at which I didn't seem able to say, 'Stop, stop, I don't want this.' Of course I *was* able to say that, but I chose not to, and I know it's lame to keep saying it was embarrassment that fuelled it, but that's what it was. It was people-pleasing of an extreme kind. When I put my hands on his back, his skin felt alien and cold. I didn't want to be there. I didn't know this man, and I didn't want this, and now I just wanted it to be over. I remain ashamed of myself, every time I remember. I'm ashamed of myself and also angry.

After a few minutes of failing to get the angle right he said I should get up onto my knees and face the wall, and so I did what he asked of me, and there was sex, of a sort, a dry and unappetising sort from behind. I was full of self-loathing and disappointment and it was completely humiliating. 'Look, I'm going to have to go,' I said eventually. I reached for my clothes and got my underwear on and my shirt and went to the table where my tights and skirt were.

Finn came up behind me and pulled my knickers down and started at me again. 'Don't move, don't move!' he shrieked. I was leaning forward, over the desk, caught in mid-reach for my clothes. It took him ten seconds to finish (and yes, he was wearing a condom, thank God). He wasn't interested in whether I might like to have any kind of a finish of my own.

I said, 'I have to go now, really.' I put the rest of my clothes on hurriedly, and grabbed my bag and ran down the stairs and onto the street, and ran to the end of it, and walked along the next one wiping tears from my face. A couple stopped and asked me if everything was all right. 'Bad date,' I told them. 'Just a horrible date.'

'Oh God, we've all been there,' the woman said jovially.

Finn had texted me by the time I got back. 'Incredible orgasm! What a night! Night night darling xx.'

What? Seriously? It wasn't possible he was as stupid as this. I didn't reply. I told a friend what'd happened, and she was shocked and said the situation sounded abusive to her. I couldn't really argue that, as I'd consented to it all, and hadn't been coerced at any stage, and had allowed it to happen. But I began to feel as if it had been intended to humiliate, in a sly sort of way. Part of the humiliation, perhaps, was this pretence that there was anything romantic about it.

The day after, Finn continued to text saying he'd had a great evening, and I continued to ignore him. Eventually by mid-afternoon his texts were becoming pissed off. Why wasn't I answering? 'You have been chilly with me since we met: why is that?' I didn't answer. I couldn't answer. The next day he texted again: 'I think I know why you're not answering, but I'm not going to know unless you answer. Let's talk.'

To this I replied: 'I don't want to talk.' Because I didn't. I didn't feel I owed him anything and absolutely wasn't under any obligation to explain myself. He texted a few more times and then he stopped. I blocked him everywhere I might see him – on social media and on my phone, and especially on Skype, and never heard from him again.

I didn't write about Finn in the newspaper column, and hesitated before writing about him here. Even now, I don't quite understand it. My best guess is that online dating culture was doing its worst. I was lined up with thousands of other faces in the digital beauty pageant, making statements about wanting to travel and world peace, but holding a number on a card, nonetheless. I lost myself, for a while, in the desire to be thought wantable.

It's all too easy to find yourself in a situation you don't want to be in. Lesson Three of internet dating: *don't be pressurised into doing what someone else wants, if you don't also want it.* It might seem obvious, but it isn't always. Women might have a particular issue with wanting to be liked, to be approved of. We need to circumvent that. We need to stomp all over it.

After this I came close to deleting all my memberships and giving up the quest. What did men really think I was offering? I looked with new eyes at my profile pages, pages that had been written entirely by me, by a woman who wanted to be chosen, but who was also confident of being treated well. There I was, chirpily confidently listed, with smiling and smouldering photographs and witty flirty copy. Online dating no longer looked like an innocent set-up in the week following the Finn episode. I said to a friend that I'd thought, in the beginning, that it was all about finding love, but now I was convinced otherwise. Why was I putting myself in danger? Why was I apparently offering myself to random strangers? The smiling rows of faces on the websites looked different. What kinds of lives had these single midlife men really had, and what kinds of minds did they have underneath the surface of polite chat, and what kinds of fault-lines lay dormant in them?

The fallout from this was that I was plunged into a period of a continual low mood. The wretchedness to do with the end of my marriage surged back, uninvited. It was like waking up with an illness you didn't have the night before. There it was in the morning when I woke, like a cold. There was a physical manifestation of grief. Grief was a pain in my liver, a backache and acid reflux. I belched grief. I was continually exhausted by it and slept a lot.

It's a human trait to want to stitch the episodic reality of life all together and make a chain of events, a continuous narrative out of it. But this was beginning to fail me. Causes and effects were becoming unhooked from one another. Perhaps I was lucky in love, in my youth, but if that was the case then my whole peer group was lucky: we met lovable men and loved them and were loved back, and got married, and had mostly happy married lives for decades before things went wrong (or didn't). That had been my parents' experience; I began to feel as if my romantic world was too inherited from theirs to cross the divide into this new one. I suppose I'm extremely conventional, with conventional expectations. Cause and effect, and people of the WYSIWYG sort – *what you see is what you get* – had always been my reality and I'd always been treated respectfully. Intelligence, education, experience, a facility for words and talking, a creative approach to living and working: these had always got me out of trouble, but now they didn't seem to count for much. Now, in the midlife dating pool, cause and effect didn't seem to work any more. There were hidden agendas. Being nice and emotionally intelligent didn't seem to be enough. Being as okay-looking as most of the men I was interested in wasn't proving to be enough either. Sometimes, being a successful woman with a fulfilling career seemed to be a drawback – and these weren't just my experiences, but those of a lot of other women, all over the world. The internet was full of women talking about just these phenomena. Most of us knew of reassuring exceptions, but most of the single men we encountered seemed to have high (or strange) expectations. Divorced men were being unleashed back onto the market and were causing havoc with the quantum physics of love. They didn't have the same expectations they had when they were on the market the first time. Online porn was widely named and blamed.

After a couple of weeks of feeling that the situation was hopeless, I realised that I needed to take decisive action. I had to put these thoughts aside. I knew that. At the end of that road there's a rancorous old crone, a Disney-drawn hag, stooped and malicious, saturated with the same poison that she thinks is confined only to the apple. I needed more positive thinking. I could feel the pull of bitterness. I could feel the attraction of joining some sort of circle, where other cynical dumped women gathered to chant contra-masculine incantations. Negativity and unhappiness were making me ill.

So I went into town and bought a book about turning your life around. I was to visualise standing on the summit of a verdant green hill on a warm day, looking down over a beautiful valley. That was my future: I just had to walk into it. Unfortunately, when I went to this hilltop in my mind, the drop was sheer and threatening, and vertigo struck. The book said: 'Think of tomorrow as a fresh white page; tear the old pages out of the book and look at all the white pages, sitting waiting for you to write your new life into them.' (It was something like that; I paraphrase.) It was good advice, but how did you do that, really, without putting the old pages in the bin and then getting up in the night and rescuing them and smoothing them out, and taking them back to bed with you and reading them obsessively?

Later, much later, in the dating quest, I had another Skype sex experience. Joseph, a man I'd been chatting to for three weeks and was supposed to be having a date with on the Saturday following, suddenly decided that we ought to

Skype. I wasn't sure. After the Finn episode I was more averse to Skype than ever. 'Aw, come on now,' Joseph said. 'What do you have to lose?' He's right, I thought. You have got to loosen up and stop being so tightly wound up about this. It's no biggie. If you don't like it, just press the red button and bring it to an end. Skype contacts can easily, instantly be blocked.

Joseph was a likeable man, down-to-earth, a big sturdy Irishman with a farm-boy look that I misinterpreted as old-school. He'd been divorced for five years, and had no children, and was as free as a bird. He talked about his freedom a lot, which in retrospect isn't necessarily a good thing when (supposedly) looking for a life partner, as he claimed he was now doing, wanting to settle down and partner up. When I mentioned the disparity he said, 'Aw, come on now,' in his southern Irish accent. Joseph was very 'Aw, come on now' about things in general. Mild joshing was his usual style. Added to which, he grinned all the time. He grinned on his profile picture. He grinned on Skype. His big wide dimply smile in his square farm-boy face was altogether heartening. He seemed contented with his life. Glass-very-nearly-full people are good people to be around. They have good life-affirming energy.

I was hampered by the usual nerves, but the video call began in a light-hearted, fun way, with a proper getting-to-know-you chat. We described how our respective weeks were going and played it for laughs. But then, quite abruptly and without any warning, Joe tilted the camera of the webcam down, unzipped his XXL mustard-coloured cords and got his dick out of his boxers (it was, I have to tell you, fascinatingly large). He moved the webcam so as to show the rest of him – his head and shoulders, and sat back on his couch, and asked if I was going to show him myself, because he really wanted to see me. This time I had more courage under pressure.

'I don't even know you,' I told him.

'But that's what makes this so exciting,' he said.

'It's just not for me,' I told him. 'I'm going now. Bye.' I shut the laptop lid with a slam, which might have been interpreted as slamming his dick in the door. It was good for me to do this. I had my usual hard-wired reaction (oh no, I fear I was just very rude to poor Joe; Joe won't like me now) and had to josh myself out of it. 'AW, COME ON NOW,' I said.

After the Finn episode I needed something much more conventional, and happy. Dating needed to be a happy experience, and fun, and life-affirming and joy-giving. That was, after all, the whole point of this exercise: to have more happiness in my life. I think that's something we sometimes lose sight of, recognising, with a sudden sharp pain, that the search for love has become a chore, an obligation, a series of badly revised-for examinations, and a war of attrition.

The Packaging

When I joined the dating site for graduates, I hoped naïvely that I'd find men looking at women their own age, with similar life-arcs and mind-sets. I hoped they'd be a little different to the panting dogs of a certain fee-free site that had made me downcast the day before.

But it was actually the opposite. It was a massive misfire, as serious a misfire as that which had occurred at a certain newspaper-owned site, which ought to remain nameless, where men of a generally lefty persuasion – and yes, a lot of them were academics – had been ignoring my emails in droves. (They talked the talk, these egalitarian and enlightened souls, but when it came to walking the walk they walked in a different direction.) The first thing that happened at the graduates-only site was that I had a conversation with a member about what he referred to as 'the packaging', by which he meant my midlife, post-wife, fleshy, bread-loving, wine-drinking self, and its deficiencies.

Writing this up, I'm immediately bombarded, in my head, by a whole stream of openly bolshy questions for men who talk in terms of women this way. Deficient in what sense? As a product, as something of use to you? Is that what

my existence means – I'm only of value as something of use
to men? I only have worth when viewed by the male gaze? I
can see that if that's your mind-set, then things are very clear.
You go out onto the internet looking for the best produce, as
if you were squeezing soft fruit at a greengrocer. If the black-
ening bananas and bruised plums speak up, you're not going
to be much bothered to answer. You're there to assess and
purchase fruit; why would you give your attention to the
protests of the over-ripe? Simple.

Generally my response to a poor start at a dating site was
to roll up my sleeves and take the project on with total dedication, and crack the nut, and that's what I did here. I
launched the campaign by sending twenty short approach
messages, a dozen to locals and eight to non-locals who were
too interesting to ignore, pointing out things we had in
common, and being funny about things that we didn't. I was
likeable, goddammit, but four days later there had been only
three responses, all of them gracious in thanking me for my
approval, and wishing me luck. In dating site code, wishing
someone luck is akin to pointing a large crucifix and a string
of garlic at them. I asked one of these repliers, a man who
lived a few streets away, why he didn't want to meet. He said:
'Not wishing to be ungallant, but there are a lot of young
and pretty girls here.' So that was me told.

When a proper response came, it was full of questions for
me to answer. Was I serious about educating myself for the
rest of my life? Did I really not watch much television? The
man in question appeared to live in a sort of hut at the edge
of a wood, 150 miles away and off grid. I answered as honestly
as I could, and received my notification of failure later that
day. He'd written the kind of brush-off I had become used
to, the kind that started by saying how much he liked me. It
was an Emotional Rejection Slip. He said that I was an

impressive person. (Uh-oh.) The distance, in miles, he had decided, was insuperable. Also, he added by way of a postscript, he didn't think I was serious enough about science and the world around us and the stars.

Well, that's a bit unfair, I thought. But 'unfair' is a pointless word in the dating game. There isn't any point trying to apply the idea of fairness to individual attraction, one person to another. Nothing could be more personal, after all, than liking. If you do try to apply the idea of fairness, you find yourself in emotional fascism, almost immediately. *Don't want what you want because it isn't fair to the not-wanted; don't like and dislike; don't have preferences because that's unjust*: it doesn't really wash in any context other than employment law. When it comes to sex, we all have our own *pillowmeter*, the highly unreliable internal gadget that registers our intuition of how thrilled we'd be to see a person's face on the pillow next to our own. Logically, we have to extend the argument (about fairness not being relevant to attraction) to men and their preferences. Having said that, I've come across numerous men using this attraction clause to account for their determination to snag a girl of 25, and others who use it to exclude all women over 35, in one fell swoop. 'I'm just not sexually attracted to women over that age' – apparently on principle – is a pretty suspicious line of argument when expressed as an inflexible rule (and not one, I'd hazard, that would survive bumping into Liz Hurley).

It had been a week of gloomy thoughts about the applicant who referred to 'the packaging'. In fact he wasn't an applicant. He wrote specifically to tell me he wasn't. 'It's a shame I don't fancy you,' he wrote, 'because otherwise you tick all the boxes.' How do you know that you don't fancy someone when you haven't met them in person? You don't. Charm, intelligence, warmth, quirkiness, wit – all of these can make plain people immensely attractive to us. It's why I never discounted a plain man out of hand, because in person the monster-faced might prove to have an inner George Clooney. This bloke who thought I ticked all the boxes, he must have thought I was seriously ugly, mustn't he, to be so rude as that; not even to want to meet a woman who *ticked all the boxes*? So I was gloomy. It was the Neville situation all over again. ('You may as well give up now, and withdraw from here and save your money.')

It wasn't a one-off, either. Another message arrived, in much the same vein, pointing out that I was plain. 'You sound nice,' he wrote, 'though unfortunately I have stringent physical criteria.' The fact is, some men are infantile about standards of beauty. (Yes, some women are too. I don't date women but I'm sure, yes, that women can be horrendously superficial.) Some men – not all of them fantastically good-looking, either – reminded me of 14-year-olds who have anxieties about what their mates will think of them if they date a … what's the word? There are various. Think of something unpleasant. Dog – I've been called a dog. There are men out there who are basically spotty 14-year-olds with pictures of Jennifer Lawrence by their beds, ones that they snog each night before going online to tell women how ugly they are.

There seems to be a gender imbalance, vis-à-vis the packaging thing. All the women I know are tolerant of middle age showing itself in a chap. We quite like a late flowering, in fact: the silvering, the smile lines, the coming of bodily sturdiness. We read these as signs that life has been lived and enjoyed. We read them as indicators of substance, of being substantial. I like the idea that in our fifties we're becoming elders of the tribe, with the stories and scars, but also with the understanding, the experience, the wisdom. These are all reasons why I was drawn to men in their fifties, but in general they weren't granting me the same courtesy. There were exceptions, of course there were – Peter had thought he was interested, for a start – but I didn't find much of the same narrative playing out in the heads of men I encountered online, about women as valued elders of the tribe, people it would be fruitful, interesting, exhilarating to partner. They were highly focused on the packaging. It was disheartening. It was really genuinely disheartening.

It didn't help to discover that a man of 51 who's online dating, a man who's nice enough but doesn't look a day younger than his age, might return from holiday to find eighty-four enquiry messages, half of them from much younger women, waiting in his inbox. He might need to apply filters to deal with this glut, and age is an obvious starting place for that. He might have an invitation to meet from a 30-year-old who has as much to offer as women his own age (he'd argue), in terms of personality and interests. He might think – and plenty of men do think this way – that a woman twenty years his junior will keep him young for longer: he could join in with her own timeline, avoid mirrors and have the illusion of living twice over. It's not a methodology for life that appeals to me but I can see how it might take hold of someone. At any rate, some kind of filter was needed by Gerald, the man in question, because who has time to see eighty-four people when you don't need to? Why go to the bother? Age is an easy, immediate, no-fuss filter.

I think this is how a lot of one-line 'thanks but no thanks' replies get written, and how a lot of painstakingly crafted approach messages get ignored. Perhaps the heart is hardened, under the force of such abundance. I tried to imagine what it would have felt like if I'd had eighty-four proper, chatty messages in a single week, and whether it would have made my world view different. It's hard to say. What's it like to be courted en masse by an enthusiastic fan base? I wonder. What's it like when far more people than you'd imagined want to talk to you, and say they're interested in you, and it turns out that they're young and vital? It's hard to grasp what that might do to your sense of what's normal, if the idea of young flesh appealed.

Gerald's sense of what was normal had changed. He hadn't expected to attract much attention on the site, as he was 'clapped out', he said (when I approached him, one of the eighty-four applicants, though he only replied after I'd sent a second message, asking if he was swamped). He was happy to chat about his newfound popularity. He was quite giddy about it. We got onto the question of age, and women, and he said he thought youthfulness was within everybody's reach. Not youth, obviously, but youthfulness. I told him that I objected to the language that's used about women in skincare adverts, which promise to rejuvenate us, as if it's actually about more than how soft and unlined your skin is, but about your womanhood and identity and purpose. (I don't need that, thank you; I'm just in my fifties; I'm not actually diseased.) He said he thought it was my duty to beautify myself.

'The word duty makes my blood begin to stir,' I told him. 'It's not boiling but it might reach a slow simmer.'

'That's how a lot of men online view women of your age,' he said. 'As dilapidated and angry; that's why they steer clear.'

'It's your age too,' I reminded him. 'It's *your age too*, Gerald.'

'It's different for men,' he said. (There you have it. The nub of the matter, encapsulated. In four words.)

'Well, I have objections to being expected to look younger than I am,' I said. 'I like my face as it is, and the years that are written on it; they're my years and I'm proud of them. I've been through things and I've survived them and I don't mind looking like a survivor. I don't mind being non-skinny, either. My body serves me pretty well, and to want to swap its features for other features, like bigger lips and bigger tits and weird squirrel-with-nuts cheek-plumping seems to me to be an acceptance of a kind of slavery. To me it says, *Yes, I am a commodity.*'

'But women do it by choice,' he argued.

'I don't always like what other women agree to do,' I said. 'Or what they appear to concede that they ought to be, and nor do I think the mechanism's really that simple.'

'But you're wearing lipstick in all the pictures,' he reminded me.

'Oh yes, I love lipstick,' I admitted, 'but I'm not wearing it for you, I promise you.'

'Women are so irrational,' he crowed.

'Listen, pal,' I said. 'It isn't irrational, it's just *complicated*; there's a difference.'

'You'll never find anyone with that attitude,' he told me.

I was unmoved by this. A man who thought that my looking my age was a deal-breaker wasn't a man I had the remotest interest in, you see.

I told the dating site veteran that I was having a poor response rate to the attempt to market my heart and soul. She was shocked that I was admitting to being 50. I should change it and say I was 40; lots of men had a search cut-off point of 40 and weren't even seeing me on their lists. I considered this. Did I want to meet those kinds of men, the ones who judge people by their numbers? Would waist measurement be the next thing? Another friend said that the first friend was right. When she was truthful and 54, she'd heard only from 70-year-olds. The 54-year-old men were all talking to the 35-year-olds, though they'd consider women of 40, at a push. 'List yourself at 40 and confess to 50 later,' she said. 'I did it. Nobody minded. They were doing it themselves, to beat the system.' I had qualms. 'Don't have qualms; it's routine. Women knock ten years off their age, and men add three inches.'

During the week that I was 40, my mailbox filled up. The trouble was, they were all messages from men who thought I was 40. When I confessed, nobody wanted to meet. One man said that he'd already guessed; in fact wasn't 50 a bit of a stretch? He thought I was probably older than that. Another strung me along a while. What kind of 50 was I? I was a spirited, cool, unusual 50, I said (somewhat desperately). I still wore plimsolls and had a silly sense of humour, I said, citing *Monty Python* as a for instance; I still bopped to eighties classics in the kitchen. 'Good for you, but I'm not interested, not remotely,' he wrote. 'I'm not ever going to embark on a relationship which began with a lie.'

A man of 44 I got chatting to wanted to know if turning 50 had made an impact on me. 'Fifty is wonderful,' I told him. 'Fifty feels like the beginning of real freedom.' The truth was that it had been shattering. Fifty was inescapably middle-aged, and death was real, and the two came together, tied with a bow. In fact I was well past the middle, in all likelihood. Contemplating this prompted me to start ticking off parcels of future time, to think about finite Christmases and finite summers. We talk about midlife as if it's really the middle, but at 50 we might be at two-thirds-life, or at an even more dispiriting fraction. Some of us will be culled well before 70, by illnesses, by vulgar little tumours or the like. Sadly, age *isn't* just a number. I'm aware, now, that my body will soon be on the turn, like a lettuce left in the crisping drawer too long. I needed a man who understood this, for whom it was normal and part of the complexity of things, because it was just the same for him. (I couldn't get my head around why someone would want a partner twenty years younger on principle; surely that just exacerbates ageing, which you have to do alone, without them.)

The fifties could be the best decade of all, if only we could get all our ducks in a row. The world might open up like a flower. Midlife divorce is often to blame for the life-in-decline mind-set, the beginning of a winding-down mind-set, because it can feel like all the good stuff is over. It can feel as if all that's left are crumbs and dregs, patching leftovers together and keeping buggering on. That is not the way to think of it.

'I bet you were gorgeous when you were young,' I was told once, via message, as if that were supposed to be a compliment. Yes, I was gorgeous (ish) for a while, in that unthinking unselfconscious way of youth. All youth is beautiful in its way, just because of freshness and newness and potential and firmness and health, but you don't realise this when you're 20 and have a bigger bottom than your friends; it's all mostly a disaster. So yes, I was lovely, and self-absorbed and shallow, and inexperienced and over-sensitive and dull. You're right, mate, I thought; you'd have much preferred me then. We would have had a lot more in common, for a start.

As the not-at-all-charming Neville had said, some months earlier, it was over for me. Over. For me. As if the (I hope) thirty years of life that lay ahead of me didn't mean much, not even to myself. What does it mean to us, as women, to be told that we're worth less than we used to be? No man I know has ever been told that his powers, his allure, his charm have faded, and that he has to face up to that, as if it means something important. Many women I know in their fifties talk about their invisibility in public places. I'm sure a case could be made for invisibility as a liberating force in a woman's life, but I was not the woman to make it, six months in to the dating game, in the week in which I'd been dissed or else flatly ignored by all the men I said hello to. The failure was beginning to make me rebellious. The experience made me want to look 50, and talk about 50, and stand firm with a whole movement of women, rejecting the pressure to try to look 35 for ever, throwing our foundation garments and hair dye away. It didn't last, as a manifesto. I had those impulses and then I went out and had my hair coloured, and stopped off on the way home to buy another stupid, snake-oil anti-ageing cream.

It was true that men didn't see me any more. They didn't see me. It was a sobering experience, to walk down the street observing how the 50-year-old men behaved, paying attention to what they were looking at as they strolled along. They weren't looking in shop windows. They weren't looking at me. They were looking at women half their age. If I was heading right at them like a car in the wrong lane I might, at best, get one of those rapid, assessing, cataloguing glances, the silent whoosh of the visual body-scanner. Otherwise, I would have had to stage a twisted ankle, an asthma attack or a major wardrobe malfunction in order to be noticed, and even then I'm not sure.

At the coffee shop, sometimes, I saw men trawling dating sites. One man in particular made an impression: he was someone I would have said yes to, if he'd asked me to meet and drink latte with him. He was mid-forties at a guess, balding but distinguished-looking, sad-looking around the eyes, tall, strong, wearing jeans and a big Aran polo-neck jumper. I had to squeeze past his table to go to the loo, and when I returned, because his laptop was turned towards me as I approached, I saw that he was scrolling through listings on one of the sites I used. I saw a row of female faces, some smiling, some pouting, some looking off dreamily into the distance, in soft-focus filters. All were much younger than him. They all looked about 30 years old.

I took possession of my coffee house chair and pretended to return to work, but covertly I was watching him, as he looked at female profiles and sent his messages to the chosen. He looked like a man who had suffered disappointments. His mouth was turned decisively down. His ring finger on the left hand bore the paler, indented trace of a wedding band that was no longer there, but had been in place recently enough to leave its unmistakable furrow.

What would it be like to become the girlfriend of this man, or of a man like this? I wondered. Would he be able to cast off the sadness of the past, and move on with optimism with someone new? Would I, myself, prove able to do that? I thought about what it might be like to marry someone who'd been dumped by the woman he would always love. I imagined the spectre of the woman he would always love following us along the street, standing with us in airport check-in queues, her hand resting lightly on his thigh in bed at night. I could see him lying awake as I dozed on, his eyes open in the dark, lying on his back sleeplessly and saying to himself, 'You need to pull yourself together, and soon.' On the other hand, how would I feel about being with a man who professed not to have any feelings for his ex at all, and who had cut her out of his life without any kind of a wound, no remnants, no scar tissue, no grief? We have to find a middle ground. It's one more thing that life throws at us.

I spoke to my friend Jack about my invisibility. I told him about the 50-year-old men on the high street, ogling the

25-year-olds. 'Men online are the same,' I told him. 'They say they're after true love but really what they're after are the 25-year-olds.'

'Maybe they think they can have both,' Jack said.

'You're not like that, though, are you? Given a choice, you'd pick the older more interesting woman, the passionate, well-read, intrepid, low-maintenance woman.'

'Nice of you to think so,' Jack said. 'But I'd go for the firm arse and tits, always, without question.' I expressed some mild disgust. 'You just have to face facts,' he said. 'Men respond visually, and we can't help it.' (He kept telling me this.) 'Well, we could probably help it, but we don't want to. Online dating's giving these idiots the impression that they can snag a honey. Most of them have no chance, of course. Don't you look at the 25-year-old men in the street?'

'I don't. Honestly. They have mothers of my age, so it'd be like randily pursuing the children of your friends. There's something inherently unsexy about that whole set-up.'

'Sexy as hell.'

'It's the 55-year-old, slightly rumpled silver foxes that I stare at, the tall well-travelled, well-used ones. But they don't see me.'

'Perhaps you should wear brighter colours.'

I looked down at myself. 'I like navy blue. What's wrong with navy blue?'

'These are just facts. Men like youth. They like long hair. They like colour. They like slender, as well. Sorry. You're going to have to lose weight and grow your hair and wear red if you want the silver foxes to see you.'

It was, disappointingly, just what Gerald had said. The question is, as I asked myself in the bathroom mirror, late that night: should I be prepared to change?

In the morning I had the answer. Physically change in order to please others? Absolutely not. Gerald's world view was still pissing me off. I decided that I'd go the other way entirely, and be more frank in the profile pictures. I took new photographs, and posted them: a make-up-free close-up and two at full length, one unedited in jeans, and another in a knee-length skirt, sans opaques. Honest photographs. After I'd done this my weight began to attract attention. Not all of it was negative. I felt unusually fondly about the man who wanted to blow raspberries on my thighs. He was a super-hero compared to some other respondents. One man who'd seen both the before and after pictures felt the need to inform me why he wasn't going to be asking me out. He was a doctor, you see, and when he saw obesity he saw death. The very old people on the streets are never the obese ones, he chided, and didn't I want to live a long time, without being a burden to my family and the NHS? It seemed a lot to put on the shoulders of a person with a fondness for marmalade. Plus, hold on a minute, what? *Obese?* I was happy to admit to roundedness. I carry a little cake at the hips and belly … okay, about twenty pounds of cake. But, you know what – I said to the laptop screen, in a defiant voice – actually, matey, I look all right. I'm heavier than I was at 35, granted, but I'm still in proportion, and I can still run up four flights of stairs without cardiac incident. My heart pounded in my ears. I pointed out, furthermore, that I hadn't asked for a date; I'd hoped that the process was as much about making new friends and widening your circle as about being invited out to dinner. (It wasn't. It really wasn't.) He said that my thinner pictures were unnecessarily coy and should be abandoned altogether. I think what he was really saying was that they're a form of false advertising.

'There are plenty of nice men who are into bigger girls,' he wrote. 'And so it's counter-productive to fail to admit to being one of them, because it won't work out and you're wasting your time. And ours, to be frank.' I looked at the honest photographs. Bigger girls? I'm a 'bigger girl'? Later he wrote again. He was sorry he'd been so tactless; he was overloaded with work. 'I'm sure you're a lovely woman,' he wrote. 'You have knockout dark eyes and sensual lips, and a very nicely turned ankle. It's just that every day I see the cost to health of obesity.' I looked at his profile pictures more closely; the one showing him on a boat with his pals revealed a hint of a paunch and the beginnings of a double chin. The bloody nerve!

'Midlife online dating is a buyer's market,' I said to a girl-friend over lunch, 'and the truth is that men are the buyers. Women are the merchandise offered for perusal.'

'It's only one guy, one joyless berk,' she consoled. 'Darling, you're gorgeous. Barely even fat at all.'

But the truth was there had been others. Two others. A bloke had already messaged saying he could see that if we got together there would have to be fruit for pudding. 'A woman needs to keep paying attention to her physical beauty,' he replied, when I told him he was rude. Then there was the diet specialist who said I should pick him as a boyfriend because he could help me lose weight. Romance is perhaps a dangerous thing, but this was a tad too far in the other direction. When I turned him down, he wrote: 'Can I politely suggest that if you don't want comments about your size, you remove references to it from your profile?' (Footnote: I'd never go out with anyone who used the phrase 'Can I politely suggest'. They're like the people who start sentences with 'No offence, but'. It's never a polite sugges-tion, and offence is always involved. It's passive aggression.)

But he was right, the doctor, that there's a market for the larger lady, distasteful though that phrase is. I know someone, an ample, lusciously curvy woman, big all over, and she's highly in demand ... though only with men she doesn't want to meet.

As is the way of things, a bad week made me vulnerable to a whole raft of bad ideas: there was a midnight ice-cream binge with Cameron Diaz, and an only just averted purchase of a run-down hovel in southern Bulgaria, before hitting the rapids, the white water, and messaging Peter asking why he didn't want to see me, if I was wonderful, and why he so very obviously regretted meeting up. He didn't reply, which was probably just as well. I was strong and deleted his number from my phone. Late night texting is too easy. Unlike email's big empty sheet of paper, it's a medium of a single thought or single question, and not enough time passes between being an idiot and pressing *Send*.

A friend, unaware that I was attempting dating, suggested I start dating. 'I am dating,' I told her. 'It's just the modern kind, when you don't leave the house. But I'm going to meet the next man who asks me out, even if he lives in Caithness and is pictured with a great big axe.'

Later that afternoon, I got a two-line email from a man who lived twenty miles away, wanting to meet for dinner. His wasn't a new face or name to me. Jonathan was one of the most persistent of the lurkers. He'd already visited my profile page two dozen times, in the manner of someone trying to talk themselves into something, and every time he had a look the site notched up his visit. He'd never said anything when he cast his eye, so it was surprising to get an invitation to dine with him, out of the blue. That's the kind of word Jonathan uses. He *dines*, preferably with a *lady* (which makes him sound like a dinosaur, though in fact he was four years younger than me). His own profile gave nothing away: he'd left all the fields blank that were supposed to be filled in with interests, biography, MARITAL STATUS. There were no words but there were lots of pictures: he was in sunglasses in every photograph and wasn't smiling in any of them, but I could forgive him that. Loneliness is a solemn business.

Jonathan was in a big hurry, and didn't want to talk before the date. He was a man for one-line messages, organising messages. Did I want to have dinner, or not? I said I wasn't free until next week. He said we could pencil in a date, although he might be taken by then and off the market. We established that he was single, and I asked if we could email a bit, to break the ice. He told me there wasn't any point. 'It'll either be fireworks or it won't,' he said. 'I'll know in the first five minutes, and so will you.' I began to be nervous. I asked if we could email anyway. He said he didn't have time.

'What do you mean, you don't have time?' I asked him. 'Don't you want to know anything about me? I could have been married nine times; I might have just got out of prison.'

'That'll give us something to talk about,' he replied. 'Give me your number. I'm going to ring you, right now.' It turned out he was an American, one who adopted an immediate authority on the phone. Perhaps he thought it was sexy to organise a woman and brook no dissent; perhaps he'd been infected by one of those masculinist directives about being manly and in charge: 'Don't ask her, just tell her,' blah blah. I wasn't attracted to the controlling manner, but it was pathetic that I hadn't had a date since Peter, and this was just going to be dinner, after all. 'So,' he said. 'We will have lunch.'

'I thought it was dinner,' I said.

'Lunch,' he decreed. 'And if we hit it off and the sex is fantastic and we have to be together, I'd like you to move in as soon as possible. It's a drag living alone. I'm going to walk round my house and tell you all about it.' He began to walk from room to room, describing each of them in detail to me, the furnishings, the views, the antiques, the open fires, which I couldn't help finding rather endearing. He was trying to impress me. He was wooing. When the tour was completed I began to tell him something about myself. He interrupted me. 'My dear, you don't need to impress me with your many fine attributes. All I need to know is, do you want a man in your life? Do you want commitment?'

'Well, yes,' I said. 'Theoretically.'

'Theoretically?' he repeated. 'Theoretically is the enemy of the orgasm.'

'I think we should have this lunch and see what happens,' I said. 'Let's have the lunch.'

'Okay then,' he said, gratified and approving. 'Good girl. That's the spirit.'

We were supposed to have lunch on Saturday, but he rang to postpone until Sunday, and when I asked if it was because he'd received a better offer, he laughed and said I was perspicacious. 'Perhaps we'd better wait till Sunday morning to see if you're still single,' I said, remaining calm. It was apparent that I wasn't the only woman he'd given the full guided tour of his antiques to, and it was further apparent that he was ranking us in order of preference, and I wasn't his first choice. Boldly, I put this to him (this whole process has made me a shooter from the hip, because who has time for games and their players?) and he said he'd been joking, and actually it was his mother-in-law's birthday dinner on Saturday, a fact that he'd forgotten. Mother-in-law? It transpired he was still married. I told him I didn't have lunch with married men. He said his wife didn't live with him any more, and were we having lunch, or not? Yes, I said. I think we should have lunch. Why not?

'You sound a bit down in the dumps,' he said. 'Is something wrong?'

'I'm just tired,' I told him, aware I was using the euphemism I so object to whenever it's used on me. 'Combination of hormones, not working hard enough, and a sore tum. It will pass.'

'Good,' he said. 'Because I prefer you when you are witty and sparkly and sarcastic.' I'm sarcastic? Then he said, 'What are you wearing? And what kind of underwear are you wearing?'

I told him I didn't discuss my Marks and Spencer scanties with married men who cancelled lunch dates. He asked what I liked in bed. Cocoa, a Kindle and blissful sleep, I said. He replied that I shouldn't be so coy, that it was thrilling to dare to be frank with a stranger. I said more details of my preferences in all things weren't available until at least the second date. I was sweating by now, so terrible am I at flirting with total strangers on the phone. (NB, I said to myself: no more cocoa talk. Ever. Kindles are no doubt also the enemy of the orgasm.)

'Question for you,' he said. 'Do you really want a man? Do you really want a man in your life? Because I want a woman. I want to cuddle up and spoon a lovely woman in my bed. Is that you, are you that woman?'

'You never know,' I said. 'But I'd like to know more about you. What do you do for fun other than spooning; what kind of books and films do you like?' He said that none of these things counted for anything, when it came right down to it, and I said that it was interesting at the least, surely, and began to tell him what I was reading.

'Yeah yeah, whatever,' he said. I told him I'd been to an exhibition and he interrupted with, 'Arty farty; I'm not into that.'

'So, what does interest you?' I asked him.

'Meeting you,' he said.

Really, this relationship was over already, following a characteristic online dating arc, beginning and ending only in cyberspace, but I was determined to have the bloody lunch. He said he would book a restaurant for Sunday. He'd choose. I wasn't allowed to have a say. He sent a text. 'I'm hugely excited about meeting you,' it said. And then a great silence fell. He didn't reply to queries about place and time. Nor did he ring in the evening. Where were we supposed to be meeting on Sunday? Hello? Jonathan? No response. So I texted again. 'Is everything okay with you?'

The reply buzzed in immediately. 'Fine thanks, just busy. Regards, Jonathan.'

Regards? Regards, Jonathan? *Just busy* is an absolute give-away. The decision to omit kisses is a big red danger signal. *Regards* is relationship kryptonite.

The following morning I tried again and sent another text message: 'Beautiful day here; how's your day going?'

Two hours later he texted back. 'Am good too. Jonathan.'

Changes in a man's mode of communicating are not usually accidental. I may have been intended to take the hint, but I blundered on, as is my way. On Saturday night, 11 p.m., and still no date confirmed, I texted him: 'Are we having lunch tomorrow or not?'

The reply was five words long. 'Met someone who can deliver.' *Met someone who can deliver?* I guessed that our date was off, then. While I was simmering, another text arrived. 'Sorry for cancelling. I need someone who can make a commitment and you didn't seem sure.' Seriously? He expected a commitment to the long haul before we'd even met face to face? I sat on my hands and said nothing, and simmered some more. By Tuesday, there he was, back on the dating site, his online light lit. He was trawling for women again. I don't think the *someone who can deliver* can have delivered. Or maybe she delivered enough.

One of the sites allowed me to limit my search to New Members only, people I hadn't seen before, and so I filled in the requirements (which had relaxed a bit: pulse, teeth, lives in continent of Europe) and pressed the search button. Some of the new men had particularly jaded-sounding openers to their profile pages. 'I don't want to walk a dog along a beach, and have lunch in a pub with a fire. I've seen all the romcoms I'm ever going to see, and have drunk enough red wine cosily on sofas. Offer me something original if you want to grab my attention.' I wondered how this irritable tone went down. I couldn't imagine replying to his invitation to offer something original, in the hopes that he'd deign to notice me, but perhaps he'd find someone equally grumpy and intolerant. What would they do in the evenings, when avoiding their sofa, I wondered – make pottery? Learn Portuguese? Well, each to their own. My sofa and I will never be parted. I should probably have mentioned, in my profile, how wedded I was to my big feather couch, and why my arse was that twin-potato shape.

I was learning to spot the men who were new to online dating. They arrived with a shiny new membership and very high expectations, as if they were going to find an order number alongside each of us and merely had to tick the box to get delivery. The man mentioned above listed the things he didn't like in 'a lady', qualities that – I suspect – defined his ex-wife. Above all, he said, ladies should only contact him if they'd managed to overcome the urge to criticise. The urge to criticise him, I admit, was strong in me.

Dating sites are Darwinian places, but not everyone has to try too hard. The people who can afford to be prescriptive – in fact they can do what they like – are the rich, successful men over six feet tall. If they also happen to be handsome, they live in a dating world of their own making. I noticed this profile page opener when I was bored one night and went man shopping, looking (though only for fun) at the uber-suave central London listees. 'Cool, happy, successful executive and international traveller, divorced and 52, looking for unique woman.' The rich man is used to living in a high-spec environment, and finding a mate seems no different. 'When I find her, she'll be a loving, unflappable, organised sporty can-do person; gentle, feminine, intelligent, tolerant, funny, sexy, honest, relaxed, charming to all and a passionate adventurer. She should have her own life, her own career, but also realise that nothing is more important than family.' Men like this are looking to breed, and they're very clear what they need: they want willowy, high-achieving goddess types of saint-like temperament, who are ready to give up the fast lane to be barefoot and pregnant. The galling thing was that I knew for sure that he'd get hundreds of responses, because although he'd have a definite physical type in mind, he didn't make any reference to it. The auditions were probably ongoing.

'Why are men like this even available?' I asked the dog. 'Why would they need to go looking online?'

He didn't say, but I could read his thought bubble. 'They must be absolute shits.'

I was almost contacted by one of those jet-set types at one point. Almost, but not quite. He was the senior version, in his mid-sixties, widowed and keen to remarry. He'd got a little jowly but you could see he'd been formidably handsome once. He enthused about having an interesting job that he loved, a creative role in international business. Although he refused to retire completely, he was winding down and was keen to find a woman to go exploring with. There was obviously plenty of cash for this – his house was vast and exquisite, his suits bespoke: in short, he was completely intimidating. (And no, I wasn't after someone with a heap of money; I'd have found the disparity between their life and mine, their normal and mine, tricky to handle.) More out of boredom than anything, I filled in his question-naire – the site offered these as standard kit – and was awarded a score: I'd answered twenty out of twenty questions as he'd have hoped. I sent him an email and was ignored. A few days later he came and had a look at my profile. He looked three times that day, twice the next. Then he filled in my own questionnaire (the site allowed you to come up with your own Yes/No questions) and got twenty out of twenty too. I sent a one-line note. 'We seem to be highly compatible. Would you like to meet?' No answer, though he came and looked at my profile again.

'What's going on?' I asked Jack on the phone. 'Is it that "I'd never date a woman who asked me out" thing again? Like we're all at a ball and it's 1825?'

It might be, he conceded. 'These men want to do the chasing, and they want to be with submissive women, and be in charge. Plus, they want a woman who will look good in a bikini or an evening dress.'

'What are you trying to say?' I asked him.

I was spending far too much time with my dog, and indoors, man-trawling. I went to the window and looked out at the street. 'I have got to get out there and dazzle some-body, pdq,' I said. 'Okay, well maybe not dazzle them. I could find a way to pique someone's interest, though, given enough props, I'm sure. Perhaps I should get a unicycle, or learn the saxophone and play it outside Zara, wearing a Kiss Me Quick hat. Maybe I could become one of those huggers who offer free hugs on street corners, and then I could hold on very tightly to the handsome tall ones. Maybe I could give out my number on the street like one of those flyer-guys offering vouchers for discount golf clubs. Maybe I could set some kind of a trap, and then they'd fall in love with me while I was tending to their wounds.' The dog looked concerned. It was true it was all getting a little bit Kathy Bates in *Misery*.

When you're single and don't want to be, there's a constant background chorus of advice. It was generally agreed that I needed, in the dread phrase, to get out there. Very few people knew that I was having relationships with people online; they interpreted my staying at home night after night in an old-world way, as being alone. People don't realise that online dating isn't just about being asked out: many of the dates start and end online, with typed words on screens, and never even make it to Starbucks.

I longed to meet someone in the old-fashioned way, but I had no idea how to put the plan into action. I'd already asked married pals if they had personable single friends, and had drawn a blank. When I told my mum I was abandoning online dating and going out to find men in the city, she clapped her hands in rejoicing. She thought there was – somehow, don't ask me how – a qualitative difference, as if finding a man online would be like finding one at Aldi. Real-world men were bound to be better quality, she thought. My mother, like many of my friends (and all too many dating gurus), had advised the joining of societies in order to meet men. Get out into the world and meet people in the old-fashioned way, they said, the fools. Generally I spared them the sad litany of failures to instigate chat in bookshops and delicatessens and with men in parks, letting my dog meet their dog. I didn't even know if I wanted to go back to that kind of happenstance. Online dating at its best sends you to meet-ups fully informed. I'd grown accustomed to the data sets. I'd grown used to self-descriptions, stated likes and dislikes, the lists of places on the to-do list, the things hoped for and feared, the all-round self-revealing that goes on in a properly filled-out profile page. Little is known about a stranger who asks you out while your terriers say hello to one another beside a shrubbery after five minutes of dog chat. You can't really subject them to the standard questions. You can't go barging in to their private lives, gung ho. *So, are you married? Oh – single, really, that's interesting, and what are you hoping for, from a relationship, something long term?* When you're used to the online way of doing things, accidental first meetings offer so little of people upfront, as facts. When you meet online, it isn't usually going to take until the third date to discover that someone is a Scientologist or a conspiracy theorist, or that he has nine children.

But there was no doubt that it wasn't working out as well as it might. 'This internet shenanigans is all very well,' my mother had already told me, trying to be modern, 'but real-world socialising has to be better.' Whether she was right or not, this wasn't really helping. 'There must be a nice dance you can go to,' was her follow-up suggestion (not showing her age at all). The trouble was that I'd already tried singles-oriented real-world socialising, and I could only attempt it a second time if I pretended the first time hadn't happened. I'd done the joining-societies thing; I'd become a Gallery Friend and had been to public lectures. Nothing doing. 'Just talk to people while you're out and about,' Mum urged me. She is an inveterate talker-to-everyone, but then she's 80 and is indulged. There were sometimes attractive middle-aged men in the café where I'd take a book to lunch, and I'd look at them out of the corner of my eye, trying to gauge whether they were attached. Twice, I'd seen faces I knew from dating sites, both of them staunch non-repliers, and had been half tempted to humiliate them in front of their peers, citing their offhand rejections, but who needs that kind of trouble? Members of the Works from Home crowd also hung out at the café, in their jeans and pinstripe shirts, with their tiny laptops and mysterious folders of papers. Our eyes met occasionally, and sometimes for a second or third time, but then they'd finish their coffee and leave. How can a conversation start in those circumstances that isn't embarrassing or obvious? The last thing I needed was to become known as a predatory woman (cougar, I think, is the charming word used) prowling about in her local coffee place, growling at men and making a tit of herself.

I'd tried the real-world pick-up, for want of a better phrase. I'd humiliated myself in wine shops, rushing in, sidling up to nice-looking men and talking to them about *vins de pays* we might buy. They'd bought their wine and had then gone home. I'd tried to initiate chat with men who stopped off in the railway station food hall at six o'clock, as they stood in front of the Meals for One section. I'd done this in an early phase, post-separation, when my mental health wasn't the best. In my head I was someone else. I was 28 again. I could see her, the slender striking-looking dark-haired girl, in the falsely reflecting mirror behind my eyes. This is what I wrote, on the second page of the dating diary: 'At 28 I was flirted with on an ongoing basis, by men older and younger. At 28 you don't see yourself at 50, thickening in the waist and loosening around the throat. It doesn't occur to you that those same men who ogled you at the office, back then, would run a mile if they met you now, even though they're all older than you.'

The next time I went to said coffee shop, I witnessed an attempt at a real-world pick-up. A man in his late fifties, lanky in Levi's, began to talk to a pretty woman of about 30 who was sitting opposite him. She was doing a Sudoku in a newspaper.

'How are you getting on with that?' he asked. That was his opening gambit. He was being friendly and introducing a topic of conversation, at the same time as signalling his interest. Easy.

'I seem to be stuck on this one, but it's a Super-Fiendish,' she said, smiling.

'Oh, I love those,' he said, coming across from his seat so that he could look at it too, sitting beside her almost knee to knee. I was amazed at his smoothness. She let him talk her through it and said his method was going to be invaluable for future attempts. If only he'd stopped there! To the wide-eyed horror of all around us, he began to test her on various mathematical problems, putting them to her verbally and talking her through them. When she understood something he told her she was smart, and sounded surprised about it. 'Hey! You're really smart!' He started explaining what prime numbers are, and when she interrupted to say she knew, he talked over her. 'Wait, listen to what I'm trying to tell you,' he said. Then he made his move, unaware it was already too late. 'Could we talk about this more over dinner?' She politely declined, and when she'd left he picked up the newspaper and didn't seem too disheartened.

There were lessons to be learned, I reflected. We could call this Lesson Four. Lesson Four is: *be openly interested, be unashamedly yourself, be bold, and try not to give it another*

thought when it all comes to nothing. Perhaps not so patronising as Levi's Man, but bold. Boldness. Who dares wins,
and all that. Yes.

A man with shaggy dark hair, Heathcliff-handsome, came
and sat opposite me and opened his copy of *A Hundred
Years of Solitude*. He had his back to the corner, and every
few minutes he scanned the room from over the top of the
novel. Noticing I was looking, he began to glance at me,
though only when I appeared to be absorbed by my own
book. Do not read too much into this, I told myself. He
might be one of the high-prestige lords of online dating, the
ones who never reply unless you meet their stringent criteria. He might not be glancing at you at all. He might be
thinking about Gabriel García Márquez, and not even
seeing you. He might be thinking about his shed, or about
his wife Claire, so young that she's still at university. He
might be wondering if you are Claire's mother's dumpy
friend Janet, and if he should say hello.

Follow Sudoku man's advice and ask what the book's like
and say you have it but have never got around to reading it,
my helpful inner voice suggested. The man was sitting eight
feet away, and was continuing to glance at me. Why couldn't
I just ask the question? He might think me forward, desperate, perhaps an unusual sort of hooker, or someone preparing to talk him into a cult or a Ponzi scheme, but so what? I
opened my mouth and closed it again, unable to speak, and
he drank his coffee down and was gone.

Next, a dating site email arrived from Jim, who was apparently unaware that we saw each other in our neighbourhood
sometimes. In fact, Jim (I thought, looking at his photograph), I saw you at the weekend, when I was buying flowers
and you were buying avocados. He was undoubtedly dashing – a blond, square-jawed man who was ageing well. He

worked for a legal outfit and was heavily into snorkelling. He had the sleek, wide-shouldered, slim-hipped body of the keen swimmer. You name a turquoise sea and he'd snorkelled there. (I hate being underwater, as it happens, but thought it best not to mention this until after the wedding.) He was a fulfilled, happy person, his bio said. He had everything he wanted in life, other than someone to love. He wasn't a player, he made a point of saying; he was one of the good guys. He found that dating sites were getting increasingly sleazy, he added.

I agreed enthusiastically to his suggestion that we meet for a drink. I wondered about mentioning that we seemed to live in the same district, but decided against. I did say that I was finding dating sites increasingly sleazy, also. He wanted very much to fall deeply in love with someone, he said in his response, and stay there, deeply in love for the rest of his life, in a marriage like that of his parents. He'd always prized his freedom above everything, he said, but recently he'd begun to think differently about his life. He saw his freedom now as a series of dunderheaded missed opportunities. There were women who had loved him and whom he'd turned away, afraid of commitment and staleness, afraid that love would end. He hadn't allowed himself to get too dependent on anyone, his whole life. He despised the whole dating site culture of one-night stands, he wrote, and short-term relationships and lack of emotional ambition.

We arranged to meet on Friday night, at a bar near his flat. I didn't mention that it was also near mine. He suggested the venue. He said, 'Let's make it after 9 p.m., as I have a meeting there at 7.' I told him nine o'clock was ideal. Once the date was arranged I went back and looked properly at his profile, and that's when I noticed something I hadn't before: that Jim was hoping to have children. I messaged him. 'You know that I'm 50, don't you? Children aren't on the cards. Still want to meet?'

'It's probably not a goer long term,' he replied, 'but how do you feel about short-term fun?' Short-term fun? Wasn't this the man who was casual-sex-averse? 'Give me your mobile number and I'll text you when my meeting's over,' he said. 'Should be by 9 but might overrun.'

Intuition struck me like a gong. 'Wait – do you have a date at 7? Is that what the meeting is?'

That's precisely what it was. 'It was arranged before I met you,' he protested. 'And I'm not one for cancelling arrangements at the last minute.'

I got dolled up, in a silver and black dress, with long silver earrings and grey heels. I was having a date! Finally, an actual no-expectations date. I waited and waited, and checked and re-checked my phone, and when it got to 10.30 I took off the dress and the make-up and went to bed. At 10.55 the phone beeped. 'Fancy a drink?'

'How did your date go?' I texted back.

'Unexpectedly well,' he admitted. 'Lovely snog at the bus stop. Are you up for another?'

The following day there was another Jim, a tanned and muscly builder, wanting to know if he could have my phone number. 'I love your profile,' he wrote. 'I barely read at all but I do like a woman who does.' (For no, I had not simplified my listing. Quite the reverse. There were something like thirty books mentioned on it at this point.) I gave him my number and he rang while I was walking along the street, just as it was getting dark.

'Well, this is weird, isn't it?' he said when I answered. He had a nice Yorkshire accent.

'It is a bit weird,' I agreed. 'How are you, what have you been doing?' I sat myself on a bench to talk to him.

'Busy day at work, just had a shower, just opened a beer, putting my feet up. You?'

'The same, though I haven't quite got to the beer and feet up stage yet. Looking forward to that.'

'You sound way too posh for the likes of me,' he said. (Posh? I'm not posh remotely. It's just that I don't have much of any sort of accent.) 'So what are you wearing?' he asked me.

'Tweed skirt, T-shirt, jacket, boots,' I told him.

'Kinky,' he said. (It wasn't, I promise you. It was firmly on the spectrum of frumpy.) 'How short is the skirt? Tell me about the boots. Are you wearing stockings? I'm getting hard just thinking about it.'

'The skirt's mid-calf and a bit dowdy; I'm altogether a bit dowdy,' I told him.

'Tell me about your nipples,' he said. 'What size are they?'

I had to catch my breath. How did this suddenly become a topic? 'Really?' I said. 'Seriously? I have to go. Bye.'

'Jim' had only posted one photograph and on revisiting it I was suspicious of the studio-quality lighting. Was Jim the man in the picture? Maybe. Maybe not. I was beginning to be sceptical about too-good dating site photographs, especially since realising, on an earlier foray into the listings, that a man who'd posted a stylish picture of himself in a black raincoat at the Trevi Fountain had lifted it from a clothing catalogue.

As it's easy to change the illustrations that we post in order to market ourselves on dating sites, I decided, experimentally, to swap mine for radically different ones, to see what happened. My pictures thus far hadn't shown even a hint of cleavage. They're what I'd call Girl Next Door Grown Up – I'm fond of a chunky jumper, a long full skirt, boots, big jewellery. I dress in the general style of what my pal Jack calls '50-year-old headmistress of a progressive girls' school'. On a good day, I might be thought to be the art teacher there, rocking her vintage Liberty boho look, though usually I'm distinctly more 'Dressed randomly by the Marks & Spencer sale'. I'm not always glad of Jack's take on things but he can be relied upon not to gild the lily, and sometimes I need that inability to lily-gild.

So I hunted through my camera files and found the perfect shot. It had been taken at a black tie do five years before, and featured a silky black frock with a low neckline, smoky eyes, scarlet lips, a bit of a come-get-me expression and lighting so flattering as to render me unrecognisable. Bingo. I went to one of the sites and posted the photograph, and sat back and waited. Within seconds, men were clicking on the photograph in order to look at my profile page, and – more to the point, I suspect – to look at that photograph at full size. My visitor numbers immediately shot up, and began to accelerate in a crazy way. 'You'll get a lot of attention if you do this,' Jack had said, and Jack was right.

Intrigued, I went across to another dating site and changed the photograph there, from the jumper shot to the cleavage one. I'd been getting about ten views a week, but when I went back half an hour later I'd already had sixty-three. Messages began to arrive that said, in short, in ways both innocuous and presumptuous, that they liked the new me. Among the approving responses there were explicit descriptions of what some of them were doing with the picture, and many invitations to Skype sex. I didn't get dates, though. No lunch offers. No offers of actual non-leg-over meetings.

I wondered what response I'd get if I signed up at a new website and used this as the only photograph. So that's what I did: I joined a free dating site, and got twenty-seven responses in twenty-four hours. I was fresh meat there, delivered to the waiting wolves. None of the wolves' messages was conversational; none talked to me as a person; perhaps I'd removed the need to talk to me as a person, by appearing to set the agenda myself. After forty-eight hours I had over a hundred responses, most of them one-line stuff: 'Mmm great tits, howsabout we get together xxx.' Some were much longer than that and detailed, and had phone snaps attached. I deleted the account and opened another one, giving myself a new name. I used a different picture, one taken when I was 40 and looked a lot younger, and was as wholesome as you like, in a field in a Fair Isle sweater. I didn't fill in the blank fields about achievements and interests, but let the picture speak for itself. By that evening there were several serious approach emails of respectful tone, requesting the pleasure of my company over lunch. None, however, was from a man within 200 miles, aside from one that was complimentary about my being a real lady who didn't wear muck on her face.

Back at the site where I'd left the cleavage/evening dress picture up, I began to get hostile messages from men I'd rebuffed. Several young ones now thought it disgusting that 50-year-old women should be there looking for sex. What did my being 50 conjure up for them? Did they see someone on the verge of decrepitude, about to be elderly, on the downward slope to the bus pass, the pac-a-mac, coupons, bungalows and yellowing net curtains? Did they foresee trouble with hills and stairs, a retreat into orthopaedic footwear and elasticated trousers, false teeth and tinned ham, bargain rails on a Monday afternoon, library books changed once a week, a deckchair on the seafront and quiz shows at teatime and death? Not that there's anything wrong with most of those things; I'll even admit to being keen on some of them (aside from death, which is a bit of a downer). The psychology was debatable, but one thing seemed really clear. When someone on a dating site appears to announce that she's ready for sex, she's treated rather differently to a woman in a Fair Isle sweater, having a picnic in a field with daisies around her.

One of the dating site men who saw the cleavage photograph, before it was deleted everywhere, was a 24-year-old called Joe, a serious-looking man with a bicycle, a flat cap and a full nineteenth-century beard. He invited me to meet him for a drink: my first hipster invitation. I responded saying I was flattered, but way too old for him.

'I'm not interested in age, and you looked stunning in that picture,' he replied. 'Why did you take it down?'

'Because I'm not really that woman,' I told him. 'And thank you, but I wouldn't feel comfortable dating somebody so young.'

'That's ageist of you, I must say,' he said. 'Anyway, who's talking about dating? I want to meet you for sex. I can assure you that I'm an experienced, generous and able lover. What do you say?'

'I say you're mad. The reality of a 50-year-old body is going to take you by surprise.'

I scrutinised his profile again. He liked European cities and historic sites and museums. We engaged in a brief flurry of friendly messaging about these things, sharing our enthusiasms. Fundamentally, he was an urban male, which was refreshing: none of his photographs showed him conquering white water. My instinct said we'd get along. My instinct also said no, NO NO NO, not even a cup of coffee, NO, NO. Partly this was self-protection, because he'd made it clear that he had no interest in anything other than sex, and I might fall for him and fall hard, all alone. Nothing frightens me more than that. It wasn't ever going to be anything other than mutual sexual gratification … which I was badly in need of, that's true, but I wasn't about to reveal my 50-year-old body to a 24-year-old male, not unless he was a doctor and circumstances were entirely professional, and even then maybe not. Despite the Sam Taylor-Woods of this world, falling in love with a man half your age seldom turns out well. Colette covered this pretty well in *Chéri*.

'Won't you at least meet me once?' Joe persisted. 'Girls of 24 bore me to death.'

'Be more discriminating,' I told him. 'They're out there, the women with similar interests to you; you just need to put in the hours.'

'I know plenty of pretty girls with similar interests,' he said. 'But I don't want to have sex with them. Won't you at least meet me, just for a drink?'

'I'm really flattered, but no,' I said. 'I wish you luck, though. It's been fun chatting.'

Closing the laptop, there was food for thought: the sweet, appealing Joe had offered, and I'd turned him down. It didn't seem to be sex that I was looking for. No-strings frolicking had been handed on a plate more than once now, and I had not taken the plate. What was it that I wanted? Was it that most cliché-ridden concept of all, everlasting love, holding hands in the street like the lovely old people who lived on my road and doddered along together holding on tight?

At a bookshop that afternoon, I dared myself to chat to a man there on his own. It's easier to talk to strangers in bookshops than somewhere people are moving, like supermarket aisles. Men in bookshops are fairly slow to react, which is a plus when you're in pursuit of them; they're standing, lulled by words and thoughts, their flight impulse slowed to reading speed; and in general, people who can't stop buying books are open to chatting with others of similar affliction. I was having a splurge, and had piled eight volumes in my hands, balancing them against my chest and chin, and then I realised that the Heathcliff-handsome reader of A *Hundred Years of Solitude* from the coffee shop was standing in front of me, in a leather jacket.

I said, 'When you can't carry any more, it's probably time to pay and go home.' I smiled at him. He smiled back. But then he returned to browsing. I swept past him, close enough to smell his fragrance, and turned on one heel and grinned like a lunatic. 'I'm bringing a Sherpa next time,' I said. He didn't acknowledge this. I went down a level to the ground floor and paid up, feeling utterly dejected.

'I don't really want a lot,' I told the universe, while standing queuing. 'I can be flexible. I just want someone funny and loyal. Everything else is negotiable, I swear.'

'The thing is,' the universe said, 'that despite what you say now, you have far too many expectations.'

Out in Open Water

Kinky Week was one of the strangest periods of the whole dating project. First there was an approach from a man who liked to wear adult-sized nappies and be treated as a baby by his lover. He was sure I would enjoy it. He wrote explaining that this isn't as rare a peccadillo as I might assume; there were quite a number of people in the UK who shared this fantasy, as he knew from the group he belonged to. He went on to explain how our relationship would work. He hadn't been happy since he was a small child, he said, and he craved the safety of being with Mummy again. (And having sex with her? I like to think I'm fairly broad-minded but this was just too weird.) He tended to write to women of 50+, he added, as there were lots of us who'd missed out on having a child, to whom this might appeal.

Shortly after this there was a one-liner from a mid-fifties man in a panama hat, his name an obvious alias, asking if I'd talk to him on Instant Messenger. He said he couldn't tell me his name as he was rather well known. 'Actor? Politician?' I asked him.

'Might be one of those,' he conceded. He confessed that it wasn't his photograph, either, and I told him that I don't talk to men who need to stay in disguise.

'No names, no pack drill,' he replied. 'Don't be a sour-puss. Let's have a fun conversation on Instant Messenger.'

'Not tonight, I'm too tired, but write to me, write me a letter,' I told him. He wanted to go straight to a porn experience; I wanted mail from Cyrano de Bergerac. Preferably, in fact, from Steve Martin playing C.D. Bales playing Cyrano de Bergerac.

'Don't be afraid,' the nameless man messaged back. 'I just want to talk to you. Five minutes. What's the worst that could happen?' It was a good question. The box opened on the screen, ready for him to type and for me to reply in real time, the cursor pulsing in it. 'Good to talk to you,' he wrote there – the words appeared on the screen as he typed them. 'Is this your first time? Instant Messenger virgin?'

'No, but I don't much like it,' I typed.

'Does it make you feel bad and dirty?'

'It didn't until then.'

There was a long pause before he replied. 'You're funny. What else are you apart from funny? Are you a naughty girl?' The light lit by his name came and went. As it only illuminated when the other person was (literally) on the same page as you, and as his was blinking on and off, my guess was that he was leaving and rejoining the conversation. My guess was that he was talking to more than one of us at once. 'Are you a naughty girl who needs a little punishment?' he asked me.

'Don't understand,' I wrote, though I had a pretty good idea.

'Will you be my lady?' he asked me. 'And will you be my whore?' I didn't reply. His little light pulsed. After a much longer pause he typed: 'I have a hairbrush here. Bend over and take your knickers off. I'm going to use it on you, because you are bad.'

'This isn't my thing,' I told him. 'Bye. Good luck. Bye.'

Some time after this, a man who had seemed perfectly nice up until then, in two or three evenings of on-screen chat, asked me if I ever fantasised about being raped. 'No,' I told him, remaining studiously calm. 'I don't think anybody does.'

'I don't mean real rape,' he said. 'Obviously.'

'What's unreal rape?' I asked him.

He told me it was the sort in which a woman wasn't keen to start with, but subsequently yielded and became aroused and had the best orgasm of her life.

And then there was Clive. Clive also wanted to go straight to Instant Messenger, without even really saying hello. This time I was armed. 'Are you a spanker?' was my first question. He said he wasn't, but that he was sexually dominant, and was looking for a woman willing to explore a passive role in bed. ('Explore' was too active a verb, perhaps, but I let that pass.) Now, passivity's not my thing: it doesn't have healthy relationship connotations, for me. But I went to his profile page anyway, because I was curious, and found it was unlike any other I'd so far seen. Clive appeared to be an aristo-kink. He'd done that whole public school/Oxford/the army/the City thing, he said, and had inherited, and didn't any longer have an alarm clock. His photograph showed him on a fine horse. I went back to the message box and asked how he spent his days. He said he was lucky in so far as he didn't need to work, aside from managing the estate. Otherwise he spent his life travelling and writing and painting, but had to admit that since his wife died, he was lonely.

Thinking back to how I replied to this, I have to admit to being deeply embarrassed. I more or less applied formally for consideration. I more or less advocated myself as a suitable wife for a baronet. I might even have said how much I felt at home in National Trust houses. Things appeared to have switched; now it looked as if it were me who was having the fantasy. Clive's response was to ask if we could have Instant Messenger sex, which would work by each of us writing what we were doing to the other, in real time on the screen, so as to create a scenario. He was going to be the lord, and I'd be a servant girl. Evidently he was going to get off on this. I, on the other hand, was getting off the internet.

It was only afterwards that I had the reaction. What evidence did I have that Clive was Clive? It's possible, probable, that I wasn't talking to the man I thought I was. He could have downloaded that photograph from anywhere; he could have made up all that stuff about his charmed life; he could have been 100 per cent a fake. The internet is a perfect vehicle for all sorts of subterfuge. He could have been anybody, an unpleasant man, an abuser, a criminal: who knows? It's more likely than not that he adopted a gentrified persona so as to enact dominance fantasies with women online, women he had no intention of ever meeting. I was gullible, and I was a snob, and I felt like an idiot. Never again, I vowed.

The feeling that the online world was becoming gradually more remote from my unquestionably rather conventional needs was put to an end by being asked out for a drink by a man who looked as normal as pie. His name was Marc, and he lived about two miles away, and he was an engineer. He was eight years younger, and wavy-haired and hazel-eyed and – judging by the site pictures – wasn't afraid of a man bag.

When he messaged me, using the dating site system, he'd only been on the website for a few days, having been single for a while after a six-year relationship. He said I had lovely eyes, and that we seemed to have a lot in common. 'In fact,' he said, 'didn't I see you at the cinema on your own, last Sunday afternoon?' He named a French film I had indeed been at on my own. He liked old French movies too. Did I fancy having a beer one night? 'I note that you like beer, which is excellent,' he wrote. 'If you also like Mexican food it's going to be a great night.' I didn't have to consider. This wasn't a man who'd asked if he could blow raspberries on my thighs, or who wanted to know what size my nipples were. We would have an ordinary date, and talk, I hoped, and that's exactly what we did. We had a beer, and ate together, and it was fine, in the end.

Marc had come straight from work and was somewhat crumpled, his hair unruly, a smudge on his face he had no idea was there. He was at a corner table, reading the paper, when I arrived, and he looked completely relaxed about meeting me. I, on the other hand, had spent all afternoon trying on clothes, and sighing at my reflection, and saying, NO NO you look TERRIBLE IN THAT. 'You look like a middle-aged man in drag,' I told myself, peeling off what had been – pre the ice-cream phase of the divorce – a dress I could once rely on to be flattering. I couldn't get my hair to dry properly; it kinked in bizarre directions. I put my thumb through my new tights, right on the shin, and had to chuck them. I wore the trusty (voluminous) navy blue frock, and put pearls on and took them off, and put make-up on in too dim a light and had to redo it, and swapped heels for flats and back to heels, and my heart beat hard all the way there in the cab. My face insisted on perspiring. I almost didn't go. I almost cancelled at the last minute because it was too hard, it was just *too hard* and why put yourself through this when you don't have to, when you could have a quiet, happy little solitary life doing your own thing with no one to answer to? This was the kind of thought spiral I got into in the cab.

Marc didn't look appalled by my appearance – in fact he looked relieved. He kissed me on the cheek and stroked my upper arm at the same time. Our eyes met and lingered; he'd been out in sunshine all day and the hazel was flecked with green, and there was something about his gaze that could make a girl blush. Our eyes kept meeting and lingering, while we talked about work, and cinema, and chat that led on from that. He said he'd only had one date so far – it had been their first and last, he added. They'd struggled to find things to talk about, he said, but nonetheless she'd taken it for granted that there would be sex afterwards, and he'd found himself saying that he didn't do that until the third date. We laughed. If I became a little manic, treating him to a perhaps overly frank emotional CV, telling funny stories in rapid fire, that was okay. I was nervous. He didn't mind. When it was obvious to us both that I was gabbling, he'd just stare at me, and his mouth would crinkle up, and he'd say, 'You can relax, you know. Shall we have another beer?'

By my reckoning we had five, spread over three hours, with lots of tacos and ceaseless talking, most of that admittedly mine. And then we split the bill, and went out onto the street, and he hailed me a cab, and kissed me on the mouth, and said, 'Sunday – are you free on Sunday for a walk?' I said I was. He said he was sure the walk would be fun. After that, Wednesday – was I free on Wednesday to go to a film? He'd get tickets. I said that would be nice. While the cab stood purring, waiting for me, he kissed me again, and for longer. He said, 'You know, Wednesday will be our third date.'

On Sunday's walk, ambling along, talking about cheese, he remarked suddenly that I wasn't anything like as fierce as he'd thought I'd be.

'Fierce?' I enquired, not entirely gently.

'Yes, he said – judging by the things you say about yourself on the profile, your academic interests, the anti-reality-TV jihad, I expected …'

I explained that I did that to save time. 'It's just a filter,' I said. 'It's getting straight to the things that aren't negotiable.' Lots of them, of course, *were* negotiable, but it was true that I was becoming more and more specific about myself, online. This, without doubt, was to do with my age. It was a way of shoring myself up. In a marketplace geared to superficial allure, it was a way of asserting other priorities and values, a way of feeling less invisible and more substantial. *This is me; I'm interesting; look how interesting and diverse I am* (I said, without actually saying it), *and if a small waist's more important to you, YOUR LOSS, BUDDY.* 'You,' I said to Marc, as we strolled along the riverbank, 'are not really there in your profile. You give nothing away.'

'Well, that's my policy,' he said. 'Bland in the profile, friendly in the email, lively at the pub. That's how the men do it.' This answer was so pat that he must have read it somewhere, I thought.

Or maybe not. It became swiftly clear that Marc was naturally decisive. Even after one date he seemed to assume that we were together, our searches over and done with, though of course it was possible he'd been the same with a string of others. (I couldn't help this thinking. It had become ingrained.) By Sunday he was holding my hand and saying things like, 'Maybe we should go away somewhere interesting for a weekend.' It's hard to react honestly to this kind of thing, this rushing ahead. The heart wants to leap with joy. The mind tells it to cool it, and slow down. In this case, the mind won the argument, and no Airbnb listings were scrolled through. But it's interesting how different life is, when – after a long drought – it appears that you might have a boyfriend. There's so much free time, for a start, when you're not obsessively trawling dating sites and trying to get perfectly ordinary blokes even to reply to you. That pursuit had become seriously time-depleting, of late, because the more they didn't want to talk to me, the more determined I became to break through. I was turning into a person who spent a lot of time trying to convince people of things. I'd spent a lot of time implying my own attractiveness to a whole host of men who couldn't really have given a toss.

But now there was Marc, who appeared to like me. Marc didn't seem to be fazed by other people's hesitations. He reminded me of a golden retriever I used to know. He didn't take it badly if you didn't want to play, but just waited stoically until you were ready. All of which made it easy, and also difficult, to navigate Wednesday's third date expectations. The difficulty came in knowing whether he was serious. It was possible I was getting myself in a ferment about something that wasn't even going to happen. But there isn't any doubt that I was getting myself into a ferment.

Third dates can be alarming things. On a third date it appears you've made a decision. Decisions are unavoidable, they're woven in – even though it's way too early to make decisions. Agreeing to a third date is usually going to be interpreted as interest in the possibility of the long haul. It's at this crunch point that a difference of evaluation might become obvious. One person's interest might tail off just as another's crystallises. The other person might need those three meetings to be sure you're a No.

I was worried that Marc might think we'd agreed to third date sex. I knew in advance that I wasn't going to be ready, not least because – in this case – the three dates had all taken place in the same week. Things had become compressed, and I really wasn't ready. Even the idea of read-

iness was a new way to think. In the old days sex had always
been spontaneous, when it happened. My ex-husband and
I got together at a student party. First date shagging ensued
(it wasn't really even a date) but we were barely adults, and
it all seemed perfectly natural then. But now – now, self-consciousness was potentially going to be a big hurdle, just as it
had been with Ralph at the beginning of all this. I couldn't
do much about that. It's one of the paradoxes of 50 that one's
fearless in so many ways, but when it comes to focusing on
the body … Being naked and saggy with a man you like is a
risk; that's just a fact. For some of us it's only our clothes that
are holding it all together. Even someone you like, and who
likes you back, might find that they mind that. They might
not be able to help it.

So, Wednesday came. We had a glass of wine in a pub,
and then Marc said he had a lovely bottle of white burgundy
chilling in his fridge (decoded: 'it's sexy time, baby'). I was
nervous about going into his flat with him, this man I didn't
really know, and the door closing behind us, and said so and
he didn't flinch. We sat out in his tiny city garden and drank
the lovely wine. It got too cold to sit outside, and he said we
should go in and warm up, and I said I hadn't realised just
how late it was, and that I ought to go. We stood at the
entrance and kissed. He said, 'Are you sure you don't want
to come in?' and I said I wasn't ready. He walked me to the
bus stop, and it rained, and we sheltered in a doorway, kissing again. Two teenage girls ran past with their coats over
their heads. One said, just as she passed, to the other, 'Did
you see those two old people? That's real passion. I want
that.'

After this I was away for five days on a long-arranged trip,
and so there was quite a gap (perhaps at a critical time) in
which Marc and I didn't see one another. Texting was only

possible intermittently. There was a lot of walking about holding my phone up, trying to get a signal, in order to receive messages and reply to them. His messages were not romantic ones, which was disappointing. I've always found affection via text and email reassuring, and heart-warming, when I'm away. There's something about it that's safe: a context for the trip that invites you home again, a loving backdrop to whatever you're doing while apart. Emotional home fires are shown to continue to burn. In this case, I hoped for a little bit of smouldering. When we'd left each other on Wednesday the promise of sex had been hanging in the air, and there'd been a passionate kiss in a doorway, one that kept returning to my mind. The scene might have been set for a little romance. His texts, however, were perfunctory.

To his own dating site motto, 'Bland in the profile, friendly in the email, lively at the pub', we should add, 'Brief in the text message'. Which is fine, theoretically. People who are digitally monosyllabic are some of the warmest people I know. Digital affection isn't their forte. But at the possible start of a possible something, on the brink of a relationship (and prone to pessimistic over-analysis), I would have hoped for more than 'Have a great trip!' and 'See you on Tuesday!' I would have hoped for kisses on the messages. I always sent two to him; we were at a two-kisses stage of things, in my own personal kiss hierarchy. Generally he sent one kiss, because I was at one-kiss status in his. While I was away, though, kisses were not offered. I continued to send the provocative two kisses on my updates from the Wi-Fi wilderness, to which he sent brief factual responses. He was working. He was fine. He was having a beer with colleagues. He was watching documentaries. He hoped I was having an interesting time. Smiley faces were used instead of kisses.

I saw him on Tuesday night, just after getting home. 'Can't wait to see you,' he texted, just before I got back. One kiss was added (apparently I was now back in the kissing zone). Come round for dinner, he said; it's only pasta, but it'll save you having to cook. I suggested we meet at a pub instead, and eat there, and he agreed. We drank beer and ate pies, and I told him about the trip. He put one hand over mine when I'd finished and said, 'You are going to want to sleep with me at some point, aren't you?' I must have looked surprised. 'It's just that you don't seem to want to come to the flat,' he said. 'I was hoping for a different kind of reunion than this. That's all.' He looked disappointed. 'I want a sexual relationship with you.'

This is one of the problems when dealing with people who are more or less strangers: knowing what's normal to them. For him, polite curtness in texts was normal, and sex after two weeks and four dates was also normal. I, on the other hand, was unhesitatingly affectionate in words, in our interludes, but cautious about rushing into bed, and Marc found that combination the odd one. We talked some more about it, over another beer. I told him that I'd begun to associate going to his flat with sex, and still wasn't ready. We were lucky to be in a pub anteroom, early in the evening, with no one else around to eavesdrop. He worried that I wasn't attracted to him physically (I was massively attracted to him; I just needed more time). He let slip that he'd been back to the dating site in my absence. Though only to answer messages, he added quickly; he always answered his mail. Not answering invitations is rude, he asserted. Having always felt the same, I couldn't exactly argue.

'So do you have anyone waiting in the wings?' I asked, my suspicion and self-loathing mounting.

'Not at all,' he said. He brought up the subject of my being hesitant again, and apologised for being pushy. He said I should take all the time I needed … but that he longed to know me better, and really knowing someone started with sex, and so he was impatient to begin. The statement started with his admitting that he'd been pushy, but ended with my feeling pressurised again. (Of course I'd been through this situation before, or one that mirrored it, with Peter, who found that I expected sex at our first meeting. Poor man. I can't help laughing.)

Sex started just at the point at which I'd slightly lost track of the number of dates we'd had, which is probably the right number, for me. I didn't feel I could hold off any longer; the weight of expectation was so heavy. And so, one night after the pub we went back to his flat and went to bed. We arrived at something, somewhere I was afraid might be the end, and that Marc was sure would be the beginning. The sex, you see, wasn't great. I know – almost all first sex isn't great. It so commonly isn't that it's almost a defining situation. I was really nervous, which didn't help. I avoided a full unveiling by ensuring that we relocated from his sofa and out of bright light at a key moment. I sent him off ahead to close the blinds, and turned the already-dimmed main light off in his bedroom (he was amused), and approached the duvet with so much haste – hoping to be a blur – that I almost broke his nose. Part under the covers, I got the chance to present myself in the only way that I could bear to, in the dark, half aware that I was shielding my stomach with a carefully placed forearm. All that self-consciousness wasn't ideal for letting go of the mind and becoming a sensory being.

The momentous event took place in a silence that continued afterwards, when I lifted his arm to put my head on his shoulder. I had to go to the bathroom, and he turned on his lamp and made fun of me for feeling the need to put my shirt on; I dressed myself in it from a sitting position in the bed. It was essential that I did so, because I needed to avoid being seen standing up, in my full glory. (I was ready for sex but I wasn't ready for that, not yet.) I'd chosen a loose shirt that falls to the thigh, for this occasion, so I could be casual about hiding myself, as if concealment were unplanned. I rushed off into the ensuite, and galloped back attempting jollity, as if it had been fun. Isn't it supposed to be fun? To be honest I just wanted to get home. When I came back to the bed he wondered if I'd like a strong drink, because he was having one.

No explicit criticism of anything surrounding the question of performance was made; we didn't talk about it. But I did wonder. There's so much written, now, about male assumptions, about extreme grooming and the necessity of being toned, and being open to experiment so as not to have Boring Sex. I didn't know how many other women he'd slept with, or if he watched a lot of porn; I wasn't quite neurotic enough to ask. But a miasma of disappointment hung around us both for the rest of that evening, drinking gin on his masculine sofa, in his masculine pad. His home was a classic of the genre: all greys and blacks, and starkly plain: it was print-free, painting-free, with expensive lighting, and was full of technology, every room wired for sound. Giant fridge with ice-maker: *check*. Shower made for two: *oh yes*. The style of his home life was feeding into my nervousness: the fact that he had a lot of magazines (consumer, motor, music), and hardly any books; the fact that his music collection was all post-1990; the fact that his stove was far too shiny and new for someone who, according to his dating profile, liked to cook to relax. There was no clutter. He had no possessions. He appeared to be living in a show home and making no dents in it. I did find myself thinking: Wow, we are really unalike.

When I got home again, the post-sex text message I sent him had three kisses on it. His goodnight message had one. 'Are we doing anything tonight?' I asked, the next morning.

He didn't answer until just before 8 p.m. 'Sorry! Just got this. Not tonight. Tired.' No kisses: instead, that smiley emoticon, one smiling so insincerely that I wanted to poke it in the eye.

I replied saying, 'What about tomorrow? Film?'

'Not tomorrow or day after; my mother's here,' he said. 'But I'm free the day after that.'

At the cinema, the day his mother returned home, we ate popcorn and he held my other hand on his lap. When we came out he asked, 'Are you coming back to mine?' and I said that I was and we smiled at each other. We drank red wine in his kitchen and trashed the film satisfyingly, and then he picked up the bottle and said, 'Come on, let's go and finish this somewhere more comfortable,' before leading the way to his bed. I was enormously attracted to him, but nonetheless more nervous than the first time, which shouldn't even have been possible. He decided he was going to take my clothes off, which should have been sexy but was actually unspeakably awkward. Somewhere along the way, from the end of a long marriage to there, I'd become more physically gauche than I'd ever been in my life. 'Hey, just relax,' he kept saying, which didn't help. He started coaching me a little bit. A 'tell me what you like' mutual conversation is good, but being coached isn't likely to make a person less anxious.

I was wearing another giant cotton shirt, which I'd dropped beside the bed, ready for reaching down to and putting on before standing up (again). I didn't ever do that with my ex-husband. 'We've just had sex; why are you hiding from me?' Marc said when I returned from the bathroom. He was looking at his phone; he was the kind of person who used natural intervals to check his messages. I asked how his mother's visit had gone, and he said it was fine, and didn't say more. He got up to put music on, an album from a band I didn't know, a series of mediocre love dirges. He said he'd been to their gig and liked their stuff. I asked if he had any old music on his iPod, and he seemed to think I meant the 1980s. He didn't like eighties stuff, he volunteered; it reminded him too much of his childhood. What about the seventies, I said; don't you like the music of the seventies? And what about Schubert? He shrugged. I asked why he didn't have pictures; he said he liked plain walls. I asked where he kept his books. He said he found paper books untidy and preferred to read on his Kindle. He rarely read books at all, in fact, he said, because magazines were all he'd got time for. I realised, looking around, that Marc was a neat freak minimalist.

On the way home I began arguing with myself. It was one of the Jims, from a few weeks back, who'd said, 'This is probably not a goer long term, but how do you feel about short-term fun?' That is how you need to think of this, I told myself. Stop second-guessing the outcome. Relax, and enjoy having someone in your life. Get to know him. Give it time. Build bridges. Learn something; teach something. Smile more. Go out to places, together. Stop thinking all the time, and enjoy the sex; the sex will improve. (People who've been married a long time before being flung out of their usual orbit into the unknown: they might have to give themselves these pep talks.)

I went to sleep feeling better, but was woken at 2 a.m. by my phone. Marc. He was going clubbing the following night, the text said, and had friends coming back to stay over. 'I don't imagine clubs are your thing,' he'd added.

'No, they're not my scene,' I replied. 'But that's okay; go clubbing, have fun, have fun with your friends.' (I was replying like I was his mother. It was a heart-sinking moment.) 'We don't have to see each other all the time,' I wrote, now absolutely miserable. 'I'm sorry I was so tense tonight, again,' I added. 'I don't know what's wrong with me; I'm wondering if it's something to do with all the trouble and rejection that I've had, in previous attempts at dating; it's been bad for my confidence.' (Here we were, being straightforward with each other via text in the middle of the night, in a way we weren't able to, face to face.)

'I don't want you to take this the wrong way,' his next text message said, 'but I'm not ready to be 50; I'm not even ready to be 42, to be honest.' I stood staring at the screen. He was breaking up with me. By text. 'You're a lovely woman,' he wrote, 'but I don't think this is going to work. To be honest, it kind of feels like you're in a different generation to me.'

A few days later, I called the midlife posse together (all of us are divorced) and met up with them for a bottle of wine. Several bottles. 'Evidently I am terrible in bed,' I told them. 'Even though I love sex; even though sex makes me happy.' My girlfriends rallied round. Of course you're not terrible in bed, they protested, eyeing each other and trying not to laugh. Why had I said that I had a boyfriend, at last? What I'd really had was an extended audition. Chief Sensible Friend said that it only looked that way in retrospect. Her view was that Marc went into the relationship in good faith and with high hopes, just like I did, but then – 'Because I am terrible in bed!' I interjected. 'Even though I love sex; even though sex makes me happy.' (This is what happens. I get repetitive on the fourth glass of wine.)

She reminded me that I'd also sensed that it was a mistake. 'You were already detaching yourself, once you'd been to his flat and saw that he had no books and that he listens to club anthems. It's your basic inescapable culture clash. He sounds like one of those perpetual boys, the ones with the Converse sneakers and skinny jeans, who are still into clubbing and drugs; it's all a big yawn.'

It was true. What had I been doing with Marc? We were completely incompatible. 'Maybe, but he's still only 42,' I told her. 'Some 42-year-olds still think they're in their thirties. They cling on to youth. I've given up the clinging. I'm ready to embrace middle age. I long for cosy sex again, like I had with my ex, before he had his head turned and went off.' (It's possible that the other woman was offering something other than cosy marital coupling, however.)

'Do you know what I blame?' Chief Sensible Friend asked. 'Porn – that's what I blame. Men have got over-visual about sex. They do sex more with their eyes now, when they used to do it with their hands.'

'Well, if they do it with their eyes we're all stuffed,' I said, and we laughed, in a sad knowing way, because we're all midlife and look our ages and don't usually have an issue with that. 'The trouble is,' I told them, 'that all this is making me visually aware of myself, too. I saw myself via an out-of-body experience, when I was in bed with Marc, and that was paralysing.'

'You didn't fit,' she said. 'That simple. A bad fit. He's never been married, for a start. His adult life has been divided into six- and eight-year relationships, one after another. He's a classic operator of the seven-year itch, and you really don't want to get into that.'

But why had Marc been with me in the first place? It occurred to me for the first time that there might be a reason that certain men favoured the menopausal. The ones who were determined never to marry or have children (to be *encumbered*, was how Marc put it) might be attracted to older women, and 50 is probably the youngest older woman there is. Whatever the case, it was clear that Marc used the culture clash as an excuse, when it was really the sex that was the issue. For me it was really the culture clash. I saw his apartment, and what it said about him, and heard him say that he disliked books because they're dusty, and knew we were doomed.

Having said that, if I'd been a woman with no qualms whatsoever about revealing her stomach to a lover in broad daylight, things would have been a lot simpler on the dating front, with Marc and also in general.

My pal Jack reacted as I anticipated he would. First sex with a new lover should be passionate and exciting, he said. It should make you blush, the next day, when you're walking to work and you have flashbacks. It should make you smile, remembering how naughty it was. You can't expect to have cosy sex with a new boyfriend, he said; everything hinges on the sex. But that can't be true for everyone. It isn't. I know of middle-aged people who've shacked up with other midlifers, both of them happy to under-achieve in bed. In dating site terms, it's another obstacle, another filter, one I need to consider. Perhaps there should be another field to fill in on the dating profile. *What kind of sex do you like? Choose. Hairless or Hairy? Theatrics or Cosy? Gymnastic or Chatty? Performance or Easy? Noisy and demonstrative, or Married-A-Long-Time style?*

A few days later I saw Marc on the street. I wasn't looking where I was going and almost bumped into him. He nodded at me, a wary nod of acknowledgement, and I grinned back. I found I didn't mind that he'd dumped me. It wouldn't have worked, and so it was actually okay. I hope I said this to him silently, through the vehicle of a wide smile, as we passed by one another on the pavement.

Needing to cast the net wider (again) I joined an expensive site that promised to deliver via the use of highly scientific (they claimed) matching software. Having used it, I can tell you that I'm fairly sure that if my parents had depended on that service, rather than meeting at a dance hall, if they'd ever been deconstructed by a questionnaire about their likes and dislikes and fed separately into a dating algorithm, they wouldn't ever have met. They wouldn't even have known that the other existed, having been prevented from meeting someone so obviously unsuitable by the selection system. He was into Beethoven. She is into Big Band dance music. He was a reclusive artist and gardener, forever in old painty clothes. She likes high heels and holidays. She eats Mediterranean, and rarely red meat, and he was a roast beef man. She reads romances; he never read fiction at all, and brought his six history books back each Saturday from the library. He liked old Westerns, and she's a family drama watcher. They had the happiest marriage I've ever encountered and wouldn't have been paired up on a dating site in a million years. Their being different what was made the marriage stimulating. It meant that each joined the other in their interests, and life was broadened. It was that unquantifiable extra dimension, unconditional love, that made it all synthesise into happiness. Compatibility can't actually be predicted by science.

I wasn't taken even with the premise of matches being delivered and access being denied to the pool. Another website I used listed candidates in descending order of compatibility, giving a percentage score. At least in that case they gave me the whole picture, and it was possible to have a look at the 35 per centers. Some of my most fun on-screen conversations were with 35 per centers. If you were to feed my old friends into the sausage machine they might not score better than that.

The algorithmic wonder site didn't allow me to see its workings at all. There were no hints or clues. I answered 250 multiple-choice questions, paid up, and the machine began to deliver people to my inbox. The results were baffling. Nobody was bookish or into art and culture and some offerings were distinctly of the UKIP sort. I know I have written in praise of difference, but this idea can be taken too far. Besides which, where were the similar people to add to the mix? There were no similar people. What was the algorithm playing at? Perhaps it was displaying a sense of humour. Perhaps its offering of right-wing philistine K2-climbers was a joke they liked to play on couch potatoes.

On the first day I was matched with an anxious-looking bloke in the Midlands who wanted 'a traditional wife', plus three Americans. One of them was a big tattooed biker who lived in Nebraska. A puzzled email to one of the site administrators drew the response that whether or not I liked the look of the guys in Birmingham and Nebraska, they were my best matches and that was that. Pages and pages of Americans began to arrive, hunched-shouldered men pictured in small sitting rooms in small towns, patiently waiting for love to be offered out of the worldwide web. Some of them were poignantly undeservedly alone, widowed by cancer, looking for help with motherless children (there's a book to be written, *Castaway* style, in agreeing to take on a stranger in a shack in Tennessee, but I am not that woman). Some were holed up in Arizona, pictured with cabinets full of guns – there were proud pictures of the guns – and some others were divorced red-pill types, in a rage about womankind. These men had serious trouble, in their profiles, in squaring their general misogyny with a friendly, wooing sort of tone. The information that you dislike and disdain womankind in general, *but are sure there are exceptions*, isn't recommended as a chat-up line.

I tried to be open to matches based in the UK, purely on the grounds of value. I was paying top dollar for this service and was determined to persist. I wrote a bland hello message to a handful of the men I'd been paired with. 'Hello, I see we've been matched; isn't this funny as we have nothing in common that I can see, but hello and how are you today?' I was interested in the responses I'd get. Perhaps an email conversation would result that would reveal that the algorithm was indeed as brilliant as it claimed, that it had bypassed the banal and gleaned deeper personal truths. But no one replied to me – not one person. They'd looked at my profile and had seen the truth, writ large.

As winter gave way to spring, a reply arrived in my inbox from Miles, a man I'd written to eight months before. Miles opened by apologising drily for the delay. Round-faced with wild grey hair, Miles was an academic and lived an hour away by train. His profile picture, I recalled, was rather dapper (three-piece suit, tie: a picture probably taken at a wedding), and he'd come over, on his page, as a glass-three-quarters-full person, consumed by enthusiasms; his only complaint about life was that there's not enough time.

Following a flurry of mutually reassuring emailing, establishing that there was conversational potential, I was invited to lunch a few days later. The day came, and after a morning of trying and rejecting dresses, opting instead for jeans, boots, a T-shirt and blazer, subtle make-up, big jewellery, I took the train nervously to his town, to meet at a restaurant he'd suggested. In fact, this was plan B. Originally he'd asked me to his house, which was in a village a further short drive away. 'Sod the protocol; come to my place on Sunday and I'll cook you lunch and we'll walk across the fields in the afternoon,' he'd written. What seems normal and sensible to one person – a few minutes' lift from the station – is impossible to others. I'm not able to get into a strange man's car unless the word *taxi* is printed somewhere on it, and even then I'm circumspect. I sometimes get spooked in a black cab, catching the driver's eye in the mirror, aware of the red light of the locked doors. I was cured at a young age of the urge to go to a stranger's house. There was a man in the children's playpark, when I was 10, who hung around to talk to me on summer evenings, and who insisted on 'helping' me swing; he'd pull the swing seat back, while I was sitting on it, so that my bum was pressed against him. He'd urged me to come to his flat one weekend to help make a cake, and wouldn't take no for an answer. I was an obedient child and so I agreed. My poor mother almost fainted when I happened to mention, after Saturday breakfast, where I was going. 'Never never never,' she'd said to me, half hugging and half shaking me. These life lessons are difficult to shrug off.

Miles thought I was being a little over-cautious. Caution will gain us nothing, at this stage of our lives, he said. As he was about to turn 60 this was perhaps a little over-inclusive, as I didn't feel I was quite at the bucket list stage of things, but never mind. I'd already checked his identity online; tenured academics are easy to check up on, at least. Maybe you could cook for me on the second meeting, I suggested, trying to be friendly and neutralise the apparent over-fastidiousness about safety. Retrospectively, I think I should have been far bolder about that, and disinclined to be defensive. Let's not ever be remotely defensive or embarrassed about safety. Let's be less tolerant of an attitude that expects us to make an exception of someone because he's obviously one of the good guys. No one should make a woman feel she's accusing a man of something, in refusing to get into his car. Anyway, Miles's reaction to the suggestion that he cook on the second date was positive. Good plan, he said; let's do that. Then he sent me another email, the night before we met, with pictures of his house, a new-build partly designed by him. Beneath the photographs there were thoughts about what he might make for lunch on our second date.

We decided to meet at the restaurant. After that, we'd mooch, he decided, around the streets. There was interesting mooching to be had, he said. 'How long can you stay?' he asked me. 'It'd be a shame just to come for lunch. Let's make a day of it: stay for an early evening drink, perhaps an early supper somewhere, before heading home.'

'I can easily do that, what a lovely idea, and thank you,' I replied. I organised a dog-sitter to cover my being away all day.

By the time I got to the bistro it was raining heavily. Miles texted to say he'd be late. I texted back to say I was already at the table. When he arrived, the man striding towards me, his wide mouth wider yet with grinning, looked a bit different to the person in the profile picture – but then no doubt so did I. He was wearing a cotton polo neck and giant plaid shirt. He was broader, and looked a decade older than in the picture, and was balding. I wasn't attracted to him, but I've learned not to make snap judgements. Sexual chemistry isn't always immediate. Sometimes it builds softly and surprises you. (I have subsequently met lots of women who agree with this, but haven't met a man who does.)

We ordered, and talked a bit about being single in midlife. He'd been divorced for almost ten years, and in the last four of those hadn't had a relationship that lasted more than a month. Perhaps you're too choosy, I told him; my mother's sure that I am. He didn't pick up and run with any of the personal cues I offered, throughout our meeting; he didn't go on to ask about my mother, or about my family or my origins, or my career. He found biographical chat dull, and wanted to talk about ideas, which was fun at the start, though somewhat exhausting over a long period. I did wonder if he was putting the lunch onto a tutorial footing. There was something vaguely interview-like about the set-up, as all the questions were his, and the ideas his, and I was the one called upon to respond.

We ate fish and drank white wine – I drank almost all of it, as he was driving – and drank coffee, and then I excused myself and went to the loo. As I rose from the table, which was the first time he'd seen me standing up, his eyes went to my hips and thighs (my belly and arse, unforgivingly clothed in denim) and his smile faltered. It didn't just fade; it actually fell away. It's safe to say that he was horrified. When I returned – his face was still grim – it turned out that he'd already paid the bill, and he wouldn't let me contribute. There comes a point at which insisting on paying half becomes an argument; I tried to insist but he wouldn't budge. I left a generous tip instead. 'This has been fun,' he said. 'It's tremendous to meet new people.' (I'm sorry to say that this 'nice to have met you' routine is almost always a kiss-off.)

We stood in the porch of the restaurant, under its awning, the rain hammering on it. He'd already made his decision. Miles, who is heavily set, sturdy in frame, his rounded midlife tummy pushing out at the cotton of his shirt, was about to make his escape. He may have had the shape of the habitual sitter at a desk, a physical flaw I'd already forgiven, but he couldn't bring himself to continue talking to me, despite having initiated the plan for the day. He wanted to abandon the date and wasn't embarrassed about it. The plan was abruptly jettisoned. Not that he said so. He just acted as if we were both in a rush. He looked at his watch. He looked at his phone and frowned. 'I could give you a lift to the train,' he said, 'but to be honest you'd be as quick to walk.'

'Oh,' I said, aware I sounded disappointed. 'So you're heading straight home? I thought we were going to mooch?' He had work to mark, Miles explained, not looking at me, and it was raining, so best call it a day. He said goodbye and went over to a big silver car, unlocking it and glancing at me, raising a farewell hand, as I opened my umbrella and crossed the road towards the station.

He didn't reply to my thank you text, sent in the early evening, thanking him for paying for lunch. Nor did he reply to the second one, asking if we were still on for Sunday. He'd said, before we met, that he was going to make me the best chicken casserole I'd ever tasted, and the best apple strudel in the universe. He'd said, before we met, planning the Sunday we would have together, that I should get a train mid-morning, and he'd pick me up from the station. We'd eat, and then we'd walk through the fields and woods near his house. After that, he'd make cocktails; he had an incredible Shetland gin, he said, and grew limes in his conservatory.

But that was all before we met, and he caught sight of my arse encased in old jeans, and decided against. He didn't reply to either of my messages. Instead, he added me to a mailing list for receipt of his daily email, a bulletin detailing the ups and downs of the day, bloopers from exam papers, a miscellany from his life. I didn't really understand what he thought our relationship was. Was it really okay, in his world, in his mind, to see a woman once and never mention it again, as if it didn't happen, and ignore her messages, but treat her like a buddy for the rest of his life? Apparently so.

Next there was an invitation from Lee (Leopold), an Austrian by birth. He was 47, divorced, childless, and said that he balanced his 'suit life', the uniform and obligations of the working week, by having Sunday adventures on a (huge muscly) motorbike. He'd only recently returned from a midlife gap year. He'd seen quite a lot of the world on his bike, travelling around it alone.

He wrote asking if we could meet for a drink. I should have said, 'Yes, that'd be lovely, shall we say Friday at 7?' That's how sane people respond. But I had to put Lee through the many hoops I had devised. He had to run round the course like a sheepdog, over barricades and jumps and through tunnels. The big email preamble hadn't worked before, but nonetheless I found myself attempting it again, because my confidence was low. Officially I'd shrugged off the summary rejection by Miles, though the truth was that the experience had bruised me.

My charm offensive appeared to work. 'I have a good feeling about this,' Lee wrote, after we'd messaged solidly for four days. 'I want to meet you soon as possible. I hope this isn't too forward.'

I replied with: 'I'm available on Saturday for dinner, and then sex afterwards. That's how you do *too forward*, hahaha.'

I thought it was reasonably funny – I wasn't actually serious, as I felt the need to point out in a second message – but online humour with strangers is always risky. Lee didn't think it was at all funny. I'm only able to assume this, because he didn't answer. It's embarrassing when this happens, when you embark on banter and find the other person isn't joining in. You can't see them, but you imagine their pursed mouth and muttered disapproval. And then you feel like an idiot. What's the female version of being left with your dick hanging out? I looked again at his profile, searching harder for hints hidden in the prose. Occasionally there are warning signs in a dating profile, like the silver sixpences in Christmas puddings that used to break people's teeth. Lee had said that he was 'self-contained', which can be a red flag. Not always, but sometimes.

Lee's pick would need to be A Hundred Percent Woman, he'd written. He'd used the word feminine three times. I intuited that my response hadn't been very ladylike. I messaged him. 'I'd like to play Q and A with you. Let's play Q and A! I'll start. Yes/no questions only. Scrabble: yes or no?' I waited, looking at my phone every five minutes, confident that a dull evening was about to be enlivened. It wasn't. Nothing. Silence emanated, noisily. I had a long bath and a soap bubble conversation with myself, out loud in the echoey bathroom. 'Why are these men so bloody wet?' I asked it. 'Why are they so easily scared off? Can't they rise to the challenge and at least be playful?'

The following day I heard from Lee. Perhaps we should meet, he said, though he felt he had to be upfront and say he had reservations about me. (Isn't that a charming thing to tell somebody? For heaven's sake. Either meet or don't meet: don't 'feel the need to be honest' and tell someone they might not be good enough.) 'Oh,' I said, 'reservations – and what are those? Is my sense of humour not feminine enough?'

'It's true that I was deterred by your apparent offer of sex on our first date,' he said, 'and though you assured me you were joking, I'm not sure that you were joking, entirely.' (This was also aggravating.) 'I like to take things really slowly,' he continued. I told him that, as it happened, I did too. 'So we should meet and have that dinner,' he said. 'Let's meet and see if we hit it off.'

'I don't know if you really want to get into anything, even a ninety-minute encounter over steak and chips, with someone who objects to their humour being critiqued as unfeminine,' I said.

'Femininity is important to me,' he said, 'and it probably is to you too; I think we're just using language in different ways.' I didn't think it was that. 'Bear in mind that I'm Johnny Foreigner,' he added (with a smiley emoticon). 'So let's have dinner.'

'Okay,' I said. 'Dinner would be nice; we'll go Dutch, which will be another nationality brought into the equation.'

'Sorry,' he messaged back, 'Dutch? What do you mean?'

'It's an expression,' I assured him. 'It means I'll pay half.'

'Oh God,' he said. 'You're not going to insist on paying half, are you?'

I stared at the screen, my mouth twitching. 'What do you mean by "femininity is important to me"?' I asked him.

'We can discuss this over dinner,' he said. 'It will make for a lively ninety minutes over steak and chips, though chicken for me as I don't eat red meat any more.' Good to know. 'Let me just say this, in case you misunderstand me,' he added. 'I'm a feminist, modern man who loves women. But I am not attracted to women who exhibit male traits. Perhaps I should also mention that I'm turned off by women who are dominant in bed.'

At this point, I was sure I didn't want to meet Lee more than once. (I mean, would you, honestly? Perhaps you would, if you think being reminded to be a feminine woman by your boyfriend is perfectly fine.) But I was curious and bored, and mildly freaked out by recent events, so I agreed to dinner. Shortly afterwards I received an email from Miles, apologising for the withdrawal of the invitation to lunch at his house. 'This will sound shallow,' he wrote, 'but I have a certain physical type, and I just wasn't attracted to you. I hope we can be friends.'

I messaged Lee. 'Let's play Q and A before we meet,' I wrote, trying again. 'I'll go first and we'll alternate with random questions. Here's my first. How do you feel about IKEA?'

His reply said: 'Why are you doing this? I don't want to answer your questions.'

'What do you mean?' I asked him. 'It's just fun. If you don't have the time or don't feel like it, just say so, but there's no need to be cross about it.'

'This is some pretty weird shit,' he said in his reply.

I was beginning to imagine what dinner with Lee would be like: it might involve a slide show of his world travels, and a lot of me-me-me. *Weird shit* was the clincher. When I said that we should probably cancel our dinner arrangement, he said it was already done. Now I was irritated, and couldn't let it go without a bit more of a fight. I wrote asking if a question about IKEA was interpreted as some sort of an assumption that I was preparing to go house-hunting with him. He replied saying that the subconscious was a powerful thing. I couldn't believe it. 'So,' I said, 'the first Q and A I attempted with you – the question about Scrabble: was that my subconscious wanting to rush ahead and buy our first marital boardgame?'

'You see,' he said. 'You're thinking about marriage. You used the word.'

I frowned at the screen. 'Are we joking?' I asked him. 'I think we're joking with one another, but I'm just not sure. Either we're joking or you're deeply strange.'

'It isn't me who's strange,' he said. 'You're the one who wants to dominate a total stranger with your demands for information.'

'Oh,' I said. 'I see – was that unfeminine of me?'

'This conversation is over,' he replied. 'Please don't email me again.'

When I logged on to a different dating site, the following day, the first thing I was confronted with was Miles's smiling face. It was a site he'd freshly joined (LOOK! NEW MEMBERS!), perhaps in the belief that he was getting away from me there and could continue his woman-hunt in privacy. I sent him a message via their system, just saying hello. He'd said he wanted to be friends. He didn't, though.

Back came the reply: 'I'm sorry again that I disappeared on you. I felt overwhelmed. To be honest all that stuff about wanting to be stitched into someone else's life was kind of claustrophobic.' But that had been a conversation about seriousness; it was a conversation about dating culture. More to the point, this fresh excuse was a straight-forward lie. It hadn't been anything to do with stitching. It had been about my body, as he'd confessed – more truth-fully – before this. But Miles had regretted being so frank, and had come up with a more gender-politically correct form of rejection. I asked what was wrong with wanting to be stitched into someone else's life, if the stitching was mutual and contented. He said that living alone had taught him that he needs to be fundamentally independent. Shared meals, evenings, nights, should be a matter of choice: surely that was a truly liberated way of life? When I argued with this, he interpreted my scepticism as a prop-osition. 'I can't offer you what you want,' he wrote. 'And nice though it is to hear from you, I can't offer you a date either.'

I wasn't looking for a date. 'I'm not looking for a date, but thanks,' I told him. 'Just saw your face pop up here and thought I'd say hello. All the best to you. Good luck.'

Then there was an email from Lee, saying that he regretted that we hadn't met, in the end, and that we should have had the conversation about femininity face to face, because if we had it might have turned out differently. We would have smiled while we argued. We would have enjoyed the debate. Good relationships need friction, after all, he said. How about a drink? Okay, I said. A drink. Why not? When, where? He didn't reply. I wrote again. 'Just name the day. Let's name the date.' Then laughed a lot at my own marriage joke.

The culmination of this series of blasts from the past was a dating site message from Peter. It was as if I'd conjured him up by thinking about him. Peter had my email address and mobile number, but opted for the formality of the site email system. 'Hello again, how's it going for you?' he asked blandly.

I told him it was going fine. He launched into an account of his life since he'd kissed my head and got on a train and had backtracked. He'd had a few short-term relationships. He'd thought he'd found the One, and then it'd turned out she wasn't. They'd got on each other's nerves. He'd realised that he needed to stop chasing the pretty girls and think about the intellectual fit.

'And so – why are you contacting me again, Peter?' I asked him. 'Have I been held in reserve until the wind changed?'

There was no answer to that.

Fundamental Ironies of the Game

SPRING, YEAR TWO

I turned 51 before spring came. I'd been doing this online dating experiment for a year, a whole year, and how much happiness had I squeezed out of it? Not a lot. The credits and debits in the ledger of love were not encouraging. There was a lot of red ink involved and my heart … not to push the point excessively but it was severely overdrawn.

'I need something!' I told the universe. The universe waited. It's a good listener, I find, but doesn't say much back.

I made a list in the dating diary of the qualities I'd really like in a boyfriend. I wanted someone cheerful, open, loving, friendly, curious, loyal, trustworthy, talkative. It flashed into my head that what I might need was an American.

I'd encountered a couple of Americans. There had been Trevor, who wasn't a great ambassador for his nation. And Jonathan, who was in some ways worse. Americans online, though: there were some fantastically nice Americans online. I knew this. And I wanted one.

Unfortunately I got talking to Todd, who said he could see he wasn't tickling my gina. 'My what? I'd be surprised if you could tickle my gina from that distance,' I replied. Then

I realised I'd heard the phrase before. It was something to do with provoking sexual interest via projecting status. Todd had been projecting status all over the place, since we started chatting, but I'd missed the whole gina-tickle objective, and had misinterpreted it completely; I just thought he was an arrogant, self-absorbed git.

The year before this, and because of a throwaway comment by an American man on a dating site, I'd found myself in what's sometimes called the *manosphere*, a sub-section of the internet where men talk about being men. (It's an international conversation, and not just an American one, but it had been Americans around whom the subject arose.) I don't know if the quadrant I wandered into was typical, but the disdain for women there was startling and vicious, and the label 'feminist' was used as a deadly slur. I started at a blog that had a lively comments section, then went off on a trail, travelling sideways into other blogs, following links into forums. There men complained that women are biologically determined to be illogical, dim-witted, spendthrift, prone to doing the opposite of what they say, and are in need of male control. I saw men advise that a woman should be denied things and told 'No' on principle, because it was vital not to let her keep getting her own way. Some men thought there were still women in the world who were redeemable if they were caught early and trained right; young women had more instinctive respect for male authority, they said, and could be more easily moulded to serve. Some others thought we were all a lost cause. As for middle age, the midlife female had no place or meaning, they asserted. The general view was that women over 50 were finished, made redundant by fresh young pussy (I quote), and should cast themselves out on an ice floe to die.

Some of these ideas were talked about in relation to marriage; in other cases, in the context of getting and managing a girlfriend. Many men complained that they couldn't get laid, entirely because (and they were confident in this diagnosis) womankind in general had become too entitled. There was a whole list of reasons why women were shunning them so very unjustly. It didn't seem to have occurred to any of them that their ugly shrunken souls were to blame.

This all started because the American, who was called Jason, accused me of shit testing him. I had no idea what he meant so I went to Google and looked it up, and spent an afternoon in silent wonder. A shit test is a provocation, vocalised by a woman in order to test the mettle of a possible or actual partner. The theory is that all women shit test (whether they know it or not) in order to determine the status of a male. I had an on-screen conversation with Jason. 'I've just looked that up. Shit tester. It seems to mean, a woman who disagrees with you.'

'Not at all. Your understanding is very superficial. All women shit test. It's hard-wired. You are programmed to want to identify the best mate, and in identifying him you throw up obstacles we are meant to overcome.'

'Do you have personal experience of this process, or is it something you've been told is true?'

'All men have personal experience of it.'

'Can I ask you something: if I had approached you, rather than letting you approach me, here on the site – would you have replied to me?'

'Absolutely not. Good women don't chase men.'

'What's a good woman?'

'You know what a good woman is.'

'Am I shit testing you now, by having this conversation?'

'Yes you are.'

'See, I would just characterise this as debate. Is debate not allowed? If I disagree with you about something, that's shit testing, is it?'

'Not always but we are in a specific environment here, in which we are trying to determine whether the other person is the highest status mate we can get for ourselves.'

'I'm not interested in status.'

'Yes you are. You just don't know you are.'

'That's the kind of comment that shuts down all debate, though, isn't it, if you are the only one in the conversation who knows what each of us thinks.'

'Well, it ought to.'

'You don't think I know my own mind?'

'In my experience women don't, in general. The exceptions tend to be masculinised to the extent that men aren't attracted to them.'

'Am I masculinised?'

'It's hard to say. You have masculine attributes, yes. But it's all about a balance. You may have sufficient qualities to balance that out. I don't know you. I'd have to meet you and see how you are in real-world conversation.'

'I don't have any interest in doing that, however.'

'Ah. I failed your shit test then.'

'No. You're just a weirdo.'

'I'm not interested in you either. I'm looking for a feminine woman, but there are very few left.'

It's interesting, incidentally, that Neil Strauss, whose book *The Game* led to a widespread dissemination of these woman-wrangling techniques, recounting his own life as a PUA (pick-up artist), has married and become a dad and believes in everlasting love and has recanted. He makes the point now that he approached the community as a reporter, while admitting freely that he got sucked in. He came to detest his seducer persona and rejected the ideas he appeared to endorse, but the online community didn't really get this message; they continue to see the book as a manual. It's also interesting that the latest cult misogynist superstar, who often goes by the name Roosh V, has disciples who demonstrate a telling irony, namely that they much prefer to socialise together and have man-conferences than to talk to actual women in the actual world. Lots of these men seem to be caught up in a contradictory vortex of yearning and hatred.

For months I'd been coming across men who bought into the idea of *negging*. That's when a man makes negative remarks supposedly designed to prompt banter, to a woman perceived as high status (and thus used to being lavished with praise), in order to project his own greater status. Men were even using it on low-status women like me, because they'd been promised it was a short cut to sex. The projecting of status is a key topic among men who think talking to women and having relationships demands technique. They don't seem to understand what a relationship is. They don't, in general, want relationships at all, it seems to me: the way they talk about *gaining sexual access* suggests getting something for free that would otherwise have to be paid for. The idea behind the concept of *game* is that men use a catnip-like combination of power and charm, triggering interest in the female target. Sometimes, and apparently without irony, the word *charisma* is used to define this.

One day I got a message that said: 'I'm not intimidated by you, but I can see that you're a waste of my time.' I hope he didn't pay a lot and go on a residential course, or anything, because I just ignored him. Another wrote: 'In general I avoid one-itis but you might be the one.' I looked up *one-itis*. Apparently it's to do with fixation on a particular woman and the belief that only she will do, when 'the truth' is that many women are all equally suitable.

I heard from a man in Ireland, who illustrated the general trend. 'Can I just say how much I like your shoes; they go with your eyes.' I'd seen 'Nice shoes, they go with your eyes' advised as a pick-up line. My shoes were silvery grey, in the picture he was referring to, and my eyes are dark brown. The compliment was supposed to intrigue me. I was supposed to write back, bemused, to point out that my shoes weren't remotely like my eyes. And I did. We were having a conversation now, which was the point. His next gambit was this: 'I like the way you wear your hair, but you'd look even better if it was long.' Thanks, I said. 'I notice you say you like modern art,' he continued. 'This doesn't reflect well on you because it's all celebrity and basically shit, and contradictory because you also say you hate celebrity culture.'

'Modern art is like modern anything else,' I wrote back. 'It needs to be judged case by case. It can't be written off simply because it's modern.'

'You're a very attractive woman, on the outside, and I knew you'd be as interesting on the inside,' he wrote.

'I think I read that line on a website somewhere,' I told him. 'A PUA website. Women read them too, you know. They don't have hormonally activated locks, or anything.' He was silent. 'Why do you feel the need to use somebody else's words?' I asked him. 'It's none of my business I know, but I'm sure you'd be far more successful if you were yourself.' There was no response. 'Okay, you don't want to talk about it and that's fine, but on saying farewell here's a piece of advice: in general women can sense when they are being fed lines, or being managed, and we don't like it, and so it's counter-productive. Bye.' (Can you just imagine the masculinist hoo-hah if women started writing manuals about managing men?)

Two days later he replied: 'You women should stay out of the manosphere. It's not for you.'

'I don't understand why you'd use these lame set approaches, when you say on your profile that you're Looking for the One.'

'Women like to hear that.'

'So it's just another line.'

'Look, you're talking to me, aren't you? If I'd written "Hi, fancy a cup of coffee?" like I used to, you would have said no.'

'How do you know that? You don't know that.'

'Women here are a nightmare; they think that just because there are search fields, they can get princessy about only having a prince.'

Another man was open about saying he was a practitioner of charisma. 'Charisma – are you a PUA type?' I asked.

'Whoa. You're very well informed,' he replied, with three kisses and two smileys.

'So why do you do it?'

'It's a way of getting badly behaved women to go to bed with me.'

'Badly behaved how?'

'Women who can be charmed into bed by a stranger.'

'Who are they, these women?'

'I meet them on Twitter. Twitter's a player's paradise. Using charisma means I get to date women out of my league. Usually I only get to date the fat ones.'

The manosphere is notably unkind to the female-and-overweight (in fact I notice that midlife women are assumed to be overweight; it's a part of our general inexplicable failure to arrest time and to put men's needs before our own). It would be interesting to read the weights in kilos of the men who frequent these discussions, and the belly-girth measurements. It's widely advised that fat women should be invisible to men, because men need to have more self-esteem than that. (They might also need bodyguards. If I see anyone wearing one of those *No Fat Chicks* T-shirts – the ones available in a size TRIPLE XL – I might push him under a bus.)

It was when I first encountered the men of the manosphere becoming enraged about women *refusing to settle* that my ears pricked up. The signs were there that these were men of 'low social value' and 'low sexual prestige' (to bounce their own cod-sociological terminology back at them). Women, they said, must stop refusing to settle and learn to take what is on offer. Them, in other words.

So now, in the second spring, there was another reader of manuals who wanted to try out his lioness taming on me. 'Does it ever occur to you, Todd,' I said, when we were discussing his pick-up artistry, 'that there's a fundamental irony at the heart of these women-handling techniques?'

'How so?' he said.

'It seems to me that a lot of the men who say that all they want is sexual access are playing out some other drama, and what they really want is to be loved unconditionally. If finding a woman to love is the goal, dehumanising her into a target so as to make her love you is beyond ironic: it makes "love" into a meaningless word.'

'Look at you, trying to dominate me.'

'Are men really threatened that much by our being self-determining? I saw advice being dished out that men should avoid women on dating sites who use words like "independent", "strong" or "ambitious".'

'Sounds sensible to me.'

'Isn't it kind of ironic that the umbrella subject of all this talk is affection, but uses such hostile language?'

'Whatever,' Todd told me.

'One last thing, Todd,' I said. 'The woman in question might be holding your hand when you die, but seems to me it's quite likely that she'd also be the one who put the poison in your soup.'

Whenever I came up against these men I felt shaken afterwards: it was like coming across a Nazi. I know that sounds extreme, but I'd read enough to know that they're extreme people whose heads have been filled with danger-ous ideology. I had to take deep breaths and remind myself that they were in the minority. I counted all the lovely men I knew, who would be horrified by this dehumanising objec-tifying crap, and all the friends of those friends and relations, and all the men in the networks of those friends, who would also be horrified, and managed to stop hyperventilating. Fascinating though it was, I had to prevent myself from doing any more reading of manosphere forums and blogs, because my adrenal gland was becoming over-tired.

I talked to Todd once more that week, and then I stopped talking to Todd. Evidently he'd gone for some sort of top-up vampire serum, or suchlike, because he came roaring back in flames of dickhead righteousness, and started calling me Princess, and asked me if I had a cat.

Thankfully a powerful vaccination was at hand. Things perked up tremendously when I got into conversation with a very different sort of an American. Cliff. Cliff found my raising the subject of the manosphere and pick-up artistry galvanising. It had been a huge media topic in the US, he said. The so-called philosophy had trickled into academia. People were doing PhDs on it. He thought Strauss had writ-ten his book as a satire, though many of his fellow Americans weren't habituated to irony, he added.

Cliff and I started talking and chatted on and off for a month. Cliff was very good medicine after the woman-haters. We had the kind of instant rapport you might develop with someone at a drinks reception: you monopolise each other for a while, and talk and talk, and you're just on the point of saying you should swap numbers and meet again, because you're convinced you've just made a new friend, when the other person says they have to go and they leave without a backward glance – because they have these sorts of conversations at parties all the time. This is their normal, though it isn't yours. That's what happened with Cliff, who lived in California, and with Paul, a man of a broadly similar type, who lived in New Mexico. I was the one who instigated contact with both of them, having decided that I needed to get out of the closed circuit I was locked into.

I'm not going to claim that American men are more dynamic and interesting than British men. I have insufficient data, by a mile. But I have to tell you that whenever I needed cheering up, I'd go and search in the American part of whatever dating website I was surfing. Usually I was cheered enormously. There was something on offer, in the US listings, that I wasn't finding at home: intellectual curiosity and a seize-the-day attitude coupled with a willingness to chat. There was time set aside to chat to me, purely on a pen-pal basis; perhaps the knowledge that we'd never meet made this easy. There was never any pressure or expectation. After a month of intermittent emailing, Cliff and Paul both treated me like their pals. In both cases their friendliness extended to invitations to go and stay, to be shown around campuses and taken to the coast. Cliff gave me his address and said if I was ever in Santa Monica … and for five full minutes I seriously considered buying a plane ticket.

What stood out about both of them was the energy with which they attacked life. Beyond the working day, the routine social pattern, there was language learning and travelling; sidelines, projects and charities. They'd undergone therapy and knew themselves pretty well, or at least could talk as if they did; there was self-imagining and self-improvement. All of which stood out starkly against the average British male's profile clichés (box sets, sofas, wine, walks, pubs, beaches, sport). Don't get me wrong: I don't practise Californian levels of dynamism either, but you see that was precisely the point. At a time at which life cried out to be reinvented, becoming the girlfriend/life partner/buddy of a man who treats each day as if it might be his last, a man truly alive in all six senses, was beyond attractive. For a while it virtually became a craving. I yearned, for a time, to be an outsider absorbed into another culture. I yearned for sunshine, literal and metaphorical.

Disillusioned by the sheer number of British men who had no wish to know me, I decided that it might as well be an international search. I was prone to the full Atlantic merger fantasy: a green card, legal alien status, and then a marriage to an eccentric, articulate loving man with a great accent: all this flashed up in my head before I'd even ticked the box. I wrote to some Norwegians, too. I had an idea that Scandinavians might be taller than average, quirky, congenially serene, bohemian and unmaterialistic. So it goes, so it went, in the personal racial mythology of one woman's head. I found lots of alluring, interestingly dressed, well-read, well-travelled 55-year-olds with Nordic cheekbones that I could project a two-nationality UK-Scandi fantasy happily onto. I also wrote to some Germans and Finns. I wasted three hours one night tracking down romantic second husbands from among the northern races, and writing them charming notes that were never replied to.

Paul and Cliff both knew how to write a profile, aside from anything. They were cool. They knew their way around a bookshop and listed unexpected genres of interest, and talked with real enthusiasm about them. The conjunction of high and low culture was refreshing. Cliff played a musical instrument and wrote songs, meditated and practised martial arts, climbed, horse-rode, cycled, swam, ran marathons, cooked to relax, mentored other people: he seemed to be living three lives at once.

But then I noticed other details. Paul said he thought life was a process of constant recalibration. He saw himself as an identity in progress, a soul in transition, a personality that was still in flux. He'd done the work on himself and was continuing with it. A voice in my head told me that people who are so driven might not be tolerant of those less so. These men might be the male dating equivalent of Tiger Mothers. They might prove to be Tiger Boyfriends, forever cracking the whip for their partner's better time management. Nor might hyper self-awareness always be a good thing. It might be exhausting, living with one of these dynamos. Their expectation of high achieving might turn swiftly into critique of the person sitting next to them. Perhaps that's why they were divorced.

Mike, a third American candidate, proved to have the supernova of all wish lists. The woman of his dreams, meticulously described, was to be tall but not a giraffe. She was to be elegant but not label-fixated. She was to be groomed but not beauty-parlour-oriented. She was to read like a whirling dervish and teach him something new every day. She ought to be able to discuss theology and theoretical physics with equal levels of competence and zeal. She ought to have read the following (list) and she had to like the same movies (another list). It went on and on. His idea of compatibility was that the other person would be identical to him other than for gender. I'm still curious as to whether the two or three women in the whole USA who fitted the bill exactly got in touch with him, or whether he's still out there, batting away enquiries from people who haven't got the right level of chat about *Being and Nothingness*. (Me for instance.)

In practice, the relationship I'd had idle fantasies about would probably have lasted as far as the first weekend. All three of the men were teetotal, and I'm fairly sure they'd have viewed the average Friday night alcohol intake of a northern European as pathological. Cliff especially, who would have fitted well into the Victorian temperance movement. I chalked this up as a negative and then I thought to myself: Why are you even having this interior monologue about a man in Santa Monica? This is utterly time-wasting and idiotic. Stop it, I instructed myself sternly. So I did. Both Cliff and Paul were losing interest in chatting, having both started dating, and the contact came to a natural halt.

I was a little bit sad about Cliff. I'd become really fond of him. It was a little bit sad not to get his slightly manic, funny messages in my inbox any more, but I was cheered up, in fact made slightly hysterical, by an episode the day after, involving mobile phones. Technically, probably a dozen men have my mobile number (it might be a lot more; I am slightly afraid of making a list), though as I write this, none have been in touch since we parted – or since things ended without ever getting going. On this particular night, the weekend after slapping my own wrist in response to my American-man addiction, I got a text from an unknown number. The number was unknown but the sender, clearly, was known to me already. 'Just got new phone,' it read. 'Can we talk again tonight?'

Now, I had no idea who this was, but it was almost certainly one of the two men I'd been talking to in the last week. Both of the phone conversations, with Greg and with

Rich, had been fairly brief. I was guessing it was one of those two, but which? I couldn't respond with, 'Who is this?' because the natural reply to that would be, 'What do you mean who is this? Just how many men are you talking to?'

So instead I said, 'Hi! Have you had a good day?'

The trouble was, now I was kind of pretending I knew who it was. Or I would have asked. And I hadn't.

'Pretty good,' the reply buzzed back. 'Went swimming after work and felt much more relaxed afterwards.'

Aha! I knew that Greg had been planning to start swimming after work. It was Greg. 'Can I call now to talk about the date?' he added in a follow-up text.

'Yes, do,' I replied.

The phone rang and I answered it. 'Greg, hi, hello, how are you this evening?' I said confidently.

The voice on the other end said, 'Who's Greg?'

In the end I didn't meet either of them. Rich was too offended that I'd called him Greg. Greg emailed to say that he had to address some long-standing issues about his sexuality, so I was kind of relieved he was bailing on me. Even though he *was* American.

Landings on Islands

SUMMER, YEAR TWO

I came across Martin when I did because of an idiot. I don't know why it is that men not interested in a woman would think to write to her to tell her so – it must be about power, of some sort, mustn't it? I received these rejection slips every now and then. The one that sticks in my mind simply said: 'Not my type, sorry.' (I hadn't approached him, nor seen him on the site, and had absolutely no idea who he was.)

On this occasion the message said: 'Just wanted to tell you that while you look lovely, I'm looking for someone younger.' He was 55 and his profile stated that he wanted someone 'under 35, preferably 24–29', so I asked what he was doing straying into the geriatric-females area of the site. 'I was trying to compliment you,' he wrote. He'd been divorced for a year, having left his wife 'when she became overweight and argumentative'. He'd spent his whole working life supporting her and their children, he argued, and now he deserved a young woman, one who was firm-breasted, flat-bellied and tight. But what about compatibility? I asked; what about going into old age with someone? He didn't plan to retire for another twenty years, he said. He was young and vital. 'As for having things in common, if she's young enough, she can learn.'

After this I craved a conversation with a regular human. Having exhausted the local line-up of men (we'd exhausted each other, in fact), I cast my net wider. Generally I stuck to a circle drawn around the accessible hinterland of my own city limits, of about an hour's travel, so that dating in a casual way was possible. Distance makes this difficult; a trip to the cinema is loaded with expectation when you've had to travel far to get there. I knew this, but I couldn't help myself. I extended and extended until I blundered into the catchments of other cities, and saw a whole new row of faces. There was one among them I was immediately attracted to. Not the handsome tanned one, nor the actor, nor the floppy-haired Peter Pan type: none of those. The potato-faced one, the teacher with the ridiculous goatee and twinkly eyes: that was the one. Martin. I went to his profile and experienced one of those immediate recognitions, the sort that tells us that someone newly met is already a friend. He'd written a funny essay about his life, breaking it down into categories (*hairstyles I have been pictured with*; *music phases I have gone through*, and so on). 'No expectations of who I'll meet, what they'll be like; no checklist,' he'd also written. I sent a one-word message: 'Hello.' Martin's online green light wasn't lit, but as I watched, I saw it light up. He'd received an alert to say mail was waiting, and in turn I got a notification saying he'd visited my profile.

Shortly after this a message arrived in my inbox. 'Hello! How very nice to hear from you. I see we have almost spooky similarities, and what's a hundred miles between friends? How's the weather looking, where you are? I've been trying fruitlessly to fix my car, which has been going URUGUGURUG when I'm pretty sure it shouldn't. I was so excited to get a message that I probably have oil on my phone.'

I asked Martin if it was really that rare, receiving a message. I got lots, I told him, though most were variants on 'Ello darlin', fancy a shag?'

'I've only been here a month,' he said, 'and none of the women who've contacted me have appealed. I hope that doesn't sound arrogant. But there's got to be basic shared language, don't you think? I'm not here just for the shags. I want a life partner. I hope that doesn't put you off. Might be bad to mention wanting a life partner in the second message.'

When he reached his laptop the conversation continued for most of the evening. He was bright and lively; it was like standing with a glass of warm white wine at a dull party and suddenly finding someone entertaining to talk to. It was rather like chatting to Cliff the American had been, in fact. When I logged off I copied Martin's profile page to my laptop and spent a while looking at it. I zoomed in on his potato head, slightly piggy eyes and squashy nose, and began to feel vaguely proprietorial about them. Just before logging off I got a message from another man, that said: 'You look young for your age; can I see some pictures of your body now, to see if you're young all over?' Sometimes an invisible hand comes out of the internet and paws at you. I got Martin's page up again, and looked at it, and immediately began to feel better.

The next morning, at just after 6.30 a.m., Martin messaged again. 'Really early, in a rush, as I'm teaching at a summer school for most of the holidays, and I'm going for a run first, but just wanted to say, what a delight to meet you last night. Very much looking forward to talking more. See you at the usual place at around 8 p.m.? If you're free that is. If you're not out on a date with some young hunk.'

'Date? What's that?' I asked him. 'Hereabouts it's a Middle Eastern fruit eaten at Christmas. I'll see you around 8 p.m.

at the usual virtual corner. Wait, this does sound like a date.'

'It is, it is,' he wrote. 'I'm bagsying you this evening. Accept no other offers!'

I looked at his page again. It was a deft summing-up of a person, of Martin's mental landscape; it gave full rein to self-promotion, and then knocked that idealised man down with a satirical second voice, as if recording his own inner reaction to it. I'd seen this attempted once before, and in that case it had come across merely as bragging. A key consideration when writing an online profile – and one of the easiest things to get wrong – is tone, and Martin's tone was just right. It made me want to tear up my own page and begin afresh. I really liked the look of him, too, in his pictures: 44 years old, sturdy, tall, with a receding hairline, he was a man unafraid to rock a checked shirt and brown cords, and his smile was mischievous. Barely half an hour after getting going with the day, I had to stop and look at his profile again. My eye ran down the questionnaire part of the page, and it was then that I saw something I hadn't registered before. In answer to the question, 'Do you want children?' he'd written, 'Undecided'. I hadn't taken that in, in previous readings. I messaged him. 'Just noticed you are undecided about children. I'm past that point. If children are a maybe we'd better say cheerio, I think.'

His reply said: 'At work but just had to say, not an issue, I promise you. I tend to the No more than the Maybe.' At 4.30 p.m. there was a follow-up. 'The point is it'd be No if my partner/wife was also a No, and Yes if she was a Yes. It'd be up to her. Left to myself I'd happily be a No.'

That evening we talked on screen again. Afterwards there was a message at 1 a.m., another at 6 a.m., then two at lunchtime. The following evening, emboldened by our growing rapport, we swapped real-world identities and email addresses, and Googled each other, and tried out comedy on one another, going into our stand-up routines about our failings – which is actually a useful way of airing some of the cons, to balance out the relentless pros of your online listing. By now it was clear we were hugely compatible. But, as I was learning, email compatibility isn't something anyone should rely on. At least, I *should* have been learning that.

It's easy to fall for someone over email. What's difficult is following through into life. The closer email conversation brought us, the greater the risk that a real encounter, in a café after a train journey, would be the beginning of a big let-down. I might not like him. It might be mutual. He might take against my middle-aged body on sight (this has happened, after all; it is not imaginary). In person, he might dominate the conversation, in a teacherish way. He might not be used to being interrupted unless I put up my hand. He might be accustomed to being right. He might be pompous and given to monologuing. He might think that I was. It might turn out that beneath the veneer of amiability there was a vicious temper and a short fuse: it was possible after all. We might find we'd said everything we were ever going to, in typed words. We might have an instant, chemical hormonal realisation that it would only ever be a sibling sort of love.

I could see that it would be easy to put off meeting indefinitely, so I suggested seeing each other at the weekend. In effect I was asking him out; I gave myself props for this. He said he was going climbing with friends, but yes, soon. Next week. Meanwhile we continued messaging. Emailing took us into our childhoods, our student days, our marriages and our sad stories. Martin had only been married a couple of years when the relationship broke down. They were separated but not yet divorced, it turned out.

This isn't necessarily a deal-breaker. Like lots of people, I started dating before I was (technically) divorced, because the divorce wasn't finalised until over two years after separating. There are people who say, 'Never date the separated but not yet divorced,' but in truth there is no fixed rule and it varies a lot. In my own case, the split with my ex was absolute and uncompromising, rather than dragging on; in reality we were divorced from that first day, from the moment of his announcement that he wanted out of the marriage. I didn't wait two and a half years to start dating, although you could argue that I began too soon. Martin was coy about the exact timing of his separation. 'I'm afraid I initiated it, the split,' he wrote. 'We wanted different things.'

'Oh, you're not divorced yet?' I asked him. 'Are you sure you're ready for this, for meeting someone new?'

'I couldn't be more ready,' he said.

He went on his climbing trip and was silent, as he'd warned me he would be, and I was twitchy and stayed quiet; it's important to know when to be quiet. I heard from him at 7 a.m. on Monday morning. There was a text at lunch, and then in the evening he wrote about his weekend, and I told him about mine. 'I feel like I'm falling in love with you,' he replied. 'Couldn't stop thinking about you, at the cottage. Couldn't stop myself rereading your messages. Never experienced anything like this. Caught up, caught up in it. Can't wait to meet you: shall we meet this weekend? I can come to you, or you to me. Don't mind. Can barely even wait until then.'

Now, our emailing became a continual conversation, and I was writing three or four long messages a day. They were beyond the usual scope of email. They were letters. He wrote back typically ninety minutes after receiving one of mine, at similar length. In other words, it was pretty much all either of us were doing or thinking about. Life was put aside. In addition, Martin had turned out to be an adept player of Q and A, the text game. He answered with verve and asked his own good questions. *Should trifle have jelly in it? Did I believe in sea monsters? Were there books I was embarrassed about loving? Were there words that offended me? What country in the world that I hadn't yet visited did I imagine I might want to live in? Did I still have any of my childhood ambitions?* Good questions, all.

We didn't talk, but the written word grew more and more intimate, without being remotely erotic. Instead, there was a dizzying deepening of friendship. Virtual romance budded and blossomed. At night we had typed conversations that had the quality of a long phone call, like those in the days before the internet, sleepily pillow to pillow. I'd done this before and it had gone horribly wrong, but this was different; this was *different* (I told myself). We found we had similar likes and dislikes, some of the same favourite books, music and films. We liked the same kind of travel, the same kind of art, the same kind of whisky. He said he'd never encountered anyone to whom he felt so immediately attracted. I said I felt the same; I said that we *really must* meet soon. Martin appeared to agree. 'Let's make sure to do that this weekend,' he wrote the next morning. 'Though I'll be quiet tonight as I have to go to a birthday party, and the likelihood is that it will turn into an epic.' Then there was a second message. It said: 'Before I go, I have a last question for today: what's the most unexpected sex you've ever had?'

Later, I wished I hadn't answered the question at all. Possibly my answer overstepped somehow; perhaps he had fixed ideas about femininity or some such, some complication, some agenda. But why had he asked the question, if he didn't want to know the answer? Was I supposed to respond,

'I haven't had unexpected sex, not yet; are you planning on surprising me?' Instead I told him about an afternoon in a meadow with an old boyfriend. I also told him that I once had sex on a desk in an office after hours. He got two for the price of one, as they'd been unexpected in differing ways. I thought we had gone into another gear, a pre-meeting, pre-dating gear, and were daring to tell our secrets to one another. Martin's question had, I thought, the beginnings of erotic possibility; he was sounding out a sexual component to our friendship, reminding us where this was going to lead. Or so I thought. Later, I wondered about the use of the word *unexpected*. Perhaps I misinterpreted the question. I'm still wondering.

So, he went off to his party, and just as he'd warned me, was not in touch that night. But then there wasn't a message in the morning either, or at lunchtime, or the next evening. Finally I texted him. 'Martin? I'm missing you. Missing our contact and conversation. Hope all is well. Is all well?' There was no response. In the late evening, still not having heard from him, I read my candid email a dozen times, becoming increasingly regretful about sending it. I'd told him my secrets – he'd invited me to – and now he'd clammed up. I felt increasingly vulnerable. What I wanted to ask was, 'Did you hook up with someone at the party? Why aren't you talking?' Instead I asked, 'Have you died of alcohol poisoning?' Texts are easier to answer if you haven't time or can't be bothered. They only require one line.

'Sorry,' his text reply said. 'Still fighting massive hangover, and backed up with work.' The disingenuousness of this was crushing. It wasn't really an apology at all; it was the cold shoulder. The open, affectionate pen-pal and prospective lover had become, overnight, a person who was neither open nor affectionate. After a sustained period of near-hourly communications (after 'I'm falling in love with you; caught up, caught up in it') it was all too likely that 'backed up with work' was a form of obituary. When a man tells you he's overwhelmed with admin and that's why he isn't talking, he isn't interested in you any more. When a man tells you, in different words, that he doesn't want to see you, it's best to take him at his word. Work is never more important than love; not really. A five-minute pause can be found, inside most days, no matter how pressurised, for a loving, apologetic note, a quick phone call, an airborne kiss, a 'missing you'. He hadn't missed me or he would have said so. He would have added that he couldn't wait to get home, to email, to call. If a man doesn't rank you higher than work commitments, you are about to be toast. His ardour is cooling fast, but he doesn't say that. Instead he says how busy he is.

Determined to meet him, to ride over this unhappy blip, I wrote that I'd looked at trains for Saturday, and listed suggested timings. 'We can do this first date entirely alcohol free,' I said, 'so as not to punish your liver further; I'm sure we're up to that stark sobriety.' We hadn't spoken yet on the phone, and it seemed imperative, now, that we did. 'I want to hear your voice,' I told him. 'I'm ringing you.' The call went straight to message.

In terms of the timing, it seemed as if it started at the party – what happened at the party? Or perhaps it started during the hill-walking weekend with his buddies. Perhaps one of them pointed out that Martin didn't really know me, that he wasn't even divorced yet, that he should slow it all down. Perhaps they looked at my profile together. Perhaps another of the friends thought I was too old. Perhaps Martin showed them the unexpected-sex email and one of them was horrified by it. Perhaps a little doubt was sown. Did he think sex in a field (or on a desk) was somehow disgusting? Was I going to shack up with a man who – it turned out – could only do it with the lights off and under a duvet? And why didn't I know that about him? I knew all about his favourite cheese.

When he asked the sex question, I'd responded, 'I have a deadline, but will reply in about three hours. Three hours, and then sex.' He'd fired back immediately with: 'I want to hear you say those last five words aloud.' What had happened to this intimacy? It had gone. It had vanished. 'I had this mad idea, in bed this morning, that I want to grow old with you,' he'd written, just three days ago.

It can't have been the sex email, I reasoned – that's not going to be it; it must have been something that happened at the party. I couldn't ask. I had to give the blip time to smooth out; I had to give him a little space. I stopped email-ing but sent a one-line text message. 'Let's have this lunch,' I wrote. 'Saturday, yes?' Martin said he was sorry but he couldn't. He was going to see his parents and wouldn't be back till Monday night. I asked if we could arrange for the weekend after.

'Unlikely, I'm afraid,' he replied (*I'm afraid* is a red flag). 'Going to be really busy, but I'll email when I can. Might not be frequently.'

Don't, please, start using *I'm afraid* on me, I wanted to tell him; don't say that the best you can do is email infre-quently; don't make me feel the weight of the obligation.

Enthusing to someone that you're falling in love, then going cold on them and turning your back: I'm sorry to say that it's well-documented online dating behaviour, though it usually happens after sex and not before. I looked back at the messages we'd sent each other before the day of the party. He'd been giddy with optimism, then. He'd written about our spending a weekend together in a cottage in the autumn; he was distracted from work by the vision of the two of us by a log fire with books and a bottle of wine. He'd written that he was missing someone he hadn't even yet met, and how was that possible? But all that euphoria was gone now, dissolved. It was gone but he wasn't admitting to it. He'd begun to treat me as if I were an embarrassment. It wasn't even that (because perhaps I was; that wasn't my call) – it was his preferring to wound someone with silence and with euphemisms: that was enough for me, in beginning to acclimatise to the loss of him. I'd already haemorrhaged far too much faith. I looked at his profile again, seeing its skilful, comical rendering of his life with new eyes. I wanted to tell him that he should be ashamed of himself. Instead I demanded that he call me. I told him that no matter how late he got back on Monday night, he had to call me. We had to talk. He said he thought it would be too late, and he'd be tired, but he'd try. (No, in other words. It's such a tell-tale thing, when people begin to be consistently too tired for you.)

He went off to his parents, and I had a tough weekend. It seemed clear that it was over, this promising thing that never got the chance to start. The abruptness of it was a physical shock. I felt fluey and ached, and didn't sleep well. I'd failed to learn both Lesson One – *men I had an instant attraction to, and who sounded like thoroughly decent people, could actually be arseholes* – and also Lesson Two – *email relationships aren't really relationships*. I hadn't even got past Lessons One and Two, but seemed to be caught in a loop of wishful thinking. *Don't get over-invested before meeting someone*: I should have learned this but I'd been an idiot. Again. The trouble is that it's intoxicating, the process of becoming over-invested.

The evening after Martin got home there was an email from him, and my heart thumped as I opened it. It was six lines, enthusing about the books he'd bought, a lovely pub lunch, the local beer. Unusually, it wasn't signed. Writing his name would have meant adding kisses or not adding them, and either way that would have been political. He'd had a lovely weekend! And now there was a six-line impersonal update; evidently he was winding things down. He could turn it off, our intimacy, and had. He'd made a decision not to be that person with me any more; I was to be denied him, that infatuated version of Martin.

But still, even now, there were mixed messages. Even now he didn't say, 'I don't want to meet you after all; I've had a change of heart.' He'd try to call soon, he added. 'So glad to hear from you,' I wrote. 'Thought you'd read the sex email and had a change of heart. I've been reading signs and omens. My confidence isn't great these days. Looking forward to talking to you when you call.'

He didn't reply to this. Nor did he phone. When I tried to ring him, the call went straight to message. I hadn't actually managed to speak to him at all; not once throughout the span of this whole brief episode.

Three days after I'd given up on Martin, I had an email from him. It had gnawed at him, evidently, his silence, or else he'd realised he had to put a stop to my expectations that our lunch had only been postponed. He told me more about the weekend with his parents. His wife had been there; a set-up job; he hadn't expected to see her. She's only 36, he added. She wanted children; the break-up had been about his not wanting children. His parents loved his wife (he no longer called her his ex, I noted) and wanted them to go to counselling, to try again. They'd offered to pay for a lovely holiday, so the two of them could be alone somewhere and talk things through properly. It was evident to me, reading this, that the break-up had been recent, possibly as recent as the day he joined the dating site. His membership, our conversations, had been a survival mechanism, one likely to go nowhere. He hadn't decided about the holiday offer, he said, but whether it happened or not it was obvious that he wasn't anything approaching ready for another relationship. He wrote that he would probably regret this, but this was goodbye: he wasn't going to be in touch with me again. He was taking this step even though he was massively attracted to me, he said; he didn't want to mess it up and break my heart. Ah yes, the I Am Nobly Going to Dump You so as to Save You manoeuvre; it was not unknown to me. I considered writing a barbed and magnificent take-down, and began one and then deleted it. Emotional energy should be saved, wherever possible, in no-win scenarios like this.

There were some things he was certainly ready for. I saw him on the dating site that very night, when I was sleepless at 12.30 a.m. and went miserably trawling. I saw the light lit alongside his name. It continued to be lit for much of the weekend. I kept the site tab open while I was doing other things, and watched, fascinated, as he came and went. Perhaps he was entering into another rapturous, manic written intimacy with another substitute woman. I wrote a four-word text: 'Go on the holiday!' But then deleted it unsent.

I was hit hard, again, by this evaporation of hopes. I'd hoped hard and extravagantly, and fell a long way from the climb. I spent the day after receiving Martin's kiss-off watching films back to back, with chocolate and ice cream, with the blinds almost closed to block out the irritating sunshine. I had a midlife DVD binge, watching films that feature 50+ love. In order to punish myself a little more, they had to be successful, rich lovers with beautiful homes. I started the binge with Diane Keaton and Jack Nicholson in *Something's Gotta Give* (Nancy Meyers), which is set in a beach house in the Hamptons. Frances McDormand is in the film too, playing Diane Keaton's best friend, and at one point she makes an impassioned speech about how her beautiful, clever, 50+ friend can't get a date, and stays at home night after night, because the men her own age are busy chasing women of her daughter's age. 'Yes! Yes!' I shouted. It was tremendously cathartic.

I went to bed thinking about Diane Keaton's character's comment that she hadn't been kissed in such a long time and thought it was all over for her. I realised that it was kissing that I was craving. Sexual hunger can be dealt with: it isn't difficult for a single woman to organise her own orgasm, if it's an orgasm that's needed. That's merely a technical matter. But kissing is something else entirely: kissing can only be done with another. There's no gadget for kissing, and no means of coming even close, desolate in your bed in the dark. I imagined a lovely man turning to me from his pillow and putting his mouth to mine, and kissing very softly, and then harder, and feeling his tongue at the edge of my lips. I saw his face in the dark, the light from the window catching the light in his eyes, and the look in them, intent on loving me. I imagined extended kissing that gradually became more urgent, probing and then softening again. There was no doubt about it: I wasn't a woman in need of a shag. I was a woman desperately in need of a SNOG. (*Basorexia*. An overwhelming desire for kissing. Apparently it's a thing.)

A few days after this a man I'd written to several months before popped up again. Roger. I'd sent a hello message to him, ages ago, having clocked that he lived along the river from me, suggesting that we might meet. This was during a radical Ask Men Out phase, when I was attempting to be straightforward. 'Hi,' I'd said. 'Do you fancy a cup of coffee some time?' Roger said that would be lovely, and left it at that. At the time I thought this was either ineptitude or rudeness, and either way I wasn't going to be the one to say more. Now, seeing his face again, and that he was still single, I thought I'd have another try. It occurred to me that it had been my turn to say something, after he'd said that it'd be lovely, and that he might have taken my silence as a sudden loss of interest.

Roger was lugubrious-looking in the photograph, long-faced and hooded-eyed, his smile tentative, like he'd just said something he'd hoped was funny. He was pictured in his kitchen, and there was stuff behind him from all over the world: an Australian painting, Asian cookware, African bowls, French plates. His profile made no real effort to appeal, but I found the unpolished style of it attractive. This time I was careful to sound interested. 'Roger,' I wrote. 'Remember me? How about that drink?'

He replied immediately. He was online. 'That'd be lovely,' he wrote. 'Let's do that some time.' *Some time* could mean at least three things. It could mean 'Never going to happen, but I'll keep saying, "Yes, lovely, let's do that," ad infinitum, in a Let's Do Lunch Sweetie Darling type manner.' It could mean 'I'm really keen, how about this Friday?' It could mean 'I agree to that, but only tepidly, so don't go getting any notions.'

How about this Friday, I suggested. I waited, and waited – twenty minutes can seem like a long time – and nothing was forthcoming. So I messaged again with the name of a dining pub, nearer his flat than mine. 'Shall we meet at 7, have something simple to eat?' I asked him.

'I'd like that,' he wrote. The enthusiasm levels were not infectious.

So, we met that next Friday at seven o'clock at a nice dark, nook and cranny old pub that does casual but pretty good food. I was ten minutes late, because I'd had an impressively noisy attack of what we should euphemistically call A Bad Tummy. There had been a suspect prawn at lunch that I should never have eaten. The pack was a few days over its date and the contents didn't smell sea-fresh, so I'd eaten them doused in tomato and chilli mayo. (Expiry dates on food are always on the conservative side, right?) I didn't think it'd continue to be an issue. I'd taken tummy settling meds, and seemed to be stable.

Roger was standing outside the building, looking handsome. His picture was as under-achieving as his profile. He was wearing a hat, and a good jacket, with a white shirt and Levi's. There was something TV historian meets Indiana Jones about him. 'Golly,' I said to the car interior as we approached. I was wearing the favourite, flattering navy frock. 'Don't you look nice,' he said, as I turned from paying the driver. He took his hat off and kissed me on the cheek. 'Shall we go in? I took the precaution of booking a table.'

As we walked towards the bar to announce our arrival, I felt a distinct, unmistakable burble. 'I'm just popping to the loo,' I said, walking and then running to the back stairs. I made it to the stall, and was very glad to be alone there. As I was on my own, I could think aloud and did. 'Come on, come on, for God's sake,' I said, after five minutes in which not much had occurred. 'For God's sake get a move on.' I couldn't sit around having ploppy intermittent diarrhoea, obviously. Ten minutes later I was back at the table, having made an executive decision that the attack was finished. I was wild-eyed and clammy, but Roger didn't notice. He was sitting looking at the menu, completely unperturbed. 'Ah, there you are,' he said.

We ordered, and we drank the bottle of wine he'd ordered in my absence, and he asked me a series of questions about myself, the kind that a stranger at a wedding, placed next to you, would ask over the baked salmon. It was all faultlessly polite. I felt distinctly feverish and was having griping pains but I ignored them. I asked Roger to tell me more about himself, and he said, with predictable diffidence, that there wasn't a lot to tell. He was self-employed these days, a consultant, but he'd been in the forces and had travelled a good deal. Did I like to travel? He was recently amicably divorced, had two sons, was perfectly happy with his life, but felt the lack of someone to share it with. As he was saying this, I felt another urgent call to the bathroom. I leapt up, almost knocking my glass over, said I'd be back in a minute, and darted away. This bout, I'm afraid to tell you, went on and on. There isn't any way of glossing over it. It was basically a war. There was gunfire. There were explosions. There were rockets. Worse, I didn't have the privilege of dealing with the episode alone. There were other women coming and going, and no camouflaging music in the Ladies' Room, either. I could hear two women chatting as they washed their hands. I managed to hold back the worst of it until the hand drier roared, and managed to hold it in again once the hand drier noise stopped. I heard the main door open and close, after which there was silence. Thinking I was now alone, I unclenched and let rip. I indulged in groaning. I said, 'This is a total fucking disaster,' to the cubicle door.

'Are you all right in there?' a woman's voice enquired.

'I'm going to be,' I said. 'I ate something I shouldn't have. Not here. I don't mean here. I'm sure the food here is perfectly ... hygienic.' The final word was drowned out by trumpeting. What the hell am I going to do? I thought. I got out my phone and considered calling my date, then put it back again. Ringing someone from a toilet is never acceptable dating behaviour.

When I returned to the table, finally and apologetically, Roger asked if I was well, his brow furrowing. He was sitting with two cold starters (once hot, but hot no longer), unable to eat his own until I had taken my chair. He was burdened with good manners, thanks to inflexible early training, he said. I noticed as he picked up his cutlery that he had nice hands, long fingers. I asked more about the places he'd been to. The conversation flowed, even after eating, but by now he was looking at his watch. 'I'm sorry but I'll have to go soon,' he said. 'My son arrives from gap year backpacking at half ten and has no key.' We paid the bill 50–50, said goodnight, kissed on the cheek, and he strode off. 'I hope you feel better soon,' he said, half turning and grinning. When eventually my cab arrived, and I got into it, my phone beeped receipt of a text message. 'That was fun,' it said. 'Sorry I had to dash.'

'Let's do it again soon,' I replied. 'Let's meet on Sunday, if you're free.'

'I'll check,' he replied. A little later a second text arrived. 'Sunday's fine so yes, let's do that.'

Roger, it turned out, wasn't the kind of man who communicated much, other than for dealing with facts and necessary arrangements, digitally, in between meetings. When I heard from him again, all the message said was: 'I can't do Sunday after all; could we make it Monday?' He ignored my attempt to start a conversation. He didn't do social media or text chatting. He associated his phone and laptop with the working week, he explained on our second date, and preferred to avoid looking at them when he was at home. He didn't do supplementary romance via typed words, and this took some adjustment in the online dating environment. I couldn't get over-invested, and, as is the way of these things, I missed it.

I took Monday off so that we could have lunch. Then he texted to say that he'd had to step in on a project that was going pear-shaped, so could it be dinner after all? He should be finished by four. Then, he wasn't going to be able to get away at four o'clock after all. At 4 p.m., armed with his address, I happened to cycle past his house, being subtle about slowing my pedalling to squint through his windows. I stopped at the corner and texted to say that I was on my bike and not far away from him, and happened to have cake. Should I pop by? You see, I had this irrational conviction that Roger was married, and dating on the sly, for whatever reason. I can't explain it. But he wouldn't have been the first married man who'd claimed to be newly single (so new that his wife hadn't yet been informed), going to his shed to write dating site messages on his phone. 'Can't,' Roger replied. 'Sorry – work has overrun, but am stopping at 7 no matter what.'

At 8 p.m. we met at a different restaurant, for a different sort of a dinner. This was more of a Fish Knife and Starched Napkin sort of establishment. His treat, he insisted; I could get the next one if I wanted. We chatted perfectly amicably, over three delicious courses and two bottles of wine. Warned it was fairly formal, I was wearing the black frock with the cunning fat-clamping panels. He was in the same black jacket and jeans as before, with a silky blue shirt open at the collar. I was so attracted to him that I could hear my heart thumping. When our eyes met I felt physically revved up. I was having trouble being calm, and consequently gabbled girlishly, and apologised for gabbling, and he said that no, on the contrary, he loved a woman with stories to tell.

When we came out, he said he'd invite me back for coffee but wouldn't this time, as his son was at home with his friends, using the sitting room for computer games. Next time, he said. He put one hand to the small of my back and went to kiss me on the cheek, and I took hold of his face and kissed him on the mouth. I asked him what he was doing tomorrow. At this point, I felt I had to combat his natural diffidence with unambiguous interest. Some people need that, after all. He was going to a concert tomorrow, he said, in fact more of a gig, in which his son was involved. Maybe I could come with you, I said. Hey, that would be nice, he said; it's boring having to go alone.

So we went to the gig together. It only occurred to me when I met him outside that his wife might be there, but he said she wouldn't be. She'd moved away; she was already living with someone else. We retreated to the bar afterwards, and when he asked me what I'd like, I said that what I'd like was to be kissing somewhere other than here. He was standing very close to me, looking into my eyes, which is how I misinterpreted the question. He threw his head back and laughed, and said that unfortunately he had to be up early tomorrow. Embarrassed, I said, 'I was only talking about kissing; I'm not going to attempt to drag you back to my lair or anything.' He nodded his head into the middle distance.

Later, at home in bed, I counted the ways in which I seemed to be doing all the work. I was doing most of the inviting and all the flirting, and he was being charmingly lovely about it all, while at the same time transmitting clear signals that he could take me or leave me. Perhaps, inescap- ably, my role was to be good enough company until a swishy-haired goddess came along. I told Jack that I thought perhaps I'd overdone it, that Roger might be fastidious about taking the lead. I might have spoiled things. I told him I was going to cool down and wait to be contacted. Jack approved. 'Though when men really want something, they're pretty resilient,' he said.

Days passed after this with no communication. If Roger was interested, he was in no rush whatsoever to put his interest into action. I decided I would ring him up. So I called him. He sounded quite surprised to hear from me. I could hear young adults talking in the background, and muffled shouts of amicable computer game aggression. Once we'd covered what sort of a day we'd both had, a silence descended. I let it run on. So, was there a reason you called? Roger asked eventually. I just wanted to hear your voice, I said – grimacing at myself – and to say hello. Well, that's very nice, he said. Another silence descended. I was determined not to be the one to bring it to an end. Eventually on the crackly line I heard him say, 'Well, I suppose we should organise dinner here, or at your place if you prefer, over the next few days.' It was my turn to say that would be lovely. That would be really lovely, I repeated. I was smiling when we rang off.

I texted Chief Sensible Friend and said I'd been wrong: Roger *was* interested. He was just diffident by nature, and preferred things to take an unhurried course; that was just his style. 'Great, that's great,' she replied warily. 'I hope you're right.'

Roger rang shortly after this. He'd volunteered to host our dinner. 'I should have asked if there's anything you don't eat,' he said. I told him I was more or less omnivorous. What was he thinking of doing? 'Well, that's just it,' he said. 'I'm wondering what to cook.'

'Well,' I said. 'I don't know. We could keep it simple and just have a chicken. Chicken's easy and reliable, isn't it – chicken and baked potatoes and salad.'

'Then that's what I'll cook,' Roger said. 'Okay, great. That's a plan. Cheerio then.'

Something about this conversation bothered me. I'd suggested chicken because it was easy, and then I thought, Why are you acting like his bloody mother? I'd had the same issue with Marc. I do, on occasion, have to fight off a tendency to mother people. This isn't good in the case of boyfriends. Other than for strange nappy-wearing fetishists, people don't usually want to have sex with their mothers.

Roger's house was actually part of a house, a small flat, somewhat run-down and chaotic, though in a nice way, with piles of books on tables, papers, newspapers, objects he'd collected on other continents, and the belongings of the son who still lived at home (who was out with his mates at the pub). Roger was apologetic about the untidiness, but actually I like it when people don't go all show home on you, in preparation for your visit; sometimes it means you're being embraced into the extended family. We had a conversation about post-divorce living arrangements, and how they can knock the stuffing out of you, something I'd had painful experience of, losing my home in the great divide. 'You understand this,' he said, looking at me differently. I was leaning against a worktop in his kitchen as he scissored the ends off green beans, as he half withdrew the chicken to put rosemary and sea salt on it. I did understand, and I was struck by a new feeling for him: empathy. I saw how a man who'd been dumped for someone else, unexpectedly in midlife, might struggle to keep up his old sense of self, his old optimism. How he might take on an Indiana Jones look, indicative of hopes of adventure, while being very careful not to get into anything new that might result in further pain. I saw the polite charm, the detachment, the silk shirt and the expensive restaurant in a new light, and the way he'd surrounded himself with objects that reminded him he'd been places and done things, nourishing this unexpected new stage of his life with icons from the past that would carry him forward.

We ate the chicken, and tidied up, and then I kissed him in the kitchen. I put my arms round his neck, and kissed him, and he kissed me back, and then we half walked, half staggered into his bedroom, falling into his bed, laughing. But then when we tried to consummate our friendship, Roger found that he couldn't get it together. He was deeply, deeply mortified, groaning and falling face down onto the bed and turning away from me. This had been a problem of late, he said. I told him it didn't matter a bit. I rubbed his shoulders and back, and he made happy, relaxed noises, and I rested my face against his neck, and we talked in the dark about other things. I was half dozing when I heard the main door opening and closing. It was Roger's son, calling out to him. 'Dad? Dad, are you here?' Roger dressed swiftly and went into the hall, and had a conversation with him about the day, and didn't say anything about having a visitor. I felt, when I left shortly afterwards, that my exit was being engineered to be covert. But that was fair enough in the circumstances.

Three evenings later Roger came over to eat. I'd been looking forward to seeing him all day. All my old reticence, all my single-lady worries about inviting strange men into my flat, had melted away. My reluctance hadn't only been to do with safety. My rented home had complicated layers of significance for me. Even though the flat didn't have marriage associations – because I'd moved into it afterwards – it still had divorce associations. It had been somewhere I'd been deeply unhappy and lost (which was one reason I was about to move; I needed another fresh start). I'd brought things with me from the marriage, things that had been saved from the shipwreck but with which I now had a love-hate relationship. A marriage is, among other things, an extended process of acquisition: every book and CD and DVD my ex and I had bought marked a season and an old conversation, a moment, a day, a memory; every chair and rug and picture had its story that used to be our story. For the first time I found myself thinking how tricky it might be to team up with someone else and his history, his belongings rescued from his own shipwreck, from his different past. How did you marry all that together?

In the event, having Roger over felt like the most natural thing in the world. 'Mmm,' he said, coming into the kitchen. 'That smells good, whatever it is.' He was wearing a tweed cap and long overcoat and looked very dashing. I'd made a warm salad with shredded duck and endive and plums; an apple crumble sat on the stove waiting to be cooked. He wandered round the flat while I finished getting the food ready, discreetly surveying my possessions (just like I had done at his place), and when he asked about the origins of things I was very nearly breezy about old holidays and auction houses and junk shops. Roger chose a CD from the pile under the television and put it on, a Brian Eno, saying he loved Eno, he hadn't known I was an Eno fan. We talked about music as we ate. We took the last of the wine through to the big sofa and half sat, half lay on it together, my head on his chest, listening to more music. I discovered he had a liking for some of the same film soundtracks I like. He told me that I'd cheered him up more than he could say, which for a man so reticent was something of a tribute, and made me happy.

I thought we were embarking on something, a relationship. I was so confident that when he'd gone, I came up with Lesson Five in the dating diary. Lesson Five: *make allowances for people who aren't communicators and who move at a different speed. Allow yourselves to align before going into a doom spiral.*

Not that the rest of the evening had gone brilliantly. We ended up in my bed, among the many throws and hundred cushions. Roger kept finding new cushions and throwing them across the room, which made us both giggly. The dog ambled in to have a look at us and had to be evicted, which made us giggly again. Cuddled up naked together, listening to the evening noises of the city, I'd assumed we were going to have sex, but this didn't seem to be happening. We continued lying companionably together like the babes in the wood. So I took the initiative. I tried to resurrect the passionate mood that had brought us in here, when we'd rushed to remove our clothes, rushing to be together, skin to skin. 'I'm sorry,' Roger said after a while. 'It just isn't going to happen. I don't know what's wrong with me. I didn't used to have this problem.' It was probably a mistake on my part to keep trying, but I felt I could beat it, given enough time and enough technique. All my efforts made no difference, though, and Roger's face had acquired a pained expression. He said he thought he should go home.

After I'd tidied up and had taken the dog out for his last pee, and had climbed into bed in soft pyjamas, my Kindle primed and ready, I began to feel that I needed to say something. So I sent Roger a text message, saying, 'What happened earlier, our not being able to have sex, it didn't matter, you know. We'll get there and meanwhile I am so glad to have met you. I am becoming really fond of you.

Night night xx.' Then I wrote the entry in the dating diary. I was satisfied, encouraged, content.

A one-word response came back: 'Night.' There were no kisses. That was odd, I thought. It bothered me so much that I had trouble sleeping. The next morning there was another text from him that said: 'You are very lovely, you know.' That was all.

I frowned at my phone and replied. 'When shall we meet again? Soon I hope. Cinema?'

He didn't reply until lunchtime. His message said: 'Overloaded this week with project, but perhaps the weekend?'

Should this have bothered me? Probably not. But, oh God, the bothering that it occasioned was really something else. I do this, though. I torture myself with others' ways of expressing themselves. I've never really learned to make allowances for poor or different communication habits. I'm tortured by bloody nuance; by often imaginary slights and misjudged tone. I have become a self-appointed expert in nuance. I was confident, when I started online dating, that I could interpret those nuances with the accuracy of an atomic clock, though often I was shown to be way, way off. It was possible that the absolute unshakable confidence I had in that ability would be my downfall over and over. Lesson Six was this: *sometimes, the things that are happening in the relationship are only happening in your head.*

Though at other times they're *not* only happening there.

'Roger, is everything okay?' I ventured to ask. He didn't reply until the evening, and then I got an email from him, the first real email he'd sent. My heart was full of dread when I opened it, and with good reason. If he was emailing, it was to explain something he couldn't say by text and couldn't bear to in person or on the phone. Sure enough, my instincts were good. He was seeing someone else on Friday, he said. He hoped I wouldn't mind too much. He hoped that I was also dating and seeing other men.

Maybe you think this was fair enough, and normal-normal and the way it works, and my qualms about it were over-sensitive. Maybe your opinion is that exclusivity – particularly after a second failed attempt to have sex – was too much to expect. I know of several people who 'date' as a permanent way of life, without ever becoming exclusive to anyone, and I can see how the thinking goes, but it isn't for me. I can't see people on a rota, not even in the even-handed spirit of having lots of friends, all of whom are equally cherished. It doesn't usually work that way, in any case: often 'open dating' entails hidden scoring and shifting rankings, until a number one is decided upon and the process comes to an end. I didn't want to take part in that game show.

I became engaged in an internal debate. On the one hand, Roger was a handsome, charming and intriguing man. On the other hand it was pretty clear to me what his message about non-exclusivity really meant. If you feel the need to announce to someone that you're seeing someone else, and hope they are too, you're signalling your waning interest. That's the purpose of it, surely. It's an announcement that's likely to offend, and people must say it in the full realisation of that. It isn't a kind announcement. Maybe it wasn't even true, that he was seeing someone else. Maybe it was a get-out clause. Perhaps he was trying to get me to finish it, so that he didn't have to. Whatever the case, my confidence in the two of us had crashed to the ground.

The week that followed was difficult in general. I was moving to another flat, a hundred yards down the road, which had been long planned but was still completely exhausting. Just before moving house, my poor old dog, who'd developed a tumour, became much worse: he was in obvious pain, the vet agreed, and uncomfortable and had lost his joy in life. The prognosis was bad and it was just going to get worse, from here on in. The vet made it clear where he thought the obligation of a kind owner lay. So my lovely boy had to go to his final sleep, which was devastating. (I wasn't going to get another dog. But then I went to the refuge 'just to have a look' and came home with one. There were too many sad old boys desperate for love, a need that I couldn't ignore.)

So, I packed up, with family help, and got a man with a van to help move me the hundred yards, and then I unpacked again, with more family help, and was confined to barracks for several days, getting everything sorted out and settling in. A few mornings later, having no choice but to resume work, I took my laptop out of the residual chaos and down the road to my usual café. And then the thing that everybody had been telling me would happen did happen: the offline real-world romcom storyline. I got talking to a stranger in the coffee shop, and left some time later feeling deeply, nonsensically infatuated. It was as sudden and unsolicited as an ambush, and the Roger debate went out of my head.

It was my neighbourhood café, and I found myself there often in that phase of my life. I liked the people who worked there and hung out there, and the occasional casual conversations; I liked the loose, relaxed sense of community, and I liked the people-watching plate-glass window onto the street. Even the coffee was quite good. As I was going in, a tall middle-aged man held the door open for me. He was broad-shouldered, strong-looking, had silvery grey hair cut short and pale blue eyes; he was wearing a suit jacket, white shirt and jeans. He had a certain presence, an atmosphere;

something personal and portable; some people do. I'd discover later that he was ex-military – sometimes ex-forces people have something about them that's hard to put into words. (Roger had been ex-military too; did I have a thing about ex-military? If so, I wasn't ever going to admit to it.) When we got into the queue I turned to the stranger and said, 'You must order first, as you were here first. Door opening shouldn't impede your rights to the last croissant.' He was trying not to order the curd cheesecake, he said, though every fibre of his being longed for some. Me too, I said, but I won't if you won't.

He was trying to get fit, he said, and was attempting low-carbing. He told me enthusiastically about the high-protein regime. He'd been pretty good and had stuck to the plan, and had lost half a stone. It was unfortunate, in the light of this, that the barista interrupted him by saying, 'Your usual?' and gesturing towards the cheesecake.

'Ah, you have form,' I said. 'Your name and your carbohydrate ways are known here.'

'I'm afraid that I do and they are.' He wasn't classically good-looking, not by any means, but he had an attractive smile … and that quality about him, one that's hard to put into words.

We stood at the waiting area, chatting beside the sugar and cinnamon. It was busy, and so coffee delivery took a while. When both cups were produced, instead of going to a table we both chose to stay there, at the end of the counter, getting in other people's way but staying put. It was a mutual decision not to move. We dodged other customers as we continued talking – about cake and diets, exercise, the use and abuse of weekends, going to the cinema alone (Aha!), swimming, the coming of autumn, dogs, books, work. He'd just gone freelance and found himself working at the café a lot. 'I'm Andrew by the way,' he said. 'Very glad to meet you.' We introduced ourselves properly. We'd finished our coffees by now, and he bought us both a second one. The barista, who knew I'd been online dating, gave me a look that was almost conspiratorial.

When Andrew came closer to me, to give me this second coffee, I had the weirdest impulse to kiss him. I can't account for it, but I felt an immediate, strong sense of … I was going to use the word *ownership*, but that won't do. I felt an immediate strong sense of belonging. What I wanted most was to keep talking. I wanted to say, 'Shall we go for a walk, shall we eat together?' But I didn't, obviously, because he was a total stranger and it might have been interpreted as deranged. (And because I'm not brave.) 'Right,' he said eventually. 'Down to work.' He'd come here to work at a café table on a Saturday, too, just like I had. It's something that single people find themselves doing, when the weekend begins to be echoey.

'Yes, down to work, I suppose,' I agreed. I walked away, holding my coffee with both hands – I found I was a little bit shaky, a little bit light-headed – and went to the far end of the room. Andrew occupied a table nearby, and I looked at him occasionally over my cup, aware that he was doing the same.

I couldn't concentrate on work, and texted Chief Sensible Friend. 'I've just experienced it, the thunderbolt. I'm not kidding. Pow! Andrew, 6'4, silver fox, charming, bright, possibly interested. Help me.'

'Oh Christ,' she replied. 'Not again.'

'No no!' I responded. 'Actual thunderbolt. Plus, seems v. nice. Interesting, cute, funny.'

'Leave the café at once,' she responded. 'Go home, never go back; avoid, avoid.'

Obviously, I completely ignored this advice. I thought it was kind of obnoxious, actually. How the hell did she know? People's intuitions can be genuinely irritating. I went on Sunday and waited for forty-five minutes, reading a paper and watching the door, and Andrew didn't show. On Monday in the early evening he came in, waved hello and sat looking intently at his laptop. A male pal arrived and they talked animatedly about politics, before leaving together. On Tuesday I wore a skirt and boots, a T-shirt and jacket, silver jewellery, lipstick, and waited for over an hour, and he didn't come. On Wednesday I zipped round there at 8 a.m. for a take-out, still in my baggy black pyjamas (which just about look like leisurewear), with a big long woolly over them, a hat over my ears, a disguising ankle-length coat, not having even cleaned my teeth, and guess who turned up? I pretended I hadn't seen him, until I had to pass by in order to exit, and then I wished him a cheery good morning, and strode home.

I hadn't heard from Roger since the dating-others email, but now felt ready to reply. 'I don't think we should see each other again,' I wrote. It wasn't me doing the dumping; the truth was he'd already done the dumping, with his apparently sincere desire that I see other people.

'I'm sorry you don't want to continue,' Roger said in his reply. 'Let me know, any time, if you'd like to have dinner again. Best, R.'

The detached, unhurried unconcern of this told its own story. I spoke to a friend about him. She saw his point of view. He'd been badly hurt and was spreading the risk. I told her how I'd listened in to a conversation between two American students at the coffee shop about dating. Neither of them was going steady. They were seeing different guys every weekend and were having fun. It was an alien idea, that it could be a process of enjoyment, rather than of neurotic anxiety, second-guessing, self-doubt, panic and nausea. But that's the way to do it. That's definitely the way to do it. 'American-style dating and seeing several people is exactly what you need,' the friend said. 'Lots of nice dates, lots of nice men and no danger of heartbreak.' I couldn't do it, though. I couldn't have been one of Roger's roster, taking turns and wondering who he was snogging tonight, just like I couldn't enter into a polygamous marriage. In any case I had my own diagnosis of his easy-come easy-go approach, one that was more straightforward. Roger wasn't actually attracted to me. He was a complicated man but I think it was that simple. Instinct was telling me that it was a hopeless case.

A few days later I got to the coffee shop to find that Andrew was watching the door. He asked to join me. 'I haven't seen you here for a while,' he said. 'It's good to see you.' I had a physiological reaction to being in his vicinity, one that was unprecedented. My pupils were probably at maximum dilation. I was blushy, stammery, sweaty, an over-excited woman trying to appear calm. We talked about food, the pros and cons of old flats versus new builds, little known parts of the city, art – he wasn't a fan of modernism – American TV series we'd seen, and then, becoming over-whelmed, feeling I might have a heart attack, I had to excuse myself and go home.

On Saturday morning I was sitting reading when Andrew came and sat – temporarily he said – in the next chair (he was parked at a table down the room). We talked about trying and failing to stay off the internet, about whether we'd go to university if we were 18 now (probably not), history degrees (he has one), and then we got onto punctuation. I'm a grammar nerd, mildly bugged by a split infinitive, and he wasn't; he didn't think it mattered; he thought language should be simplified. As we were having this conversation, a mother and adorable blonde tot of about two came to sit on the sofa opposite. The little girl made a grab for my phone and I had to swap it for her toy one, and negotiations were complex. When they'd gone, Andrew said, 'Pretty child.'

'Do you have children?' I asked him.

'No,' he said, looking away. He kept looking away, as if thinking about something challenging. Then he said, 'Well, I must get on. Work to do. Have a good day.' He returned to his table, but only for five minutes, before packing up and leaving. Clearly the query had been a faux pas. But of what order?

The following Sunday, while doing some work at the café (I'd begun to do a lot more work there), I became aware that Andrew was standing in front of me. I was in a quiet corner where there are only two tables, and after looking around at the options he sat down at the other one, unpacking his laptop. He began to chat to me as he did so, and we got talking and lost all track of time. Our laptops sat open and dormant while we chatted. We had several coffees – I can't be sure how many – at intervals, still talking, and then glasses of water, and didn't stop. I was amazed to find afterwards, looking at my watch, that we'd talked for over three hours.

Initially I'd had the same physical response to him, but after a while I began to relax. This time we talked about ambition and money and fulfilment. We talked about time, and how different it seems in your fifties (he was 55) and about infirm parents. We talked about going to live overseas in our old age, and about unspoiled corners of Europe, enthusing about the Mediterranean way of eating. He said that cooking was his main relaxant at the end of the day, and that he lived alone. He'd never married. I told him a bit about my divorce, and said that I'd been online dating. He said he was trying it too, but with little success so far. He thought he might buy a little house in France, and retire there, and it happened that I knew of one for sale, so Andrew asked if I could send him the internet link, and gave me his email address. I had his email address, now, which was hugely encouraging. This could be the beginning of an email romance, I thought – though the incredibly exciting thing was that we already had a connection with the quality of that: we'd talked to one another, in three-dimensional space, in ways that I'd only experienced via email with Peter, with Martin. That had been email and illusory, but this was real; this was happening!

I can't tell you how excited I was. I was having all the good and happy feelings. My antennae were picking up reciprocal feelings. This was going to build up a real head of steam; it was going to develop into a sexual and intellectual intimacy, I was sure of it. I'd seen in his eyes the same reali-sation about me as I'd had about him. On the way home, still euphoric, I thought, This is it; this is the man I've waited for and wanted. It's done. I've found him. The minute I got back to the flat I wrote that in the dating diary and under-lined it. Next, I emailed him. 'I'm sending this to you before I forget,' I wrote. I attached the link and sent the email with-out pondering any cunning additions. I wrote it and sent it. He had my email address now.

Late the following afternoon a reply arrived, thanking me for the info about the French house. He might go window shopping, looking at other houses in the south of France on his laptop as a work-avoidance strategy, he said. He was in the café, he added, and having trouble concentrating. He was in the café! That had to be an invitation, or else why had he mentioned it? I dropped everything and ran down the street, before slowing to a casual stroll as I drew closer. Andrew was standing in the queue for another coffee. 'I just got your message as I was coming here,' I lied, holding my phone up illustratively. 'I didn't see you here at all, until recently, and now I see you here all the time!' That was because he was finding the freelance life lonely, Andrew said. I sat at a nearby table to him, reading a paper. It wasn't too obvious or smothery a thing to do, I reassured myself, because it was the only table that was free. My phone buzzed with an email from Roger, saying he was sorry that it hadn't worked out. He'd realised he wasn't ready to enter into a one-to-one relationship that would lead naturally into a partnership. He needed to see lots of people first, make friends, have fun, take his time. I said I understood, and wished him luck.

Midlife hesitancy about commitment is a big topic. Sometimes it's complicated. Sometimes it masks another truth (in other words, it's another form of the kind lie). Someone on Twitter told me of a friend of hers who'd been seeing someone she met on a dating site. All seemed to be going well; in fact it had been going really well for six months when he felt he had to correct a misunderstanding. He felt the need to point out that they weren't really a couple. 'Oh, but we're not an *item*,' he said. Some people are able to live in a permanent state of impermanence. I talked to a psychiatrist friend about Roger's freedom issue. He concurred with the kind lie theory. 'He's chocolate coating it, this Roger person,' he said, 'because actually it's just that he wants to dick around – and why do men dick around? Easy. Because they're terrified of death.' Whatever the case, there's no doubt that 50 is dangerous; 50 is a neon sign in your life that reads *Last Chance*. There's still time at 50 to change everything, still the last remnants of an illusion of youth and potential. At 50, that's a time to take serious stock.

Better ask yourself at 50 if you are happy with your life, because it might be the last fork in the road, the last time we can convince ourselves that we're still in our prime.

Once Andrew had drunk down his coffee, he packed up his things and came across, saying he hadn't realised how late it was. He was going to the gym. 'Core strength, weights, they're the thing at our age,' he said. In response to this I expressed invented enthusiasm for the prospect of using machinery to improve my fitness, and he said I should join, and I said I would. (I had absolutely no intention of joining.) I began to realise that he was a fitness-oriented person. He asked me what exercise I did, and I said swimming and cycling (though the truth is that most days it was limited to walking an undemanding dog around the park). He asked what kind of bike I had and I said it was a silver and red one. He asked which pool I went to and I named the one I'd been to twice. The conversation was disappointingly pedestrian after the life-ambition-disappointment one, in which I'd felt we were making strong headway.

I told him – truthfully – that what I wanted was a dance exercise class, and he told me about the zumba classes that were held at the same gym, and added that he went to salsa classes, and I said that I love salsa – which is true, though I've never done it. He asked me if I danced, and I said I did, but not very well, and he asked what kind of salsa I did. I had no idea what he meant (there are different kinds?), so I said 'just the standard kind' hoping there was a standard kind, and apparently there was, so that was fine. 'You must come along to the class,' he said, 'to the same salsa club I go to; it's really good.' My heart pitter-pattered, and I said I'd love to. He said that I should join the beginners, probably; he was an intermediate, and loved it. (Oh. He wasn't actually asking me to dance with him. We wouldn't even be there at the same time.) There wasn't any need to take a partner, either, he added encouragingly, because people paired up at the classes. It was obvious that I needed to become an intermediate dancer of salsa as fast as was possible. I went home and spent the rest of the evening following online tutorials on YouTube.

After that, aware that I might be on the point of becoming absurd, I had to administer a reality check. Andrew had been given an opportunity to follow up, to email, to suggest we do things outside the coffee shop, and hadn't. I needed to slow down, I told myself sternly. So I stayed away from the café until the following Saturday. I made myself stay away, though it wasn't easy. On Saturday morning, there he was, and we had a conversation about being middle-aged, and what it might be like to live in a non-English-speaking country at 60, and then, quite unexpectedly, he began to talk about love. He said that he'd been alone for most of his life, and had never married, but that he thought it was time to change. I asked him why he hadn't married, and he said the answer was that he wasn't a very nice person. What makes you say that? I asked him. I thought he was joking. He said, 'Because it's demonstrably true.'

'But why, what have you done? You say "demonstrably": is it other people who've made this judgement about you?'

'No, no, they don't need to make the judgement,' he said. 'It's my own.'

'Have you behaved badly in your life and made mistakes?' I asked him. 'We've all done that. That's normal life stuff.' He smiled, shaking his head. There was something, something he wasn't admitting to, but he wouldn't say any more.

A few days later I sent Andrew an email. It said: 'Trying to work but appear to be distracted. Only pretending to be working. If you are similar, message back and we'll play truant together. A walk by the river? A bike ride? A glass of fine ale? Here's my mobile number.' There was no response. I had a clairvoyant vision of Andrew in a panic, Andrew saying, 'Jesus, what have I done, giving this woman my email address?' Andrew drew in his horns. He went into emotional lockdown. On Saturday morning he came into the café at a purposeful stride, got his coffee and went to the soft chairs where I used to sit, down by the window. I was up in what was now our usual corner, at a table getting varicose veins. He sat in an armchair with his back to me, and drank his coffee, and then he left.

Twenty-five minutes later, an email pinged into my phone. It was from him. It said: 'Sorry – missed this yesterday; just seen it, far too late. Hope you had a lovely walk and beer.' Ah yes, I thought, the *somehow managed to overlook your message* gambit. I know that one. It was a shame because I'd gone out and bought a new bicycle. It sat forlornly in the apartment block hall, looking shiny. I'd spent three hours trying to teach myself salsa in my sitting room. I'd gone swimming, hoping to see him. I'd looked at fitness classes at the gym he goes to. I'd started sitting on hard chairs that I hated at the coffee shop.

The next day he turned up, looking solemn, and sat solemnly typing away at his laptop for a while, and then, his rucksack already in place on his back, he came and chatted to me, standing at my table. He'd just bought a book about working fewer more efficient hours. He'd just read another one on how to stave off ageing, how to live a long time. 'Course, it's not always worth living a long time,' he added, laughing. 'I think the key thing for me will be to leave the country and start again.'

The following day he found me sitting reading and – for once – not actually looking out for him. He was wearing a dark suit and looked good. 'How's it going with you?' he asked unenthusiastically, looking rather melancholy. I told him I was having trouble; my mind kept wandering from the book. (It was him that preoccupied me, though I couldn't say or hint at that.) I asked him how his day was going. 'Ask me later,' he said. He took his coffee and laptop bag to the other end of the room.

I had to stop what I was doing and breathe deeply. I was having the usual physical reaction. My heart bumped and raced. My cheeks grew hot. Either I'm deeply infatuated, I thought, or else I'm allergic to him. The idea took hold that I could probably make myself allergic. All I had to do was to push him into showing less friendly colours. What I needed, I decided, wasn't to avoid him but to crowd him a little, in the hopes of panic and disdain. I needed to find the trigger to my own disdain. I needed to puncture the whole bubble.

On the way out I stopped to speak to him; his laptop was still closed on the table and he was reading a paper. I had a pretext for my visit: I had news. The friends had sold the French house he'd asked about, at a knockdown price. Apparently the market's flat, I told him; there are serious bargains out there if you're still interested in France. He nodded and we conversed in a stilted fashion for a few minutes. He made little eye contact and looked absolutely miserable. Eventually I was dismissed with the words, 'Well, I must get back to my newspaper.' The message wasn't a subtle one.

Jack thought it was even less subtle than I did. 'The man thinks you're stalking him,' he said.

Back in the Fray

Next, I had a dating site message from someone called Bill. He was pictured on the site with his spaniel, and they had a similar kind of look – wild auburn hair, brown puppy eyes. 'I know I'm not obviously a catch,' Bill wrote, 'but I like the look and sound of you, and I'd like to have a conversation. You will note that I live 200 miles away, but distance is probably all in the mind. No, I know, it isn't when train timetables are involved, but let's have a conversation, at least.'

On Saturday, avoiding Andrew, I had coffee at another café with a girlfriend, and told her about Bill, who wanted us to meet halfway, after a hundred-mile journey each, and have a date that started with jumper-buying in Marks & Spencer. (An ice-breaking activity can work well, the gurus tell us.) I hadn't yet replied to him because I couldn't decide. 'Go,' the friend instructed. 'Why not? You could do with a break, and you always need a new jumper.' Cycling home, I realised that I could see Andrew walking towards me along the pavement, so I swerved to the left and screeched to a halt to say hello. He told me the bike looked new, and I told him it was, that I'd treated myself. He looked particularly alluring in the cool sunshine, in good jeans, a white shirt, a tawny tweed jacket. He'd caught a light tan and his eyes looked bluer.

'Nice jacket,' I said. 'I do like tweed on a chap.'

He raised his wrist and smoothed his cuff with the other hand. 'Meeting someone, a woman, so I'm dressed up a bit.' My heart sank. He hadn't wanted a date with me but he was having a date with someone else. It wasn't that he wasn't dating.

'Hope it's fun,' I said, pulling my bike straight and preparing to ride off again. 'Got to go, there's a newspaper waiting for me at home,' I told him, riding off with a merry wave. I told Jack about this small incidence of payback, and he high-fived me by text message.

On Sunday morning at the café I ignored Andrew and sat elsewhere. I wasn't in a great mood, and didn't care whether he talked to me or not, so I took possession of a small sofa, got comfortable and began reading. I didn't glance towards where he was sitting. A friend had advised me to appear to be passive in my pursuit. This works like catching a reluctant horse does: sit in the middle of the field with a rustly bag, and eventually it will come to you. Half an hour later, Andrew got a second coffee and came and sat at my table and asked me how I was today. I didn't seem myself; was anything up? (He'd diagnosed the absence of my usual manic-squirrel manner as something wrong with me.) He touched my arm as he asked if I was all right.

We got talking about people who pretend they take exercise, and I admitted to being one of them. In terms of the nervous reaction, I seemed to be right back at square one. I got over-excited and gestured wildly. I could feel my cheeks burning. I could feel sweat forming on my upper lip, and mascara settling under my eyes. Water began to drip off the ends of my hair (this was how I got when excited, now that the menopause was with me). He took this in his stride, as usual, and said that he had to go; he was supposed to be somewhere. 'Let's have a proper catch-up next week some time,' he said.

How was his date? I asked him. Oh, he said … it was fine. It wasn't going to be repeated, though, because they hadn't found anything to talk about. *Nothing to talk about?* No marathon conversations, then, that spanned several top-up coffees and glasses of water, and took three hours, while laptops and deadlines cooled their heels? No lengthy conversations that covered a dozen topics and seemed to collapse time and space? I wanted to leap to my feet and shout. Could he see me, the woman he'd spent hours talking to, who'd told him she was online dating and had given him her mobile number? Could he see me at all? Was I visible? Was I not in the reckoning, not even there in the field from which women were chosen? Apparently not. We'd talked and talked – we'd probably talked for a dozen fervent hours, and we'd formed a real connection (I thought), and yet he couldn't join that form of intimacy up to his search for a woman to share his life. It wasn't the same order of connection, it seemed. I wasn't a woman he could envisage being naked with. Andrew thought of me as a buddy, and that was that.

As I write this I'm casting my mind back to the few really stand-out conversations that I've had in my life with men, and I can't recall a single instance in which that intellectual fit hasn't led to attraction. For me, it's the mental fit that's sexiest. (*Sapiosexual*. Turned on by an intellectual connection. Apparently it's a thing.) I was becoming steadily quite offended that Andrew made it so obvious he wasn't interested. And no, I'm not saying that he had some kind of a duty to want to date me, and that he was a bad person for not wanting to. Obviously not. People are attracted to the people they're attracted to, and there isn't any point trying to massage the situation into something else. But when he'd complained several times about not being able to find a woman who'd also be a soulmate and friend and co-conspirator … it was hugely disappointing that my physical self seemed to be such a deal-breaker.

Having nothing to lose, it was time to push him a little. I asked him about his guilt; what was it that he felt guilty about? All sorts of things, he said; I haven't treated people very well. In what way? I persisted. Just not very well, he said. It was clear that there were experiences he wasn't ever going to talk about. Our conversation had been wide-ranging and it had also had depth, but there were nonetheless walled-off sections that were no-go zones. I went home wondering whether he thought me straightforwardly unattractive, and when I looked at myself in the mirror found I had a huge smear of newspaper print across my cheek, make-up that had sweated off and lipstick on my teeth.

Meanwhile, I'd had another email from Bill. 'Let's do this jumper-buying trip,' he wrote. 'And let's have lunch afterwards. It'll be fun. Let's both look at train times and figure it out. Maybe next weekend? The one after this? I've got football this Saturday.' Football, I queried – do you play? 'I watch it,' Bill said. 'I'm a live sports fan. I travel to see certain tournaments. Golf. Cricket in the summer. Wimbledon always. But don't get me wrong. I like BBC4 science docs, and French films, and read history and other proper books. I'm not a goon or a jock. I'm an Oxford graduate and not an idiot. But I find going to sports events relaxing.' Bill was ten years younger than me, and thought my age was a plus point. He'd more or less given up going out with younger women, he said, because he kept finding that they were looking for

sperm donors. 'I know I live far away, and distance relationships are even more challenging than usual, but I'd like to
buy a jumper with you, at the least,' he wrote.

Having avoided the usual café for a week, my return
found me standing right behind Andrew in the queue.
Nothing had changed. I felt the old unsolicited flipping over
of the heart. 'Hello!' he said, turning to me and beaming.
'How are you? I'm only here for a takeaway coffee today, but
let's catch up soon.' He looked at his watch. 'I have a meeting in twenty minutes. Good to see you though … er …'
And then it happened. 'I'm really sorry; I've forgotten your
name.'

'Don't worry about it a bit, Adrian,' I said.

This man I had so obsessed over: he didn't even know my
name.

Things got weirder. Four days later, an email arrived.
'Finding work dreary. There's a lot of sighing and internet
distraction. Coffee! Soon?'

'Name the day and the time and I'll be there,' I said.
Andrew didn't reply. I messaged him again. 'That catch-up
coffee: let's have it today. Let's have it right now if you're
free.'

So we met. He told me he'd been suffering a bad case of
the blues. He'd been Googling cheap houses in the hills in
southern Spain. He'd decided that he was going to do it: he
was going to up sticks and relocate overseas, country of resi-
dence to be determined. He could work from anywhere
there was internet provision. Perhaps he'd find someone, a
woman, in the town he relocated to, he said. It might turn
out to be fate. I told him about people I know who live
abroad, and my own period of living overseas, and how
homesickness had been a huge, unanticipated problem. 'I
could communicate with people,' I said, 'but only like a

child would, and even when I got better, when I spoke the same language as my neighbours, we didn't really speak the same language.' I jokingly listed all the things I thought he'd miss. 'You'll like the lack of high street sameness at first, you'll be smug about it. But then it will bug you that there isn't a Marks & Spencer, that there isn't anywhere obvious to buy underwear, or woollens. You'll miss Boots the chemist; you'll miss British newspapers, the colour supplements at the weekends; some things have no equivalents in Europe.' He said that sounded good to him: all these problems were just what he needed, so as to feel more alive. 'So, are you still planning to vamoosh?' I asked, in a jolly tone, making zigzag motions with my arm.

'Yes, absolutely.'

'Oh no, when?' (Could I BE any more obvious?)

'Just for the winters, I think. November through till March. Otherwise I'll be here. But I can't stand the winters any more.'

'I know the feeling,' I said. 'I might be doing the same in two years or so.' Not the tiniest stirring of interest in having the same life-plan was evident. Not the faintest.

'I bought that book you recommended, by the way,' he said.

'How did you like it?'

'I couldn't get to chapter two. Do you think it might be more of a book for women?'

I went home and began tidying old files off my laptop. There was a folder in which I'd copied and saved the profiles of men I'd messaged, so that I'd know what they said about themselves and what their interests were, if we began talking, without having to return to their online profiles. Dating sites chalk up each visit, and such returns can become, on occasion, political. It's disconcerting when someone starts looking at your site profile again, after you've agreed to part, or have agreed not to meet or take things further. If someone you're seeing suddenly consults it again, that too can be tricky: what are they thinking, what are they checking, what are they comparing it to? The profiles I'd put in the file were all out of date, from the year before, and had led definitively nowhere, and so it was time to bin them. As I was putting one of these into the trash, I realised that it was the profile of a man who looked rather like Andrew.

I scanned the page. The man who looked like Andrew was six foot four, ex-military, silver-haired, self-employed, single. He wrote that he was generous and considerate. He said he was looking for a woman he couldn't help falling in love with. She would be optimistic, individualistic, good at conversation, perceptive and kind. He wanted someone to flirt with, to travel with, to have adventures with. He invited women to be bold and email him. He didn't mention anything about her age, her size, her looks. No wonder I'd contacted him – he was exactly what I was looking for, and lived nearby, and I must have thought I had a real chance. If he'd asked me on a coffee shop date, we'd have talked for hours, we'd have got along like a house on fire. I would have assumed so much, after that, walking home. I'd have walked on pillows on marshmallows on air. But then, I think, there would have been a kindly worded knock-back. (*The truth is, I have a certain physical type …*)

I'd written to him, a long email. I'd made a copy of the message in case he wrote back, and read it again now. It was a warm letter that he hadn't bothered to reply to. This had all happened well over a year ago. I remembered him now. I remembered the excitement, when I found him, the proper astonishing exhilaration of it: the instant attraction to the smiling face, the attraction to the warm and hopeful profile statement that invited contact. Here was an ideal man, I'd thought, who lived literally down the road, a man I thought I might like, and who might like me. I'd tried twice to get in touch with him, and then I'd sent a follow-up note, and he'd completely ignored all three attempts. So – now I went back online, back to the same site, and did a fresh search, using the same profile name he'd used then (which wasn't anything like his real name). He was still active there, and he'd posted new, better photographs of himself. He didn't just look like Andrew; it *was* Andrew. Andrew was one of the men I'd written to and who hadn't replied. He hadn't even been able to bring himself to say, 'Thank you for that – you seem lovely but I don't think we're compatible', which is all it really takes. REALLY. It's all that it takes. He was one of the rude men who couldn't even be arsed to be kind, and I hadn't realised, all the time that I was talking to him in the coffee shop, all those hours.

Which brings us to Lesson Seven: *often, people have fixed ideas about what they want, and it won't matter how nice you are.* Try not to take this personally. The situation is rather like directors casting a film. It doesn't mean you're not a good actor, if you don't fit their preconceived brief. All it means is that you don't fit their preconceived brief.

The news that was at first grim began to seem funny. The next time I saw him at the café, I said, 'Here's something that'll make you laugh: I've just realised that we're on the same dating site and that I messaged you once, a long time ago.' Oh really, he said, his eyes betraying that he was instantly on alert. What was I going to say next? 'Yes!' I said. 'I messaged you and you didn't even reply to me; how hilarious is that?' He didn't look as if it was remotely hilarious. 'How's it going?' I asked him. 'On the dating site, I mean.'

'It's going fine,' he said grimly.

I don't know you at all, do I, Andrew? I thought. I'm not sure I'd know you even if I knew you for a very long time.

Sometimes we realise afterwards that we dodged a bullet, and sometimes the bullet's a big man-shaped one.

I asked Bill if he'd like to talk on the phone. This was fairly radical for me. I'm on the record as a phone-disliker; I'm easily flustered when nervous, and (though this might be hard to believe) I'm naturally shy, and the phone fills me with dread, always has. But Bill was easy to talk to. Bill filled in my own awkward silences with self-confident, tangential chat, and made it seem easy. He said that he thought we should meet. He thought a distance relationship might work. 'After all,' he said, 'there are trains. After all, there is phone sex.'

After having that conversation, I began one with myself about what I really wanted. We all make assumptions about our own needs, and it's good to interrogate them, once in a while. Bill's list of the joys of a distance relationship (he'd had one before) was quite persuasive. There was the (theoretical) romance of train travel in the mix, the anticipatory pleasure involved in whizzing along the backbone of England on a Friday night towards an escapist weekend in your lover's arms. There was the not seeing each other much thing, because according to Bill anticipating is exciting (it works well with Christmas). No supermarket runs would be involved in the relationship. There was also the fact that we were both ridiculously busy and independent and might not want someone else to have to relate to all the time, and to bend our lives around day to day, and to negotiate with 24/7.

You see, in the mouth of a man of lesser appeal, lacking Bill's blunt northern charm, that list could look quite selfish. He was selling it to both of us as a lifestyle choice but what he might really be saying was: I am not good at sharing, I'm set in my ways, I am not prepared to defend all the live sports I go to, and the many beers I have afterwards, and actually what I need is a bit on the side.

Even apart from that possibility, I wasn't sure about an arrangement that skimmed all the cream and custard out of the trifle and left the stale cake behind. What kind of a connection would that be, fundamentally? It made me think hard about relationships and what's vital about them. We're often told – not least in the constant drone of the mass media – that it's love that matters, that it's the spark that counts in sexual dalliances, and that there are ways of keeping the sparky element alive under domestic duress, so that we can all have the sort of love lives that mimic the train-based one (romantic, anticipated, fresh). Is that really ingredient X though? Or is it something else? These questions are highly personal. We all like different ratios of stuff in our muesli. Personally I'm big on that dried chewy pineapple that no doubt leads to pretty instant dental caries.

So, having considered Bill's well-honed, well-practised propaganda, I realised that the one thing that was missing from it and that he delighted in having excluded, was one that I might value: the domestic life. I missed being part-nered up like two little water rats, cosily just above the water line. I missed the day-to-day things Bill didn't: supermarket conversations, having someone there at night to tell about my day, snuggled up watching box sets together, with wine (the worst cliché there is, in dating site terms); and I missed the fact that when you're contentedly paired up and living with someone, sex isn't so performance-oriented. I had a subsidiary fear that the alternate-weekends plan he described – seeing each other twice a month; each of us travelling once a month – was going to bring high expectations with it. In my (admittedly incomplete) survey of middle-aged

British men, they'd lined up in two basic groups: those who were tired, like me, and wanted fulfilling but unpressurised, non-try-hard intimacy, and those who'd been watching a lot of porn and were all revved up for a woman as unlike their middle-aged ex-wife as it was possible to find; men who were highly focused on depilated nights of marathon hot shagging. It was possible that Bill was among those who inhabited camp B, I realised.

It was with Bill that I had my first phone sex experience. (Don't judge me.) It was okay. I mean, it works, it really does: it really is possible to heat someone up to explosion just with soft words and unexpectedly frank but poetic descriptions of what's happening – I might actually be a phone sex goddess – and to be heated up, in turn, by the other person's being so heated up, and to find that you come like a train, but … it's like eating a lot of the chewy dried pineapple. Gorgeous, trippy, a sugar high, but there's a bit of a comedown afterwards. There was no one's hairy chest to rest my head upon, no heartbeat. And that's what I missed. That's what I really, really missed.

When we had phone sex a second time, I wondered if it was going to feel just the same, and it did, and that was the problem. It was exactly the same. It felt like it might be exactly the same forevermore. Having nothing to do with anything tangible, it could be recreated over and over in exactly the same prompted, cued and processed way. Fundamentally, it wasn't anything like an authentic event. All it had anything to do with was the achievement of an orgasm that could just as easily have been manufactured by a machine. *Cybersex* is a better name than it intends to be, because of its sci-fi associations. There's more than a whiff of the robotic about it. It travels from one brain and one nervous system to another, down an interplay of wiring, both human and technological, bypassing the world and its happenings entirely. It exists out of time: it has no past, no future and no present tense. It's a fiction, one we step aside from our lives into. In the case of Bill and me, it was all about our both being lonely. We were not only the substitute people for one another, but substitutes for the substitute people. I felt virtually romantic about these limitations.

Once we were having phone sex, I became less and less sure that Bill still wanted to meet. When I tried to take him up on the meeting-halfway idea, there were always issues: he had his son and couldn't; or he had a work deadline; or he had a cold. I had a long non-sexual phone conversation with him one weekend – he seemed an intelligent man, sardonic, sane, sensible – and asked about his previous distance relationship. He and she had love-commuted for a while, and saw each other twice a month, just as he'd suggested we might do. 'Right – so what brought it to an end?' I asked him.

'Distance killed it,' he said. 'The end of the relationship was mostly down to the distance.'

'That being the case, I don't know why you're even bothering to talk to me,' I said (though I had more than an inkling).

'Just because that attempt failed doesn't mean all attempts would,' he argued.

'But you said it was distance,' I reminded him, 'and we can't do anything about the distance; I'm embedded here, for work and family reasons, and you're embedded there, to be close to your son.'

'I know,' he said, 'you're right, you're right.'

'Why make things so difficult for yourself?' I continued. 'There must be lots of women in your own city.'

'I'm probably on the phone for the same reason you are,' he said. 'I'm casting the net wider.'

I got a sweet, funny email from him later that evening. He was an attractive man, in many ways. But 200 miles away. I didn't think I could even embark on it. I was having trouble believing in it.

But our erotic phone connection continued. Bill rang one evening and said he was a little drunk. He'd texted earlier asking what I was doing, and I'd told him I was reading on the sofa. I was feeling a little low, and I'd drunk a whole bottle of red wine, having started at 4 p.m. When he rang I was making a Spanish omelette. The conversation proceeded like this.

'I've been thinking about your sofa,' he said. 'One of my favourite post-coital moments is reading aloud to one another. You like?'

'I do like. What else do you like?'

'Other things. Don't get me going. You'll regret it. I'm thinking about running my tongue along the inside of your very long legs. And then …'

'And then …?'

'Nibbling the inside contours of your thighs, and then …'

'Oh God. I'm trying to chop garlic, here.'

'I'm standing behind you and spreading your legs. Don't mind me, carry on. I've lifted your skirt and I'm squatting down to kiss you through your underwear, and then …'

'Can't cut straight.'

'You know, I could just get on a train. Just say the word.'

I turned off the gas and drank the dregs from the glass, and sat in the kitchen staring out of the window, unsure what to do. I'd already had a conversation with someone who'd had a distance relationship. It was a disaster, she told me. They got themselves into a spiral of suspicion. They'd made themselves unhappy imagining the other being unfaithful, and then that suspicion began to cloud the actual meetings, and after that it was hopeless: the whole thing had imploded.

I saw Andrew the following morning. He came and sat at the table with me. 'Hello, stranger,' he said. 'So how are you?' I told him I was wondering whether to say yes to a date with a man who lives far away. 'You should,' he said, 'you should – it'd be good for you.'

How easy it was for him to be my buddy and advise me to see other men; it was crushing, even now, after all hope of him had ended. I asked what he'd been up to. I began to notice that as we talked he was glancing repetitively over my shoulder. There was, from somewhere behind me, the sound of someone getting up from a table, a chair being pushed back, and then a slim blonde woman of 30 or so, in skinny jeans and heeled boots, walked past me and into my eyeline. Andrew's eyes followed her; they followed her into the bathroom before returning to me. A few minutes later, as another young woman got up to leave, he appraised her rear view as he was talking. He was multi-tasking. I went to get more coffee, and watched as he scanned the room. Another young woman had her rump evaluated as she went to join the queue I was standing in. I'm fairly confident in telling you that Andrew's an arse man.

Right, I thought, it's now or never. When I returned to my seat I asked him if he was dating. Not really, he said. Are you hoping for someone young? I asked him. Our eyes met and he considered his answer. Well, I've decided that I want children, he said, and so it ought to be someone young-ish. You *should* have children, I said; it'd be good for you. It's tricky, though, he continued – appraising the blonde woman again as she passed – because most of the 30-year-olds I chat up in here think of me as elderly, at 55. That *is* tricky, I said. It wasn't that I was surprised, because why shouldn't a man of 55 have a word with himself about last chances to be a father? I have complete respect for that. But this was someone I'd had long, long, intensely personal conversations with, over weeks and weeks. We'd done a course in one another; we knew one another. We'd covered hopes and fears and dreams and nightmares and he hadn't mentioned once, in all those hours and hours of talking, that he wanted children.

On the other hand – really, why would he? Our intimacy had been something huge for me, but was something routine for him. I've seen him in operation many times since, sitting with his laptop open, not working, talking nineteen to the dozen to a woman at the next table, leaning towards her and gesticulating with his hands, in full flow. It was possible she'd become rapidly infatuated, that she'd go home and write in her diary, as I did: *This is it, I've found him, it's happened at last.* He likes to talk to women. He likes women who have something to say and can argue a case. That's basically all it was about, with the two of us, all those weeks I was obsessed with him. He wasn't infatuated. He was socialising and practising work avoidance. I wasn't someone he'd found after a long search for compatibility – I was just a part of his coffee-time clique.

'You should mention on your online profile that you want kids,' I told him, when his attention returned.

He shook his head. 'That might look desperate,' he said. 'And I don't want to scare anybody.'

'What was it you did that you feel bad about?' I asked him. 'You said once when we talked that you're not a good person.'

'There's a list,' he said. 'I won't bore you with it.'

'I hope when you find your 30-year-old that you bore her with it, the complete list, before you marry her,' I said.

'Okay,' he said, looking me in the eye at last. 'Do you really want to know?' He warned me he was going to shock me. 'I jilted someone once, when I was young,' he said. 'At the altar. Changed my mind.'

'Oh God,' I said. 'Oh GOD. Tell me you didn't. You don't mean at the actual altar, on the day?'

'I'm not going to do that again,' Andrew said, 'and so I need to be 200 per cent sure.'

Later that day, Bill rang again. Look, I think we really have to meet, he said. Let's just meet. I think I'd be nervous, I told him – but when were you thinking? Tomorrow, he said; let's seize the day, I'll come to you. I can't do that, I said, because I have a friend staying and we're going to the cinema. Oh, well, never mind, he said; another time. I don't really have a friend staying, I confessed, but I feel nervous about meeting you and having real sex. Has to happen some time, he said; we can't just have phone sex for the rest of our lives. I do this, I told him; this is what I do, I defer – and then people lose interest; we talk ourselves to death and then they lose interest in me. I'm not losing interest, he said, but we can't continue like this. I know, I told him, but do you really, really want a distance relationship? It didn't work before, remember, when you tried it before. I know, he said; it isn't ideal.

I spent the evening trawling through more bold statements by men who'd declared themselves available. There seemed to be a theme emerging. 'I'm not prepared to go to a supermarket on a Saturday any more.' 'A woman must be able to grasp that I am a free spirit with my own life.' 'Feminine woman wanted, who understands that a man is an imperfect being, who needs to see his friends and to watch sport.' 'Beautiful woman wanted for urban life of hedonistic pleasure; the time for DIY, children and animals is over.' Researchers of the male midlife crisis should look no further.

Meanwhile four new approaches had arrived in my dating site mailboxes. None of them had really tailored their messages so as to start a human conversation.

1. 'I'd be good for you, I promise, here's my mobile number.'
2. 'Here's my email address, tell me all about yourself and what you like in bed.'
3. 'How about it babe, love ur sexy pix.'
4. 'Tell me what u r doing right now. George xxxxx'

George hadn't answered most of the profile page questionnaire. Answering the question 'What makes you unique?' George had written: 'Wot makes me unique? My DNA. LOL LOL.' George, to whom I had never spoken, with whom I'd had no contact before, wanted to know what I was doing right now, and attached five kisses. Get a grip, George. It might take a little more effort, finding the love of your life. You can't order women like chicken.

I was feeling low again. I'd been trolled on dating sites several times that week, by mean-hearted men who enjoyed taking a brave anonymous punch at a sad middle-aged woman who had the temerity to need love. I'd got myself into an email cycle with a nice-seeming man of 36, who wooed me for forty-eight hours, drew out all sorts of personal details and confessions, asked for my real name, Googled me, and then wrote me a one-line message that said: 'I have looked you up and I've seen your pictures, and I hate to be rude but I won't be doing that again, I can assure you.' What was most obvious was that he really didn't hate to be rude.

The week after this, I went away for the weekend to a coastal village with my friend Anna, who is also a divorced midlifer. We were going to do a lot of walking and spend our time reading. In the end we did a bit of walking and spent our time eating, touring quirky shops looking for presents (mostly for ourselves), and reading newspapers in the pub. Anna liked to hear about my romantic encounters in gory detail. She'd never done online dating. She hadn't needed to. She fell in love with a male friend who was also divorced, and her love was reciprocated, and she made it all seem so damned simple.

Late on the first night I got a text from Bill, just as I was nodding off, asking if I wanted to talk. He couldn't sleep, he said, and, strange though it was to say, he was missing me. This is one of the gifts of the internet revolution. You don't need to have met someone physically in the same three-dimensional space to feel that you know them, and like them, and have admitted them to the tribe of your people.

In the morning when I checked my phone, I discovered that I'd had an email from Bill at just after 2 a.m. He was still awake, he wrote, and he was imagining I was there with him. He'd become aware of my turning and coming to lie right behind him. I'd kissed his neck. He'd felt the soft press of my breasts on his back. He'd arched himself and half woken, feeling the flush of desire. He'd turned and kissed me. He'd taken my hand and put it gently over his hard balls. He'd run his own hand down over my lower back and arse, and then between my thighs … It was quite difficult to concentrate on what Anna was saying, over breakfast.

I know of two women – successful, midlife, single women – who have what one of them calls *digital boyfriends*. Friend A, the one who *has* met the man in question, told me, 'It's like we're married; we talk about our days, what to have for dinner, what film to watch afterwards, as if we're together on the sofa. We're together on the sofa via a phone line.' Friend B (who hasn't met hers) told me that her man was invaluable for help with ringmain fuse catastrophes, and IT advice. 'He's like my own personal help desk,' she told me perkily. 'That, and very steamy late night sexy time, baby.'

'How do you know that it's mutual, the way you think of these sessions?' I asked her. 'How do you know that these Skype sexploits aren't making you into a phone sex worker that he doesn't have to pay?' (This question had bothered me a bit.)

'He wouldn't do that,' she said. 'He's a nice guy. Besides, you could say that about all relationships, really.' Is there a script, I asked her – I don't mean an actual script, but are the things you say to one another more or less the same every night? She said that was true; they'd found what worked for them. 'And of course,' she added, 'we can do it four times in a row, in nine different positions, if we feel like it, because we can talk it, even if we can't do it.'

Perhaps I should add that I've never met Friend A or Friend B. I got to know both of them via Twitter. A case can be made that digital love has a lot in common with friendships entirely played out on social media. Asking if phone-based romances are real isn't that different from asking if social media friendships are authentic or not. It's quite difficult to argue that they're not.

A relationship that goes on only at a distance might be a lie, but it's an easy and delicious lie, and has built-in safety mechanisms. If Bill and I never met, we couldn't really separate. If we didn't risk physical sex we couldn't fail at it. Despite never meeting we became intimate, and got to know each other's preferences in bed. It reached the point where we could make each other climax from a standing start in ten minutes flat. I was a train and he was a volcano. He'd work himself up to a pitch and demand to see me soon, in the real world, insisting that we had to meet, and then he'd have an orgasm – boom – and let the subject drop. I let the subject drop too. I didn't have any feelings about being used or about using someone, because we both chose to be in the bubble. It was fun, and mutually supportive, and that was all. We avoided having contact on Skype. I didn't want to, and not just for my own Skype-historical reasons. I can't speak for Bill, but in my case it was because that eye-to-eye contact is too persuasively but synthetically real. So much is said by the eyes. So much might be revealed, or let slip; so much might prove to be lacking.

We had the ending-things conversation during the final evening of the seaside break. It was just before 1 a.m. and I was sitting up in my cottage bed as I spoke to him, so I could see out of the big rear window. I was looking out at the dark sky, the black sea, the lights around the bay. 'I don't think we're going to meet, are we?' I said. 'Neither of us thinks this situation will be improved by meeting.'

'Probably not,' he said; 'it's been spectacular, but either we'd see that we peaked on the phone, or we'd meet a few times and then we'd have to face up to the fact that neither of us really wants a distance relationship.'

'That being the case I think this is the last time we do this,' I told him.

'Oh God,' he said, 'you're breaking up with me! You're not even doing it face to face!' We both laughed at this. 'I agree,' he said; 'I'm sad but I agree.' It was time to break up, even though we weren't really together.

And so I was properly single again. After a longish period of not investing much in dating site chatter, preoccupied by

Andrew and then by Bill, it was disheartening to go back into the fray. It was almost nostalgically like the old days of eighteen months before, when there was wave after wave of mostly sex-oriented approaches. Something else that was immediately noticeable was a tweaking of the status categories. At one site, when I returned to it, there was a new box to tick, to add to the usual Married, Single, Divorced, Separated, and it was 'Seeing Someone'. In other words, *shopping for something better than I have*. It is a category for those addicted to the constantly replenishing supply, and who, to put it in executive terms, are looking to get an upgrade.

A blandly blondly handsome, 1960s-styled man of 35 (thick dark-framed glasses, extreme side parting) messaged asking for my number. I told him I didn't give my number unless I felt that trust had been established. Tell me more about yourself, I said. No, let's just skip the niceties and get to the sex, he replied. What's your real name? I asked him. Lars, he said (I bet it wasn't). He wouldn't give me his surname. We had a pointless message argument about why I wouldn't meet a surname-less man for a drink. Let's skip the drink and go straight to bed, he wrote: I'll give you my address, how's that, and you can get a cab and come over. Wear a fur coat if you have one. Skip the underwear.

The day got worse. I'd had an offer of marriage from a man I'd not yet spoken to, on the basis that we could change our minds after meeting. Kevin explained that he just wanted me to know that he was serious about the long term. He made his living by buying flats, putting cheap furniture in them, then letting them at as high a price as possible to people on benefits. I don't know about you, but I wasn't attracted into this orbit. When I didn't want to meet him, his parting shot was to send a picture of his erection. At least he claimed it was his. It's difficult to say if it was intended to be appetising or to punish. I'm pretty sure that – at least in some cases – the sending of dick pics expresses a bizarre sort of hostility. It's a mystery but it's possible that it's more to do with power than sex. (At which point I can hear a whole cluster of dick pic survivors chanting in unison, 'Really, you think?')

The next day when I heard from Tony, a Spanish man of stout middle age, I told him about the dick pic I'd had the night before, and how unappetising it was (how unappetising they always are). It was reassuring that Tony sympathised. He told me that I was hanging out with the wrong class of people and that I should block anyone like that, and focus on the quality men, like him. He was undoubtedly a monumental snob, keen to ensure I knew he was wealthy, a successful business owner. He'd been in touch, on and off, for months, and kept popping up to tell me how much trouble he was having finding 'quality women'. He would describe the women he'd met in disparaging terms. They were fat (he didn't seem to have registered that I was non-slender), or unattractive, or wore too much make-up. They wore 'lesbian shoes', he said, or 'had no class'. Like lots of other men online, he wanted *a lady*. 'I can't believe how difficult it is to find the second Mrs Tony,' he'd say, expecting me to sympathise. At a low point – around the time that my dog died – I gave him my mobile number, and he'd rung three or four times, usually to tell me that he'd had another bad date. One day he said that we ought to meet. I told him he wouldn't like me. 'It's just lunch, for God's sake,' he chided. 'Don't take everything in life so seriously.'

Still I dithered, even though he was a heavy smoker, and had no interest in giving up, and the smell of fags on someone's breath makes me gag. Dammit, I thought, I'm tempted to have lunch with this awful man who says outrageous things about women: this won't do at all. But he seemed to think I was a catch, which was an unusual enough situation to warrant consideration. He hadn't referred to my body once, nor mentioned sex, nor suggested Skype nudity. Perhaps the smoking didn't have to be a total deal-breaker. There are strategies and even hypnotists for ending people's addictions. Perhaps Tony's openly judgemental streak was really just a kind of social coping, a way of getting a rise out of people. I was having an internal debate about it.

And then, the next time we spoke, he told me a racist joke, and when I probed a bit it became clear that he was a white supremacist, the real McCoy. (In general I'd say, in retrospect, and we could call this Lesson Eight: *if you have to talk yourself into seeing someone, presenting lists of pros and cons, you've reached a desperate phase and should probably avoid them.*) At the end of our brief encounter Tony was convinced that I was the one who was a terrible bigot, for saying I found smoking intolerable.

I went to the coffee shop looking for Andrew, wanting to balance things by talking to someone I felt comfortable with, and sure enough he was there, reading an article about George Osborne. We blundered straight into a huge argument about austerity. It turned out that Andrew thought we needed to slash the welfare budget further. He thought poverty was a necessary social tool and that welfare was bankrupting us. I was genuinely taken aback by this. How had I not known this fundamental thing about him? The argument grew heated, though only on my side; he confined himself to nodding, before presenting me, coolly, with what he insisted were indisputable facts. On the way home I suffered a serious attack of midlife anxiety. How can we get to know people, new people, in middle age, how can we feel that we really know them like the people we've known a long time, without issuing and consulting a thousand-question questionnaire?

I was nervous and on edge. When I got home I rang Bill and told him about my weird horrible day, and how I'd had two surprising arguments with two different men. I told him that Tony was a racist and what Andrew and I had argued about; Bill was horrified by both, and that cheered me up immediately. 'Listen,' I told him, 'I think you and I should meet halfway. Let's do it. Let's meet halfway and have lunch and buy jumpers.'

'I have news,' Bill said. 'I've started seeing someone.'

I said to a friend later that night that I was thinking of throwing in the towel. There was no doubt about it: my milkshake was NOT bringing all the boys to the yard. I didn't even know any longer if I wanted it to. There was no question that I needed to get on with life and redirect my energies. I was aware that the terms and price of the search were making me narrow, and miserable and odd. Why did I need a man to be happy? The friend said that if her own husband were to leave, she would embrace the single life with relief. 'I've done my stint. I think I'd pack up my kit and bid a rather grateful farewell to sex and sexual relationships, and compromise.' A world without men. Happy celibacy. Why wasn't it enough? Partly, for sure, it was the need I felt to be part of a team. I'd had a hard time, and one person to deal with life didn't seem like enough. I liked the idea of being happy to be alone, but couldn't make myself want it. I'd see women's magazine happiness pieces at the hairdresser's: *You Can Get Happy! How to Get Happy in 12 Easy Steps!* There she was, the Happy Woman, a radiant skinny woman on a country lane on a bicycle, sticking out her happy legs and laughing uproariously – in a way that, frankly, might have been dangerous to other road users. I was afraid I wasn't a 12 Step woman. I was afraid that 12 Step plans for happiness might be the psychological equivalent of 12 Step plans to get fit: something to feel stressed about and to fail at.

The *Mad Men*-styled 35-year-old got in touch again. Lars. All I could winkle out of him was that he lived in a rural suburb and worked in the banking sector. He asked me what I wanted, before having sex, and I said a drink was traditional: a drink and perhaps a little conversation. He didn't want to meet for a drink. What was the point of delaying things? People should just meet and have sex, and do the talking afterwards, he said. Dating was a waste of time until it'd been proven that the sex was good. 'Let's just skip that and go to bed,' he said. 'What do you say? I could come over right now. Just say the word. The word is Yes, by the way, in case you were wondering what the word is.'

'Very nice of you, but I like to know more about a person before I sleep with them. Their last name for instance.'

'My last name's irrelevant.'

'Not to me. Your reluctance makes me 95 per cent sure that you're married.'

'I've never been married. I have no intention ever of being married.'

'Why are you on the dating site, Lars? Why are you talking to me?'

'I want to have sex with you, and like everybody I'm looking for lurvve.'

I thought it likely that only half of that statement was true. 'Let's sext, at least,' Lars wrote. I ignored this and went off to do something else, and when I returned to my phone he'd already delivered his opening salvo, a deeply unsexy account of our getting together that featured lots of *knob* and *cum* and *hole*.

Shortly after this another dating site hopeful sent me an unsolicited dick pic. It seemed to have become fashionable, commonplace, a *thing*, to send photographs of your thing. Perhaps it came about via morphic resonance, afflicting men simultaneously across the world. Perhaps someone was in possession of a cultural megaphone somewhere, and was telling men that it turned women on, that it encouraged them to meet you to see the dick in person. Maybe they thought that a dick pic acted as a letter of introduction. It's hard to say. Or maybe men just like to get their willies out and take pictures of them, like that sub-culture of women who can't stop taking snaps of their own cleavages. Pride might be at the heart of the dick pic phenomenon. I have to tell you, though, chaps, that lots of us aren't anything but startled (and, I'm afraid to say, repelled) by an unexpected erection arriving in our mobile phones, so you might be having the opposite effect to the one intended.

On this occasion there was the oddest sequence of events. I got an approach message from Lucas, a man who lived eighty-five miles distant, asking if I'd like to have a conversation. He was lonely but not ready for a relationship; technically he was still married, though they'd been separated for a while, he said. So for a couple of weeks we were basically pen-pals. Typically, I'd get an email from him at around 9 a.m., and I'd reply in the evening. It was platonically friendly, amiable chat. Then, quite suddenly, he sent an intimate picture of himself, very late at night. It's difficult to know how to reply to one of these, if you don't want to respond with the aid of a camera. If you have no intention of joining in, what do you say? I went for, 'Whoah, that was unexpected, was that really meant for me?' He didn't reply. Instead he sent two more, taken from other angles.

Then, in the morning, he emailed as usual as if it hadn't happened. Only now he had quite different things he wanted to say. Now he wanted to talk about his unhappiness – partly, no doubt, to account for the emailed erection. He said he'd been bullied in his marriage, which made it difficult to trust women, which was an odd thing to say, given the photography exhibition of the night before. That hadn't come across as a lack of trust. He asked if he could call me and talk it over, and during this call he mentioned that he was having trouble convincing his wife that their marriage was over. She seemed to think they were just on a break, he said. What?! Well, in that case, I told him, we can't take this any further, because you're not really free.

Next, I had a dating site message from a man called James, a round-faced, twinkly-eyed mischievous-looking man in his mid-forties, who wanted to invite me to lunch. I know I live twenty-five miles away, he said, but I have a very fast car. His profile didn't divulge much – it was a generic listing that could apply to most people: he liked the things everybody likes, and asserted that he was easy-going. For him, a good sense of humour was most important in a date; the craic was far more important than the physical look of someone, he said. He addressed himself to the world in these abstract terms, offering nothing specific or individual to latch on to, apart from one detail: his love of fishing. I've never been fishing so we had a chat about it by email, and then he said he'd like to phone. I gave him my mobile number – it's easy to block callers on your mobile, and so it's fairly low risk – and James rang, and he was warm and friendly, though somewhat chippy.

First of all he worried that I sounded posh. 'I'm not remotely posh,' I told him, 'I'm just English' (he was Scottish).

'You sound posh to me, but then I'm a poor boy from the projects,' he said. 'We don't call them that but that's what they are.'

'I'm not posh at all,' I said. 'I just don't have much of an accent, thanks to living in different places as a child.'

Then he worried that I read too much, and was too highly educated for a boy who left school at 16. He worried that I liked Scrabble and crosswords and made me self-conscious: was I expected to apologise? It felt a little bit like I was. I began to wonder why he wanted to talk to me. 'I'm a bit of a pleb,' he said. I was sure that he didn't think so at all. What he was really saying was that he thought I would think so. I asked him why he wanted to meet if he'd already decided I wasn't right for him.

'There's something in your eyes,' he said huskily. 'I want to meet you and ask you two questions.'

'What are the two questions?' I asked him. He wouldn't tell me. He said he had to go, and rang off. Then he messaged me asking if he'd passed the test. What test is that? I asked him. 'I have no idea what's happening here,' I told my new dog, who grunted and rolled over. The new dog was commendably lazy and this suited me fine.

After this I went out food shopping. As I was walking back my mobile rang and Lucas's name appeared on the screen. When I said hello a screechy and irate female voice told me that it was Lucas's wife. I didn't quite grasp, at first, who this was. 'Who?' I asked. 'I'm sorry, who?'

'Lucas, you know who Lucas is, I'm sure,' she shouted. 'He's the one who's been sending you pictures of his dick.'

Lucas's wife rang twice more, in the following two days, to rant at me. It turned out they still lived together. She wasn't interested in my 'story' that he was on a dating site, nor that he'd said he was separated. He'd sent me explicit pictures and that was evidence enough of my guilt. Evidently I was some sort of hussy, predating on her husband. I don't know if it really got through to her that it wasn't like that, and that he'd signalled, very loudly and clearly, that he wanted out of the relationship. The next time she rang I pressed the red button as soon as I heard her voice. Then I blocked the number. After that the emails began arriving, warning me to stay away from her man. I'm more than happy to, I said, in my five-word replies.

James rang again, suggesting lunch. 'Meanwhile,' he added, 'can you tell me why you're divorced – did you have an affair?' No, I said. 'Did you lose interest in sex?' he asked. No, I told him. 'Did you rack up huge debts,' he asked, 'and are you a mean menopausal nag?' This wasn't encouraging. 'My wife was sexually dull,' he added, 'are you the same?'

'Perhaps you bored her,' I countered. 'Do you watch a lot of porn?'

'Of course, of course,' he admitted.

'Perhaps you had performance-related aspirations that turned her off,' I suggested. 'Perhaps your lovemaking became unaffectionate.'

He didn't get it. 'Let's have lunch,' he said, 'and spar a little more; I'm feeling quite turned on by your argumentative side.'

I told him that I didn't want to.

He didn't take this well. 'I'm not stupid, you know,' he said irritably. 'Just because I left school at 16 doesn't mean I'm stupid.'

(Here we go, I thought: here's the trap that the pleb comment was supposed to set, a trap I was now being treated as if I'd fallen into.) 'Of course it doesn't mean you're stupid; why would that mean you were stupid?' I said, becoming offended.

'I probably know more than you about Italian food and modernist architecture,' he said, 'and I probably speak better French – how's your French?' He started speaking in French, and I replied, haltingly. He told me that my grammar was rubbish, which was true. I told him that I had to go. 'Oh, you have to *go*,' he said dubiously. 'Somewhere urgent to be?'

'Yes, urgent soup-making to do,' I told him. 'Very, very urgent. Bye.'

The next morning he called again, wanting to know if I was a rich woman looking for a gigolo. I wish, I said. 'You don't have money, then?' he queried. 'Because you sound like you have money.' (Presumably it was the lack of an accent, again, that was to blame.)

'I don't have much money at all,' I admitted. 'I chose a path that only just keeps the wolf from the door.' That's a pity, he said. He told me he was having to sell up and rent somewhere, as part of the divorce. 'I sympathise,' I told him. 'I've been there – it's physically shocking when everything gets divided up and half of your life disappears.'

James told me that he could tell I had a fantastic body and that I'd be fantastic in bed. Christ, how I hate this kind of schmoozing. He didn't think that at all. He was just trying to score. I was steadily becoming pissed off. 'Hold on, hold on there,' I hectored him. 'You're making quite a leap here; why would my body be fantastic? That doesn't follow from what we've been talking about, and no, since you ask, I don't have a fantastic body, by anyone's reckoning; you can see my pictures on the website.' I was openly irritated now. 'Don't go telling me I'd be fantastic in bed, either,' I told him. 'I'm not interested in having sex that's evaluated, nor in having my physical self rated, not by you or by anyone. Sorry.'

'Aw, come on,' he said, 'I bet we'd hit it off, I'm the best kisser you'll ever meet, and I have other skills that'll make you dizzy.'

'I'm not sure I want to be dizzy,' I told him. Still he insisted that we meet. I don't want to meet you, I told him, and I have to work, so I'm going to have to say goodbye.

'There are so many women with heavy baggage out there,' he said. 'I can't tell you how much baggage there is, how many sad stories I've had to listen to; I went to bed with a woman six times and every time it turned into a whole saga about her ex-husband – they pour their little hearts out, these women – but you're not like that are you, you haven't mentioned your ex once.'

'I have my baggage, believe me,' I told him, 'and it's unrealistic to expect people who've lived half a century to be able to discard the past completely.'

'But that's exactly what we need to do,' he said. 'That's why I left my wife.'

I had a last message from Lars, an unexpected one. 'You're not going to believe this,' he wrote, 'but I'm in love. I met a girl in a bar, and fell for her, and we're seeing a lot of each other.' I said that was marvellous, I was thrilled for him. His reply to this surprised me. 'Can we still meet and have sex some time?' What? No, I told him, no we can't, and hang on a minute there, I thought you were in love. I am, I am, he insisted, and I'm about to mute my profile (he wasn't deleting it entirely, just in case it didn't work out). 'I still want to have sex with you,' he said. 'I still imagine it.'

'Please don't cheat on her, this lovely girl,' I wrote. 'Be faithful. You'll feel good about yourself.'

'You're right,' he replied. 'So, let me know if you change your mind.'

* * *

I went back online a few days later feeling lower than I had for a long time. A message was waiting. 'Hi I saw ur profile, thought was gr8, let's meet, I have a GSOH, work hard and play hard, that's my motto, keep fit. I like most things, love to cuddle up on the sofa with a DVD and a bottle of wine, if you want to know more just ask me, now tell me all about you.'

You need to stop this now, my inner voice said. Something in me that had been holding on tight relaxed and gave way. Clenched stubborn hopes gave way. Determination loosened its grip on me. I've had enough of this, I thought. Enough. Why am I doing this to myself?

The Day I
Decided to Quit

I decided that I'd cancel my memberships at the rate of one a week, starting with one I rarely went to, the fee-free site that had proved to be full of fuckwits of various sorts. I couldn't remember its password, but found it eventually, written in a list on a laptop document I'd made at the beginning. I'd added other passwords as I'd gone along. All the passwords were here and there were fourteen of them. I'd joined (and in some cases unjoined, and in some cases unjoined and rejoined) a total of fourteen dating sites.

So, I found the password and logged on, and went through the whole rigmarole of convincing the site that I wanted to leave it (they don't usually make this easy). The inner voice said, *Just one more look before you go*. There on the first page, lined up in the row with all the faces I'd seen before, was a new one, a serious face, looking out pleasantly but seriously from among the grinners, the poseurs, the scowlers, the uber-filtered, the intentionally blurry, the sunglasses-wearers, the boys-night-out shots, the wanted posters, the naked-chested, the pictures taken beside cars and at office parties and while barbecuing and at weddings, and scuba diving and on Ben Nevis.

His name was Edward. He had a long symmetrical face, and sad intelligent eyes. He was a very tall man (six foot five apparently) pictured in a checked shirt and a grey V-neck jumper. The photograph wasn't flattering – it was flattened out and a little bit jaundiced, like a bad passport snap. Edward lived in the next neighbourhood to mine, though, and he'd written a short but appealing autobiography in the space provided. He was a scientist interested in physics and the cosmos, history and culture, as well as *Dr Who*, action thrillers, hills, cycling, beer, cooking, weekends away, the south of France … I decided to message him. 'You're way too normal to be here,' I wrote. 'Did you get lost on your way somewhere else?'

A little later he replied. 'I could say just the same about you. Shall we meet?'

Then he visited my profile four times. I knew this as the visits were chalked up by the site and communicated to me via exuberant emails. *Good news, Stella Grey: someone just had a look at you!* (Oh yippee, I had taken to saying to the screen sarcastically.) The first time he looked was immediately after I got in touch. Then, half an hour later, he looked a second time. That evening there was a third visit, and after midnight a fourth. 'Oh, so here you are again, Edward,' I said, when I got the final exuberant alert. 'What are you looking at?' I asked the screen. The fact that he'd looked four times made me want to look myself, attempting objective fresh eyes. What was he seeing there? Did I do myself justice? Had something put him off, so that he had to return, to decide whether the positives outweighed the downsides? Or was it – as had happened to me, more than once – that he'd had an experience of recognition, and he was excited and couldn't resist revisiting? The evidence, I'm afraid to say, pointed to (a). I'd replied enthusiastically to his suggestion that we meet, perhaps too enthusiastically. (You see? Online dating had filled me with self-doubt.) As yet there had been no reply. Only silence had resulted from the Edward direction. As I waited over several days, the silence grew noisy. I forced myself not to write a second time, and waited.

As I've already mentioned, writing a really good profile is difficult, without being dull and generic, or sounding as if you got a PR company to spin you in the best possible light (spin is always suspicious). Right at the beginning of this story I shared a first attempt at writing a dating site profile, and critiqued it with today's eyes. At the time, I didn't follow the advice I'd give myself now. I didn't whittle and weed. My reaction to a lot of rejection, and things going wrong, was to go the other way and make my profile more elaborate, and more detailed, and to appear to demand more (though that was never the conscious intention). I think this was a lot to do with not being picked. The men I'd picked weren't picking me. The message I received was that I wasn't good enough. My reaction to not being thought good enough was to make it clear that most of the people who viewed my page weren't going to be good enough for *me*. There was quite a bit of FUCK YOU involved. Though I hid the FUCK YOU deep inside long, specific lists.

When I reviewed my old out-of-date spiels, ones written at earlier times, on earlier days, I was always horrified. Oh my God, I'd been known to shout – making the dog look anxious – that's terrible; you sound desperate, self-aggrandising, prescriptive; you sound like one of those people with a wish list, when the truth is you don't have a wish list, not beyond ordinary decency, a bright mind, warmth in the eyes, a general wry optimism and lack of cynicism, a sense of the absurd, a love of reading and cinema, and – *oh no, there it is; it's happening again.*

Scottish James rang again to say he thought we should have the lunch. I said I didn't think so. He asked what I was doing and I told him I was frying onions for a curry. I'd come over and join you, he said, but I've had half a bottle of wine. Really, I said – so who had the other half? Ha ha, he said, no no, the other half is for tomorrow; it's just me, just me in this big empty house that I'm going to have to put on the market. 'I can't shake the feeling that we'd have great sex,' he said. I told him he was projecting like mad, that it was unlikely, and that if it was a pick-up line – seriously, he needed to stop. He rang off. Later, he texted asking what I was doing. I said I was reading on the sofa. He said he wished he was on the sofa with me, because he could distract me from a book very rapidly.

'Maybe I don't want to be distracted,' I told him.

'Let's have lunch and sex afterwards,' he said. 'We're middle-aged and need to grab opportunities and live a little, what do you say?' I said no thanks. 'You need to become a yes person,' he told me. 'I'll get you saying yes; you'll be shouting it.' (Oh, good grief.) 'À bientôt,' he said, making his husky voice huskier. 'I'll call you.'

At 11.30 p.m. he rang again, sounding as if he'd drunk the other half of the bottle. 'There's something I want to do to you,' he told me. Oh, I said wearily, what's that? 'I want you to bend over the table,' he said. 'I'm going to run my hand up your thighs and up into your scanty little pants.' I told him they weren't scanty, as it happened; they were more like the kind of navy blue knickers we used to wear under our hockey skirts. He said my sternness was sexy as hell; was I the hockey mistress? He'd always had a thing for female games teachers; he'd like to back me into a sports cupboard and have me against the wall. He texted me immediately I'd rung off to say he was hard. I texted back to say I didn't want to talk to him any more. He told me I was a bitch like all the other bitches, and then I blocked him. So that was nice.

I went back and looked at Edward's profile. I'd copied it onto the desktop, knowing that if we were going to meet I'd want to look at it multiple times. I didn't want the site to chalk up an embarrassing number of visits. 'Hello, Edward,' I said aloud, feeling suddenly hopeful again.

Edward was back in touch the day after this, apologising for the delay. He'd been in the USA for work, he said, and he'd still like to meet, and did I have a preference for an evening, a time, a venue? 'Oh, hello again,' I wrote, cool as you like; cooler than some cucumbers. 'I assumed you'd looked at my profile and changed your mind.' (If he had really been in America, he'd been looking at it from there, too – the visits racked up had now reached double digits.) It was clear we might not naturally be in sync. I was dating-site-paranoid and had a tendency to catastrophise. He was cautious and had a tendency to ponder. This combination, I recognised, might not be ideal.

There are people in the world who understand that going quiet can be interpreted as an ill-mannered lack of interest, and there are those whose answer to that is basically, 'Er – what??' Half the population of the world is puzzled by the rest misreading significance into things. 'Your profile is lovely; what could possibly be wrong with your profile?' Edward offered gallantly. His Red Alert button, one that might go off in the presence of neurotics, could easily have begun to flash at this point. Even over email I could sense him frowning – after all, he'd only gone quiet because he was away. It seemed best to him to wait until he got home, to fix a date for a day or two later. He was right. Casualness is potentially a lifesaver in a world of heightened expectations and rampant delusion like semi-blind dating. After all, generally it's just an arrangement to drink an astringent red wine in a busy pub with someone you'll meet only once.

While Edward was in America, being silent, I'd had two dating site messages. One was from Alec, a knowing-looking, self-satisfied-sounding man. 'Have a look at my profile,' he'd written, 'and let me know if the woman I'm looking for sounds like you.' He didn't use my name. It was obvious that I was included in a mass mail-out, in which an unknown number of us had been invited to pitch, so that Alec could assess us. Alec wanted somebody strong, self-aware, productive, funny, politically literate, able to converse on most topics fluently; someone with emotional intelligence, adept at expressing their feelings, someone prepared to work hard at the relationship. Alec made me tired. I told him I wasn't that person; I hate the idea of having to work at love. Love should be easy, like Sunday morning (thank you, Lionel Richie). Love should be a refuge for both people, from everything that's hard about the world, as soft and comforting as an old blanket. What would 'working hard at the relationship' entail? I asked him. Would there be a lot of talking about how we were doing and progress reports and homework? I'd overstated the case, he told me, but yes, of course there needed to be honesty, there needed to be monitoring; couples should keep the other person in touch with how they were feeling and what they needed. It sounded like continuous assessment and marks awarded and vows to do better. That's not me, I told him, but good luck, I wish you luck.

I'd also had a message from a man called Michael, a bald man with a middle European look and round glasses, and a suspicious-of-all-comers expression. Let's meet for coffee tomorrow, he suggested. I felt I ought to declare that I was talking to someone else and about to fix a date. He said it was just coffee, and what did I have to lose? I said I'd let him know next week, if I was still free. I mentioned that I'd prefer to meet in the evening at a pub somewhere, as daytime first dates made me nervous, and dimmer light with wine to hand was better. He replied asking if I had an issue with alcohol, as he was wary of that. Nor was it going to be a date by any stretch of the imagination, he added: it was a cup of coffee and some carrot cake, not a date as he understands the term, but whatever. *Whatever*.

I'd always said that I needed someone serious-minded, but Alec and Michael were both serious-minded, and they were the wrong sort of serious-minded for me. That wasn't the kind of humourless seriousness I needed. I wondered if these things came in threes and if Edward was going to be the third.

We had arranged to meet the following Sunday night. His thinking was that we should eat something, rather than just meeting for a drink. Our places of work were twenty miles apart, so lunch was difficult. I agreed to dinner; I'm in favour of eating during first dates, as it gives you something to do. Menus have to be studied, and cutlery has to be deployed, and spearing and cutting has to be done, and food has to be selected and dealt with and chewed. Talking is done during a physical activity, which is always better than dealing with a social vacuum (it's why I've always been keen on dates that are also walks, or museum/gallery visits). A date without food is one that's more under pressure. There are no natural distractions if you're sitting opposite one another in a wine bar and there is nothing to do except look one another in the eye. Dinners have a natural shape and come to a natural end: the complimentary mints are eaten, the bill is paid, and

you go out onto the street. There's no international agree-
ment as to how many beers are the norm, on a drinks-only
date, and breaking off and going home can be difficult to
initiate. Dinner would give us something to talk about –
whether our steaks were tough, for instance, leading into the
story of the best one we ever ate, should the chat threaten to
run dry. I had a memorable-steak story.

He suggested that we meet at 7.30 outside the bistro. He'd
reserve a table but we should meet outside. 'You'll recognise
me because I'm taller than most people,' he said. 'And I'll
be wearing a red woolly hat.' (He was. An appalling hat,
pillar-box red and acrylic.) What to wear to a first date is
always a tricky question. I always tended to employ the full
make-up armouring to a first meeting, because it made me
feel, yes, protected, and had the secondary benefit of weed-
ing out the disapprovers, the asinine real-women-don't-wear-
lipstick dullards: win-win. The weather wasn't good – it was
chilly, damp and blustery – so my thinking was this: the
trusty navy blue dress, a big military coat, heeled ankle
boots, smoky eyes and pinky-brown *This Bugger Won't
Budge*™ lip colour. I was reasonably confident that Edward
would be in the checked shirt and grey jumper, or one of its
near identical wardrobe-mates; I thought it likely that he'd
have a cupboard full of variants of the same reliable uniform,
one that he'd wear for work and also for social evenings out.
Males I know who work in science/technology don't really
see themselves aesthetically.

I'm not saying that this put me off. Quite the opposite:
I'm far more drawn to a man who looks like a geography
teacher than I am to a dandy in a silver suit, his hair gelled
into points. Plus, there was another huge upside. It might
also mean that Edward would have a natural tolerance for
the deficiencies (by now well catalogued) of my physical

self, and that thought made me a lot less nervous. Nonetheless, I was unsure what to expect as I set off from home. Perhaps he wouldn't be very good at talking, because he wouldn't be able to stop thinking about the Hadron Collider and how beautiful it is. Perhaps he'd be sadder even than he looked in his photograph, with a palpable sadness that made normal interaction difficult (perhaps still in love with someone who'd treated him appallingly: that'll prompt unquenchable melancholy in a person). Perhaps he'd want to 'talk ideas' like Miles had done, ready to issue a pass based on apparent intelligence, but would tear it up again when he caught sight of the size of my behind. Perhaps he'd have no conversation. Perhaps he'd dominate the conversation with dull work anecdotes. Perhaps he'd want to talk in detail about the Cybermen and other *Dr Who* matters, and would have strong views on who was the best doctor ever (I'd had this conversation, on-screen, with someone else, and, to be honest, after twenty-five minutes my attention wandered a little). Perhaps he'd be misanthropic and the whole evening would be taken up with saying how doomed and hopeless the future of the planet was, and that humanity is a plague on the face of Gaia that needs to be eradicated (I remembered, suddenly, an early dating site conversation along these lines, with a depressed biologist). Perhaps Edward would turn out to be a practical joker, one who wasn't really six foot five, and all the tall chat was a joke, because he was short. He might be that guy from ages ago who was angry because I was heightist; he'd said look out for someone taller than everyone else, but in reality he'd be five foot two and he'd spring out with a serves-you-right TA DAAA; *fuck you, you heightist bitch*. Would he be who he said he was, at all, remotely? A rumble of fear always went through me when I set off to meet someone I didn't know, and didn't know if I could trust, even if we were meeting in a crowded street and confining our contact to a crowded room.

Edward was waiting for me outside the bistro, in spitty rain, looking as melancholy as his profile shot suggested. So that was a little worrying. This was supposed to be fun, upbeat, a treat; I didn't go out to eat often and didn't much fancy having to field Marvin the Paranoid Android, one of Douglas Adams' *Hitchhiker's Guide* creations ('Brain the size of a planet, and all they give me to do is make small talk in a restaurant, when I could have stayed at home stroking the Hadron Collider'). I could tell it was Edward who was standing outside, because he was genuinely a head and shoulders taller than the people passing by, and was looking up the street in the direction he knew I'd be coming from. He greeted me unsmilingly but verbally warmly, and opened the door for me and in we went. He was wearing a jacket that was pretty much a high-class anorak, and dark baggy chinos and policeman shoes – and the unflattering red hat. He was wearing the dating-site-picture jumper, but when he shed the coat I saw that there was a crisp white dress shirt beneath it, with the knot of a tie visible under its V-neck. He'd made an effort.

I was expecting someone lanky, but though he was undoubtedly very tall he also had broad shoulders and took up physical space (a man with a smaller waist than me makes me feel like a heffalump). He had long hands and fingers, and a well-shaped domed head; his hair had receded so that his brow looked high. His nose was long and straight, his ears big but flat, and his eyes (a sort of air force blue) quite deep-set. The whole effect of these proportions made me think of a carved knight on a medieval tomb, and it turned out that he had Norman invader heritage. When we got onto this, over the second bottle, the subject morphed rapidly into *Monty Python and the Holy Grail*. Edward and I were the same age and shared the same cultural references, and it's funny how important that can seem when trying to bond with someone. (Millennials who think the 1980s classifies as *vintage* – don't the older men who date them have trouble with this? Shared frame of reference is important, surely.)

There wasn't any trace of performance, of rehearsal, of an angle, of attempts to appear cool or impress. It was rather like beginning to talk to a man sitting opposite you on a long train journey, as if our being at the table together was somehow accidental. When he bent to pick up his stray napkin there was a hint of an incoming bald patch at his crown, in greying brown hair. His hair was military short (but no, he wasn't ex-forces) and his eyebrows a little wild, though not the full Denis Healey. He maintained steady eye contact as he talked to me; his mouth had a deeper lower lip and his bottom teeth were uneven. His chin at the side bore a tiny nick from a hurried pre-date shave.

We talked about my work, and his work, and ate steak and drank red wine, agreeing that the meat was tender but had little flavour. I told him the story I'd prepared for just this eventuality (isn't it good when you get to tell the story you wanted to?), about the best steak I'd ever had, a rather ragged-looking escalope in a pepper cream sauce, at a scruffy village café in France: the steak of my life, I told him. He took it well. He was quietly amused and tried to think of when his own best ever steak had been. But we couldn't seem to move sideways from there, and reverted to autobiography. He was more comfortable with abstract chat than with the personal. He talked about artificial intelligence and I tried to ask good questions. He mentioned quantum physics and how strange it is, and I was genuinely interested, and

I could see that this pleased him. He started to tell me how weirdly matter behaves at the quantum level, and how little we understand about it, and his focus and engagement went up a gear. He leaned forward and began to gesture, when he was allowed into his comfort zone. He was keen to share what he knew and what fascinated him. He was a man with genuine enthusiasms.

After a while, though, he began to look ill at ease. I wondered, afterwards, if he'd begun to have to deal with an inner voice, just as I have to sometimes on dates, when you begin to register the greatness or otherwise of what's happening, and how you're behaving, and how the other person is reacting, and lose a little confidence, after which self-consciousness can threaten to engulf you. He might have realised that he'd done all the talking for quite a while, and that we had strayed into an area (how light itself is used to transmit data) that might not be of interest to everyone. I did find it interesting: I just didn't have anything to contribute, but it was possible he interpreted my facial expression as having begun to glaze over. Hoping to help alleviate his nervousness I asked relevant questions, and because he was uneasy he dealt with each query at length, which made me smile, and he saw this and became more self-conscious. I could hear his mouth becoming dry and felt fondly about it: I wanted to say, 'I have been there; my God how I've been there.'

Eventually I broke in and changed the subject, and he might have been relieved. We talked about places we'd been in the world: he knew the USA well, and I could talk about other places. Towards the end of the second bottle of red we got the big conversation briefly over with, the one about heartbreak and separation. We confined ourselves to the headlines and not the full stories, but there was enough to establish that the circumstances and timelines surrounding our break-ups were broadly similar, and that our subsequent relationships with our exes were equally neutral. It's always good to find a rough equivalence.

Trying to keep expectations at a normal level, I'd managed not to subject Edward to daily emails. In the past, of course, I'd insisted on lots of communication before meeting. I'd been cursed by it and had cursed others in turn. It's a thing women do that men don't always understand. I've seen some man-chat on the internet about it. I've even seen men stating upfront in their dating profiles that they have no interest in emailing. Some commenters diagnose a female need for a lot of attention. For many women, they say, online dating is a vanity project in which we try to get six candidates to email us simultaneously, thereby revitalising our self-esteem, without needing to go to the bother of going to bed with any of them. (In some cases this argument is reverse-engineered by dull men to explain why they can't pull, but we'll let that go.)

It might be more complicated than that. Often women push for a lot of email contact, just as I had done, to reduce a sense of risk or foolishness, trying to avoid a glaring mismatch – but it's also done to footnote any immediate lack of attraction. It's something that the not-beautiful do, to create a positive context for their not-beauty. I didn't always come off as terrifically alluring during a first date, to say the least – I knew this about myself. An email friendship lead-up (so long as it doesn't stray into premature sex chat) can be a positive, establishing that this other person is someone you'd like to talk more to. I hadn't done any of this, though, this time. As we paid the bill I suffered a creeping awareness of having failed to be properly myself, and began to wish that I *had* done it. I wasn't convinced that I interested him.

Perhaps he'd registered that I wasn't really of his tribe, and wanted someone more similar. Perhaps he'd found me trivial. I enjoy triviality sometimes – my love of whimsy is well-documented – but he might not understand that it was a way of relaxing, and an ice-breaking mechanism. He didn't look thrilled to have met me, when we came out onto the street, and I felt I might have failed my audition. His face was inscrutable as we stood outside together. When we parted I decided against shaking his hand or kissing his cheek. I said I'd had a nice time. Me too, he said. That was all. I waited – would there be an invitation to meet again? There was not.

There was on-paper compatibility, heaps of it. But no apparent mutual attraction, no 'spark'. This didn't bother me. Personally I don't trust either the spark or the idea that its presence or lack means something definite. People who won't agree to a second date 'because there was no spark' are … I hesitate to say they're idiots, but they're discounting something that could prove to be a slow burner. Personally I find the idea of the first date spark being a prerequisite to love a bit infantile. I mean, come on: not every successful romantic partnership has started with an immediate attraction. I've experienced the spark twice in my life, and neither time did it lead to anything happy or fruitful. You only have to look back a few pages to see how the spark that sparked into life when I met Andrew turned out. The other time, I was young and the man in question was married and it was a disastrous mutual infatuation that I was mature enough (but only just) to put a stop to quickly.

The spark is massively unreliable. A little electricity between two people is less meaningful than we often assume. It's heady, and misleads us, and our brains fill in the gaps, trying to complete the picture. Nor is a lack of instant electricity particularly significant. When people complain there was no spark, as they do so very often in newspaper accounts of first dates, explaining why they don't want a second date, quite often what they're saying is that they didn't pick up immediate sexual interest from the other person. It seems to me they're talking about charm, and not everybody has that on tap. Not everybody is immediately comfortable with a stranger in such an artificial situation. Not everybody goes into flirting mode, and that's quite a lot of what a spark is: it's interest, body language that reflects interest, intense eye contact, the chemical hormonal soup beginning to bestir itself. It's also to do with having a similar bantering style of chat.

Sometimes a spark doesn't even look like a positive. It might look like incompatibility. Lots of people who have paired up for life started out by having strong feelings of dislike. Consider the Benedick and Beatrice model, in Shakespeare's *Much Ado About Nothing*: they use their natural banter to disdain one another, for much of the play. Look at Belle and the monster in *Beauty and the Beast* (setting aside the whole Stockholm Syndrome question), Ron and Hermione in the *Harry Potter* books, and Han Solo and Leia, in *Star Wars*; not forgetting the best possible example of dislike that turns into love: Lizzie Bennet and Mr Darcy in *Pride and Prejudice*. Lizzie doesn't come away from first meeting him at the Meryton ball feeling that they had a spark. She thinks he's insufferable, but all that animosity can flip over, sometimes, into a much more positive energy.

But I digress (again). At any rate I was pretty sure this meeting was a one-off and that Edward wouldn't be in touch again, other than to send a brief 'thank you for having dinner with me' message, perhaps. (What had Miles said? *This has*

been fun. It's tremendous to meet new people. I thought it
might be something like that.) In any case, it wasn't clear
what the date was *for*. Were we friends now, but avoiding the
second date conversation because romantic rejection is
embarrassing? Or was I just one of a shortlist and he still had
more women to see? It was possible Edward might be dating
in a more American style, meeting a different woman in the
bistro every week, as it had turned out Roger was doing.
Edward was a rational person, and might consider that a
logical approach to finding someone.

But as I strode off down the street I half turned my head,
and saw that he was still standing there, watching me walking away.

I didn't hear from him for forty-eight hours after our date.
My phone cover began to fray, because of the constant opening and closing. So I sent a message saying it had been lovely
to meet him: a formal enough response to minimise the
awkwardness, should a 'Look, here's the thing' reply be
fermenting in his brain (*Look here's the thing, I think you're
great, but ...*' It had happened before). 'Dear Edward –
thanks for dinner on Friday; it was lovely to meet you,' I
wrote. Pride was saved by the use of *lovely to meet you*; he
could be reassured that I wasn't going to be devastated by his
not wanting to see me again; he could surmise, if he wanted,
that I too was dating in the open no-strings manner, and
seeing various people. I'm not needy at all, I thought it said.
I'd written that it was lovely to meet him, as if we'd met at a
business dinner and had chatted all evening, but now,
because we were flying in different directions from the
airport in the morning, were unlikely ever to run into one
another again. Dignity was saved by the form of words. If
he'd wanted a second date, he would already have asked for
one, after all. I added that I'd like to do it again and then

deleted that part, feeling the need to wait it out. I hate the whole 'make him do the running' narrative, and – even worse – the 'leading isn't feminine' one. Nonetheless, I felt the need to wait it out.

Why wasn't he replying? What was going on? I thought we'd had enough of a rapport to warrant basic good manners, even if Edward was one of those dating site arses (admittedly a cunningly disguised one) who thought silence could be used to say goodbye. (*Ghosting* is the name of this practice.) The salient question was this: did he know that silence was rude? It was entirely possible it wasn't intentional. It was also possible that he didn't really want to date anyone. Maybe, I thought, beneath the skin, Edward hated the whole world, and was only going through the motions of reconnecting with it. Some men do feel they are obliged to reconnect, after a divorce (perhaps it was worse than he admitted), and they do this obediently – obeying their parents, friends, inner voice – even though the eye they cast upon woman-kind has become a severely jaundiced, wounded one. More likely, he was One of Those Non-Verbalisers. I'd come across the type before, and even knew some; some of them were people I loved dearly. They tended, like Edward, to be social media refuseniks, who made happy ruts between work and home, and while at home minimised their digital presence to the essential. Roger had been thus, and this could be another Roger.

Then Edward's reply arrived. It said that he'd also had a nice evening, and thanked me for being such good company. I can't quote exactly because I destroyed it. I didn't just delete it. I put it in a plastic bag and whacked it with a hammer. Metaphorically. (Because – completely failing to take the tone of my own post-date message into account – I considered his to be rude.)

So, what I needed was cheering up. Moaning to girl-friends wasn't going to help, but I did it anyway, despite knowing that I'd become a heart-sinker around my pals with my constant tales of dating woe. They say that a problem shared is a problem halved, but sometimes a problem shared just gives everyone else the same problem. Chief Sensible Friend thought Edward might turn up again. 'He's a nerd, a geek, a Brainiac,' she said. 'And he might not be great at communicating, and he might take a while to readjust.' I grunted at her. No, I said, it's not that. 'He might be think-ing,' she added, 'Wow, I really liked that woman, but I don't think she felt any sort of attraction for me, and why should she, and so I should wait a few days before enquiring if she'd like to meet again because I don't want to look like a prat by rushing at this like a bull at a gate.'

But, obviously, it wasn't that.

In need of further cheering up, I checked in to the websites where I still had a presence, though I rarely insti-gated contact at any of them any more. It had become a leave-the-door-open policy; you're unlikely to find some-one if you close all the doors they might walk through, and I had few enough doors available in my narrow and narrow-ing life. There were two messages waiting for me online. One was from a doctor in Paris (supposedly) asking if I'd like to take the Eurostar and have lunch with him. A French doctor, really? The English idiom was authenti-cally slightly off ('Are you been visit in Paris?'), but would a Parisian obstetrician really use so many emoticons? Plus, he could turn out to be Kristin Scott Thomas's ex-husband, which would be way too much pressure for subsequent women.

'Perhaps I will,' I responded, 'though I have to warn you that my French grammar is officially atrocious.'

'You can wright [*sic*] to me in French,' he replied, 'and I will correct you, but only your French **wink emoticon**. It is far, but why not, we can do it.'

The other message was from a man called Alex, who lived in a pretty market town three hours away (too far), and had written one of the best profile pages I'd seen. We had a quick on-screen chat, in which I accused him of getting a female friend to write it, and he admitted that his younger sister did. I like men who have good relationships with their sisters. Alex's pictures looked a bit like those done for an actor's agency (though he was an engineer of some sort) and he wasn't the handsomest in the world, but he had that something about him – intelligence and humour in the eyes and natural warmth – that reminded me of Steve Martin, and anything that reminds me of Steve Martin is generally a good thing. 'It's a pity we live too far apart to meet for a pizza and a film,' Alex wrote. I asked the French doctor why he didn't come to me instead: he could catch the Eurostar and we'd have lunch. He didn't reply to this invitation.

Alex was one of the few men I came across who wanted to spend time establishing a friendship via email before meeting. Generally, as I've said already, it's a thing that men complain women want. Alex, though, wanted to wait and form a bond, as if lunch were really sex and we shouldn't rush into it. He'd found waiting worked for him. Combined with the fact that he was a 51 who looked 41 in his profile picture, this was winningly charming. So we spent four days emailing, and he seemed … I was going to say a nice man, but that can come across as damning. (My mother has a tendency to say, 'He's nice enough,' of the widowers who woo her at tea dances and it's plain there's a great big BUT coming.) Alex had all the qualities that make men successful online. He was articulate, if a little earnest; he wanted to see

the world, and do things and learn more; he was straightforward about his emotional life and needs, and frank about
mistakes made in past relationships, and sensitive to my
potential vulnerabilities – and I just didn't fancy him at all.
He wrote saying he wanted to grow and change, and I admit
that my spoken response (to the dog) was, 'Yeah, I had a
husband who wanted to grow, and he grew into someone
who wanted a divorce.'

My relationship with Alex, if you could call it that, took
place over a week, virtually and in speeded-up time, like the
birth and death of a flower in time-lapse photography. On
day five I decided to ask if there was a reason he was shy
about meeting women in person. He sent me a photograph
of his dad. At least I assumed it was his dad, because it
looked like Alex, but a lot older, and of course that was Alex.
Alex wasn't 51, the sort of 51 that looks 41. Alex was 63 and
looked older, and had serious health problems, and had no
confidence.

At this point, I noted with passing interest, I seemed to
have stopped being a person who wanted a lot of email
wooing before meeting. I seemed at last to be learning
Lesson Two (*email relationships aren't relationships*). I
seemed to be in transition. I wanted to skip the detailed
preamble and the fifty messages and meet people. So I
decided Alex and I should meet, on the basis that you really
never know. What I'd do was surprise him. I was on my way
to stay with my mother for the weekend, because it was my
birthday (I turned 52 and was Eeyorish about it), and as it
happened Alex lived not far away from her. So I messaged
him: 'Surprise! I'm half an hour away from you; why don't
we have lunch? It'd be great to meet you.' Alex's reaction,
I'm fairly confident in telling you, was to freak out. He went
into silent mode, pretending he hadn't read the message

until it was already too late, something that's a classic avoidance gambit. There's often an over-long and overly detailed list of reasons a message is 'missed'. *I'm so sorry, my internet went down, and then a dog ate my cable and I've been in a coma and now my fingers are broken.* Once I'd left my mother's house on a train and had returned to a safe distance Alex popped up again, saying how busy he'd been. I replied, apologising for the impulsive gesture. I might have got a bit ahead of myself, I admitted; I do that sometimes. He responded immediately, saying it was okay to do that sometimes, as long as it *was* only sometimes. I caught a strong whiff of habitual critique. I told him I hoped to hear from him when he was less busy, but realised afterwards that I didn't hope for that. Perhaps, I thought, I should take the hint and give up this search, properly give it up instead of talking about doing it. There's nothing wrong with being a radiant spinster, too busy with her fulfilling life to miss having a partner. There's a lot that's right about it. It just wasn't what I wanted.

Then Edward texted. Was I free for a drink on Friday? Should we go to the pub? It was such a brisk enquiry that I wasn't sure whether he was suggesting a second date or whether he wanted to tell me in person why my application had failed. But yes. I said yes.

The wood-floored traditional alehouse that Edward invited me to was in a quiet nook in an unfashionable part of town. It had a random assortment of drinkers, most of them men. Probably he chose it because he thought it would be quiet and we'd be able to get a table (or – and I couldn't help having these thoughts – he wasn't known there and his wife wouldn't see us) but it was packed, and so we had to stand at the bar. He looked uncomfortable about this, glancing around the room as if it were something he felt he ought to fix. Finally, people left and we swooped. A small brass table had become free, sandwiched between geezers talking about football on one side, and two women discussing their divorce travails on the other (oh joy). The stools were uncomfortable and the lighting glaring.

I had an attack of paralysing second date nerves and couldn't think what to say to him (partly, of course, because I was unsure what this was). He, too, seemed edgy and out of sorts. We had one of those dull chats that people have when they're too tired to socialise and would rather be at home with mugs of cocoa and the Netflix powered up. We talked about our days, our working weeks; we even talked about the weather. He told me a long story about a work problem and how it was solved. I knew that my eyes were genuinely glazing over this time – I was too tired to be able to stop myself from looking bored – and became aware that he'd noticed. His nervous reaction was to provide even more detail about the solution to the work issue.

The question is, I asked myself when I went to the Ladies' Room, why did he invite me if he didn't want to see me again, and why was he so ill at ease? After all, the man had been brisk, monosyllabic, absent, since last we met. He had my email address and hadn't used it. He had my number and hadn't called. (Not that the businesslike 'So can we have sex on Friday?' text that a friend received after a first date would have been preferable, but still.) The evening wasn't a great success, and we both wanted to cut it short: that much was clear. It wasn't even that it went badly. We both tried; there were no awkward silences, but honestly (I thought, somewhat peeved about the sense of obligation I perceived flowing out of him) if there doesn't seem to be a natural flow to the chat on the third beer on a second date, there might be something amiss. In the bathroom I gave myself a pep talk. Was it me? My eye make-up was uneven and had descended at the sides, and my lipstick had greased off, leaving only an outer line of red. That was easily sorted out, but the pep question wasn't so easy. Why had my social pep deserted me? 'Cinema, books, TV, nature, human nature, politics,' I said to my reflection, reminding myself there were topics I could instigate. A woman came out of a stall and smiled at me. Perhaps she'd had the same problem, one in which her head emptied abruptly of all thoughts, during a second date that might be a mercy date.

When we came out onto the street, Edward and I waited at the same bus stop – he lived on my route but further along the line. I wrapped my wide scarf so that it covered my mouth (no points, Mr Freud) and buried my hands deep in the pockets of my coat, and looked doggedly in the direction in which double-decker rescue would come. Edward got out his phone and texted, and I couldn't help wondering if he was telling his wife that he was on the way home. We had to stand, once we boarded the bus, and were separated by a pair of giggling girls who got on after us and settled in the space before we could close it. 'Well, bye then,' I said, as I got off at my stop. Just look at him, I thought, as I did so. He's so tall, so striking-looking; he has such melancholic, expressive eyes, and there's something there; possibly loneliness. When he looked back at me, it seemed to be with regret of some sort. There might have been something imploring in his expression. I felt attraction for the first time, but I was sure it was too late for that. He'd shown no signs whatsoever of reciprocating. He'd seemed to me, all evening, like a man who didn't really want to be there. 'Bye,' he'd mouthed, raising his hand as the bus rumbled away.

I got out my phone and looked at it. It occurred to me that it might have been me he was texting, saying something his mouth couldn't. 'Well that was a weird evening. We both seemed tired, off our game, but should we go to the cinema or something next week?' There was no message. So that's that, I thought; I won't hear from him again. Or … perhaps this is all happening in extreme slow motion and I will, but not for a while. At the risk of posing a Carrie Bradshaw-type question: was he behaving in a strange fashion for a man who wasn't interested (I mean, why ask to meet again?), or was a drink every two weeks – with no communication in between – his equally strange way of courting a woman?

The evening after the second date, not having heard from him, I grumped round the kitchen engaged in deeply unconvincing rationalising. The dishwasher was unloaded with excessive energy, resulting in the cutlery box spewing arrows across the room. The retrieval of knives and forks was accompanied by a rant of determined disregard. 'And so, Edward, you're not keen, but that's all right, that's all right, because I'm even less keen,' I announced to plates as they were stacked with crashes into the cupboard. 'It's fine,' I told the dog. 'Sometimes you have two dates with someone and recognise that the conversation has come to an end. It's fairly vital to be able to keep talking, after all. If there's not much to say, nor a burning desire to rip each other's trousers off –'

My phone buzzed, and my first thought was, It's Edward, wanting a third date, and I take it all back. It wasn't Edward. It was a dating site message from a man called Gavin. I recognised Gavin. I remembered the dating site conversation we'd had the year before. We'd been larkish pals for two or three days, mischievously sparring and insulting one another before the banter ran dry. Gavin was 59 and had written on his profile page that it was best to be straightforward, because his picture would speak for itself. According to him he looked like Frankenstein's monster. He was one of the ugliest men in the world, he'd written (this wasn't remotely true, though he did have a very large chin, and hair that stood up on end), but on the other hand had an interesting life as an artist. He stood out among the sea of the bland, and that's how we got talking. He'd referred to me as the 'Water Buffalo', insisting that I had the exact determined expression of one, and a little bit of the sturdiness too (and I'd be the first to agree). Now he wanted to take me to lunch at a rather swanky hotel, and – thinking this would be fun, that we'd revisit our bantering brief chat of a year ago – I agreed.

'You're not going to back out, are you?' he asked nervously. 'You're definitely coming, aren't you?'

'I'm definitely coming,' I said. 'Definitely.'

The next morning, working away, absolutely not thinking about Edward, I had a sudden thought about Edward. I looked back at the messages I'd sent him and saw that they were the under-eager communications of a woman determined not to be hurt. 'Oh God,' I said aloud, looking at my phone. 'Edward doesn't think I'm interested.' There was every reason why he wouldn't. There it was in black and white. I'd sabotaged it. After the first date I'd said, with terrible, fatal politeness, that 'I had a nice time' and that had set the tone. I'd sent a message saying, 'It was lovely to meet you', a self-protective phrase that positively reeks of non-keenness. He thought it was a kiss-off. (Remember Miles? I'd written this, after Miles told me how nice it had been to meet me: *I'm sorry to say that this 'nice to have met you' routine is almost always a kiss-off.*) Edward thought our second date was a mercy date. He might not even be debating asking for a third. I was aloof and fearful and he'd interpreted that as indifference, and was self-protectively out-aloofing and out-fearfulling me. Nothing could really be more British. So I decided that I'd text him. I was going to have to use a deadlock-breaking phrase. There was really nothing to lose at this point.

'Look – Edward – do you want to meet again? It's okay if you don't. Just say. But I'd like to.'

I couldn't let Gavin down, so I had lunch with a man who wasn't a day under 70, a man who rolled his own and had tobacco-yellow fingernails. He tried to play footsie under the table, and grab my hand. He'd brought me a present, a painting done in acrylic of Pan playing his pipe, and he wanted to know my exact time of birth so he could do my chart. It was your basic blind-date nightmare. This may sound a little snotty and I'm sorry if it does because Gavin is in many ways a great guy and heaps of fun; bear in mind that I'm trying to entertain you. But having said that – notwith-standing his great guy status – I don't think it's really on to ambush people at the revolving door of a hotel on a first date. There probably shouldn't be what we used to call 'French kissing' during an ambush, either. Gavin caught me off guard and lunged at me without warning, and his tongue tasted of bacon, even though we'd eaten fish. He texted me later asking if I would be his girl. It was awful to have to confess that I'd met someone else. 'What, since lunchtime?' he said.

There were three women of about 60 standing behind me at the coffee shop when I answered this message. They were well-groomed, silvery women with a look of quiet affluence, so similar in size and shape and style that they might have been sisters, though probably it was just some sort of conformity-provoking friendship set. I realised with a jolt that they were talking about the online dating one of them was engaged in. She'd had first sex with someone the week-

end before, I gathered, listening harder – they were whisper-
ing by now. 'He said he was 62 but I swear parts of him were
older,' she whispered, sending them all into giggles.

That's where I was standing (in the coffee queue) when
Edward responded to the deadlock-buster. Of course he
wanted to see me again, he wrote. He'd just wondered if I'd
be interested in that. He'd thought perhaps I wouldn't.
HE'D THOUGHT PERHAPS I WOULDN'T. Friday, he
suggested – what about Friday? Another drink, at a different
pub, somewhere nicer? 'That'd be lovely,' I replied. 'I'm
looking forward to it.' My mind travelled over and over our
exchanges, after this was arranged, and I had another look
at my cucumber-cool messages. Edward hadn't taken the
lead either, not assertively, but perhaps there were reasons
for that. What I'd taken to be diffidence, a lack of interest:
perhaps it was just a manifestation of seriously low expectations. Perhaps he doubted that he'd have another romantic
chance in life. I understood this, because I'd had identical
doubts, though mine had manifested in very different ways.
We were both playing it so safe that we almost didn't meet
again. Perhaps there needs to be another lesson inserted
here. Lesson Nine: *use positive language and be unambiguous if you feel positively about someone. No self-protective
hedging! The road of indecision is paved with flat squirrels.*

Andrew was there, at the coffee shop, talking to a young
blonde woman. He was in full performance mode and said,
'Oh, hi there,' when I caught his eye. I got the coffee, and
then – because I could do this now without gibbering or
palpitating – I stood by his table waiting to say a proper
hello. He didn't break off or look at me, and I began to feel
as if I were waiting to talk to a teacher talking to another
teacher, and walked away in the end. He thought I was still
in pursuit, I assume. (I was not. I was cured.) As I passed the

window of the café I saw that he was still in full flow. He thought he had a fish on the line and was patiently reeling her in.

And Then
He Kissed Me

AS WINTER TURNED TO SPRING,
AND YEAR THREE BEGAN ...

The third date pub was just as rammed as the last one and we had to stand at the bar. I had a plan, for when things didn't go well: I was going to say that perhaps we should stop dating and be friends. (Of course in the romcom narrative that would be an indirect route to true love, though I've never found that life coincides with the romcom narrative.) When Edward turned to me to hand over my beer, I told myself to stop feeling that this was an interview, and relax – not something I'd ever found easy in the two years I'd been on the quest. I decided to pretend that he was someone I'd been at university with. We'd known each other 30 years ago, I decided, and were comfortable with one another, and could be subversive as well as newsy.

One of the killers of any authentic process of getting to know someone is the weight of expectation. Too often, midlife dates are like waking up on Christmas morning with a stranger. (Where do you start? What shall we do, what's your tradition, and who *are* you?) It came to me that that was the question to ask. 'So who are you, really, Edward?' I asked. His face softened and his posture relaxed. I'm fairly certain he was as anxious as I was. I said that I'd start. (Nothing to lose.) I summed myself up, using some pungent Anglo-Saxon, and he laughed and joined in with a pithy summing up of himself. A table became free and we grabbed it, and I realised I was hungry.

'Do you have any really unhealthy bar snacks?' he asked the barmaid. We ordered the gourmet platter of terrible bar snacks and retreated to our corner.

'If you could bear a fourth date, I'd like to cook for you,' Edward told me.

My heart jiggled happily. 'Are you a good cook?' I asked him, surprised.

'Not really, but it's basically chemistry, and I like doing chemistry.' There was a brief diversion into how we'd changed as people since our marriages ended. 'We change, and change is fascinating,' he said.

I found myself watching his mouth as he spoke, and met his eyes again. You know the way a person looks at you, that look in their eyes when they're thinking of sex? It was possible there was that. His expression was warm and intense. 'What would you cook for me?' I asked him.

He told me he'd been trying to imagine what my favourite meal was, aside from a French steak in peppercorn sauce. After he'd said that, we were off; we talked and talked. I'd been sure this was a man I wasn't interested in, and that he was even less interested, but what I thought now was, Perhaps I haven't blown it after all. It was as if we were meeting properly for the first time.

It was much chillier when we came out onto the street, and we put on our hats and scarves, buttoning up against the cold. 'What I'd like to do, if it's all right, is walk you to your door,' Edward told me. 'Let's not get the bus; let's stride out – come on. I love walking through the city at night, don't you?' It was something else we had in common, because I do love it: that feeling of ownership of the place, in the dark when the city's off duty, when it's dormant: the cars whooshing by and the buses and cabs, the silhouettes of magnificent buildings and the million lights. I was still rooting around for my gloves when Edward said, 'Here, take my hand.' He removed one of his enormous padded gloves, his winter cycling gloves (he isn't a man who has more equipment than he needs), and took my hand in his much bigger one. His was warm and soft. He squeezed my fingers lightly and said, 'That's better.'

The thought that came to me then – I'm confessing this – was, Oh my God, this is a Mr Darcy situation … well, okay, maybe just a Mark Darcy one.

We talked more as we walked along and it seemed, now, that there was a lot of ground to cover. I don't know if he was excited. I was excited. Something was happening to me; something was cranking into life. Interrupting our stream of conversation, we paused at lit-up shop windows and amused ourselves discussing the merchandise with brutal honesty. Eventually we got to my corner. Ordinarily I ran from the bus stop, on ink-black nights, because I got spooked by the road's being lonely and deserted. I didn't tell Edward this, but nonetheless he insisted on going out of his way. We walked along the empty street, still holding hands, and stood at my door saying goodnight. When goodnight had been said several times, and we had both added comments to it, necessitating saying goodnight again, and had come to a halt and had nothing else to offer, when I expected Edward to take his leave, going off with a wave … he remained standing there, looking down at me. He didn't move. He looked more serious-faced than ever, like a man with something important to say. He took his other glove off and unbuttoned my coat – it only had two buttons, so this wasn't a prolonged event – and put his hands around my waist. This took me by surprise; I'd associated his general reticence with probable sexual reticence; I hadn't thought of him as likely to be even this physically assertive. He made deep eye contact, throughout these rather erotic few moments. (*You know the way a person looks at you, that look in their eyes when they're thinking of sex? It was possible there was that.*) Moonlight glanced off the warm intensity of his eyes. He said, 'I've enjoyed tonight. What are you doing tomorrow? Can I cook you dinner?' And then he leaned down and he kissed me.

I went upstairs and into my flat, and closed the door by reversing into it, and stood with my back against it, laughing. I grinned while I took the dog out for his last pee of the day. I wished passers-by on the street a good evening, with perhaps excessive chirpiness for the lateness of the hour. As I stood in the kitchen and made peppermint tea I joined Alison Moyet on the iPod in singing 'Dido's Lament'. The song always moves me, but that night there was something transcendent about it. Time seemed to slow. I was alive, my senses fizzing, feeling all the feelings at once. My life has never flashed before my eyes, like they say happens in near death experiences, but I had a sort of concertina of flash-backs, standing there and singing along. My brain was growing hectic and I had to calm myself. I took the tea to bed, and sat up with the duvet pulled up to my shoulder, and laughed some more. 'Oh my God,' I said aloud. 'Well, that was surprising.' I chuckled softly to myself, from time to time, as I lay trying to sleep.

So, the morning came, a fine Saturday morning, and Edward and I were all set. We had a plan, cooked up via text message at 8 a.m.; he'd warned me already that he was an early riser. We'd meet straight after lunch, go for a mooch, have coffee, read papers, do the crossword – we were both crossword fans – and look at paintings. He was more than happy to go to a gallery and have me talk at him, he said (I'd warned him I might; I get enthusiastic in museums). He didn't visit galleries much, he'd told me, not on his own, but he'd been to a cinema showing of a film made at an exhibition, and I'd been to the same one. I wasn't ready to go to his flat and be cooked for, so we were going to end the day at a small Indian restaurant. Crosswords, art, curries; similarities were being ticked off. The plan was all set.

I left the house shortly after we'd finished texting, pulling on clothes before washing because the dog was restless and couldn't wait – and brought coffee and croissants and newspapers home. I had a leisurely breakfast, and then I went into the bathroom intending to have a shower. But when I opened the door things were not as I'd left them. Water was spurting out of the inlet pipe of the toilet, out of the joint in the pipe leading into the loo. I'm not just talking about a drizzle of a leak. There were fountains. There was already a lake on the floor. My first instinct was that I should call Edward. It didn't occur to me to try to find a plumber – a plumber could easily have taken hours to arrive; even a job classified as urgent might, in reality, have been fourth or fifth on his list. It was perfectly possible, likely even, that Edward was going to tell me I needed to call a tradesman, and that was fine. I thought that he might have good ideas about what to do in the interim, though. As I dialled his number I was already heading for the kitchen to find the floor-washing bucket.

'Help, there's water spurting out of my toilet!' I said without preamble, when Edward answered. 'Not the pan, I mean, but the pipes, and I don't know what to do.'

'Let me find my tools and I'll be right there,' he said. 'Turn off your water supply; I'm coming.' A little while later he arrived, on his bike, and parked it in the downstairs hall of the flats, and raced up with his tool bag. It transpired that he'd re-plumbed and rewired his first home; it was the kind of challenge he enjoyed.

And so Edward spent most of our fourth date on his hands and knees in front of my water closet. The fault was tricky to get at and the repair didn't go smoothly. He cursed and twiddled and cursed some more. 'The pipes don't line up,' he said, 'and the plastic thread has largely been stripped and PTFE tape isn't holding it, and also I notice you need a new ballcock.' This last comment wasn't said with any innuendo – he's not an innuendo kind of a guy – so it was only my mouth that twitched. I confined myself to nodding knowledgeably. He went off on his bike, twice, to get parts, and I hovered intermittently at the bathroom door saying how grateful I was, and how I *really must* learn some of these skills, and would he like a bacon sandwich? (He would. He ate two, and had three cups of tea.) He didn't finish the job to his own satisfaction until just after four. Then he had a shower with a borrowed towel and drank more tea, and sat at my kitchen table in his now grubby clothes, looking strangely wildly attractive. Don't tell me that I shouldn't have felt this attraction, and that it was only down to a conditioned female response to men good with spanners, one that obliterates centuries of feminism. For one thing, so what: my feelings were mine; they were feelings, and weren't pushed through the fine mesh filters of gender politics. Furthermore, and far more importantly, what was really happening in my mind, in my heart, was more of a response to his selflessness.

Edward ate a lot of biscuits and then he ate most of some leftover cake. We did the crossword and I held my own in helping solve it, and felt totally relaxed around him. I was relaxed around him in a way I absolutely hadn't been with any of the men I'd seen since my divorce. It was strange. The whole episode had marked some decisive sea change. Both of us, in the course of the day, had stopped trying to be ourselves with one another, and had abandoned all effort to please, and just *were* ourselves. It was as if we'd survived a disaster. The loo disaster had brought us together. All the usual date-related anxiety had vanished and there had been some sort of reset, so that being around one another felt completely normal. It was a bit like being married again and spending a lazy weekend afternoon at home, and it was a good feeling. As I was thinking this my phone buzzed with a text message. 'Are you still coming at 8 p.m. for drinks?' it asked. 'Oh God,' I said, 'I completely forgot, I'm supposed to be somewhere tonight for somebody's birthday.' Edward took this in his stride. He hugged me at the doorway, holding me close for a good long moment, then kissed me and said we should do something tomorrow. I heard him whistling as he wheeled his bike out into the street.

That evening, I might have annoyed my friends by talking about Edward a lot. The conversation kept coming back to him. I had been dismissive of him, I imagine, in the way I'd spoken about him previously, so now I felt the need to set the record straight. There needed to be a stark and total corrective. I had to account for the way things had changed, via two moments: the way he'd taken his glove off on Friday, to hold my hand, and the way he'd come to my rescue today.

'Oh my God,' Chief Sensible Friend said. 'You're falling for him, aren't you – you're falling in love with him.'

'No, no,' I protested. 'It's way too early to talk like that; but he spent *five hours* cheerfully fixing my loo.'

The group is all midlife and separated/divorced, and conversations at these get-togethers with wine aren't ordinarily oriented towards admiration of men. We've all dated and we have our stories. My obviously being smitten might have been a bit irritating. I intuited this after I was told, 'For God's sake, will you just shut up about Edward?' In the week that followed there'd also be some divorced-women's-group eyebrow-raising about how many evenings we were spending together. I saw him on four of the five days that followed the Great Plumbing Incident. We went to the cinema, the theatre, did more crosswords in pubs, and talked more about our marriages and their implosions. We found we shared a retrospective distance. Like me, Edward wasn't the instigator of divorce. As in my case, his long-term relationship was the victim of midlife concepts of newness, the great midlife restlessness that had infected both of our exes.

But then the next weekend loomed, and its yawning unscheduled time was making me a little anxious. What would happen if I stopped initiating conversation? What if the ease of the previous weekend deserted us? Dating experience had brought falls onto hard, unforgiving surfaces, when such social pedalling failed. I needn't have worried, though. When Saturday came, Edward turned up looking completely relaxed. The grey V-neck was off and tied round his neck, signalling playtime. He said, 'I have this car I hardly use; let's go out and about in it.' We went to see some very modern art, and I was confident he'd be a traditionalist, but he surprised me by being interested in the installations and the big conceptual stuff, more so than I am. He stood looking at things I'd walked right past. He was interested in the construction and the engineering, he said.

We went back to his flat on that Saturday night, and my heart was skipping nervously, because I'd discovered that sometimes sex can mark the end of the affair. He lived in a classic divorced-man pad – he was renting and searching for something affordable to buy with his settlement 50 per cent. The flat was dismal, tired, tiny, with technology in abundance and leads stretching across the floor. He'd bought himself a new bed, though, and had dismantled the rental one. He'd been to John Lewis for nice new bedding.

He decided he was going to cook for me. I sat on the sofa drinking wine, and he sang along to Lou Reed and the Alan Parsons Project while he made dinner. He came back and forth with the wine bottle, and lost track of time, so that by the time we came to eat, the chicken was tough, the potatoes had disintegrated and the mangetouts were soggy. 'I'm better when I have a recipe,' he said. 'I tried to wing it and lost confidence.' We ate, and he tidied up, and then he came back into the sitting room, and kneeled solemnly in front of me.

I'd wondered, as I've already said, if Edward would prove to be as hesitant in matters sensual as he'd been in other areas of his life. I'd thought that perhaps, being a person who lives so much in his head, he wouldn't be particularly sexual. But I was very wrong. That's all I can tell you. Very, very wrong. Anticipating that this might be the night, I was wearing the Sex Shirt, the one that also acts as a baggy cotton dress and is invaluable for post-coital bathroom visits. I did my usual whole disguise routine. Edward read the situation instantly. 'You don't need to hide, you know,' he said. 'I approve of every inch of you.' He kept marvelling, in bed, at how soft my skin was and how good I smelled. He had the smooth palms of a man who'd spent his life working at intellectual problems rather than with his hands (other than days fixing people's toilets, obviously). Nor did he have a boy-man's porn-fan's issue with female body hair. It wouldn't occur to him to judge. You're incredibly beautiful you know, he said, and though I'm not, not remotely, he seemed to be completely sincere. I could sense that he was smitten, that there had been a collapse of his defences, that he might already be mine, and I felt the first spasm of fear.

On Sunday we drove out into the country and walked through the gardens of a manor house and ate scones in their tearoom. I cooked for him that evening, and because I had people staying with me he was plunged into meeting members of my family, who of course were all madly curious. Edward was adept, coolly friendly under their scrutiny, and survived; he wasn't remotely rattled. For the three nights that followed this we cooked and ate together and lay in bed afterwards, talking in the dark, discovering more about each other's music collections. Meanwhile, the work days were interrupted by intermittent (text only) Skype chatting. Edward was having trouble concentrating, he said. He was happy; was I happy? I was. And yet … I was having trouble adjusting. Suddenly it was all full-on. It was moving at top speed into something settled, into the rhythm of a partnership. In the space of a month, two shy, unsure strangers had begun dating, had become a couple, and were now more or less living together, even though they hadn't yet spent a night in the same bed.

By the following week Edward and I were in constant communication. Some days I had to say, 'Stop, stop talking, I'm getting so far behind.'

'Me too,' he'd say. 'And isn't it great?'

'I'll get stressed if I keep being interrupted,' I had to say. 'I'll see you tonight, so tell me then.'

He stopped Skyping but continued to send texts, telling me about funny things that'd happened, and work frustrations, and random thoughts and how he was missing me.

Which was truly, deeply, lovely. But I began to be afraid. Was this it? Dare I be this happy? It wasn't asked consciously but the subconscious started to nag. The conscious mind was horrified that I could be so ungrateful. It occurred to me that Edward wanted very much to be settled. He needed his domestic life to return to a contented, predictable state, so that he could function properly. He hadn't been good at being alone. He'd been worse at it than I had.

What happened, under this pressure, was that eventually we had a row. Like most rows, it wasn't about what it was apparently about. That would be like saying that earthquakes are caused by the ground rising up. What really caused it was that I was scared. I was afraid of declaring the search over and another phase of life beginning. I was afraid it wouldn't last. I was continuing to wonder if I should have cancelled the memberships – for yes, I'd cancelled them. I'd been around the dating sites and had deleted my profile at every one.* (*Though somebody told me several months later that I was still listed at two of them, where people who'd cancelled remained on show so as to boost their numbers, which is a shameful practice.)

I was feeling surer about what I wanted than I had in quite a while. I knew that if this didn't work, I was finished with online dating. I had no more energy to give. I couldn't be attractive and available and fascinating any more, nor have any more over-sharing email conversations with men. A sudden repugnance had struck me. I think this was to do with the naturalness of my friendship with Edward, and the way he and I had started to be when around one another. I'd begun to be repelled by the idea of being listed at all. I'd begun to be repelled by the emailing, the attempts to woo by written word, and embarrassed by how much of it I'd done. It had seemed the obvious way to deal with the system, and the problems it presented, but it'd been time-consuming, and often defensive, and much of it had been a total waste of effort. Mostly, though, I was afraid of heartbreak. I was afraid that Edward would have a revelation, that one day he'd sit down next to me with a look on his face and say, 'Look ...' and I'd know what was coming. I had no confidence in permanence any more. I began to worry about the responsibility we'd apparently taken on, the responsibility of making each other happy. Did I want to be married again, or at least coupled-up and behaving like we were married, rattling around in a department store Home section discussing bowls? (We'd already done this, restocking his woeful rental kitchen.) What if Edward had a dark night of the soul and thought, Wait, what am I doing? This isn't the woman I should settle for; why am I settling? He might go into retreat and find he couldn't move forward again. In short, I was a neurotic mess.

There were things I loved about being single. I did what I wanted, when I wanted. There was no one to object to how I lived, scheduled, prioritised, behaved: no husband-audience, no husband-editor. I didn't feel the need to say why I couldn't see someone tonight, composing a defence in advance. I didn't have to think in the constant first-person plural. Do I really want that? I asked myself. I wasn't sure.

And so, when the first misunderstanding arose, when we disagreed, I had an exaggerated reaction to it. Edward made a joke about my being upset, using humour so as not to confront the issue (his words, afterwards, and not mine). He tried to joke me out of being distraught, not realising how serious it was, and how much thinking and insomnia lay behind it. I went quiet, which is my own way of dealing with suffering. I found that I was shaking. What on earth is the matter? he asked, still thinking that it was half a joke, or at

least something fleeting. We'd found our first incompatibility, at exactly the wrong time. I began to have extreme
thoughts, and come to extreme conclusions. This isn't going
to work, I thought, talking to myself, and you had better end
this now, while it's still all reversible. There was spiralling
panic and intensifying fear. His ability to joke about my
upset had made the fear worse. *None of this really matters to
him*, my inner voice said; *he's given the impression of being
embedded, but actually he can take this or leave this; he'll
recover quickly and move on; better get out of this now before
you get seriously hurt*. The spiral accelerated, but Edward,
unable to see this invisible escalation, was still trying to jolly
me out of what he'd characterised as *a bad mood*. We didn't
understand one another at all, I decided. At the first real test,
the relationship had proven to be as much an illusory bubble
as my unrequited passion for Andrew had (I told myself). I'd
been caught out again, and this time I'd gone deep – I'd felt
trust and hope, and had made my trust and hope obvious,
but it had all been as idiotic and self-deluding as before, the
panic voice told me.

I stared at Edward and he stared back, smiling, because
(innocently) he thought smiling would help. I said that I
thought we should slow this down. He was shocked. I saw a
tremor pass through his face, though he was on top of it
instantly. He didn't give any sign of his own fear. He didn't
want to fight; he didn't even argue the point. He just said,
'What?' His surprise seemed quite neutral to me. He's a man
of extreme self-control, of mental discipline. I'd admired this
in him, up until then, but now I saw its implications. I said
we were too different. I said it wouldn't work. I said I could
see the signs. 'What signs?' he asked, infuriatingly calmly. I
told him he was too Spock-like. He frowned at me in reply.
I told him I couldn't do this, rush into this; it was all moving

too fast. He stepped forward and took hold of me, and
wrapped his arms round my shoulders, pressing my face to
his chest. 'I'm sorry if it's moving too fast,' he said. 'I thought
you were happy.'

I extricated myself – why was he hugging me, as if that
made everything all right? Why do men take physical charge
of women when we're upset? I thought. Is it comfort, or is it
a way of blunting our responses and shutting us up? I was
stirred up and felt unwell, and the row could have been far
more decisive. I told Edward, while stepping back to a safer
distance, that I needed a break. What kind of break? he
asked, stepping forward again and looking down into my
face. I saw it then – his own upset, the shadow of it. His
mouth looked less certain than it had, and his eyes were
hurt. Just a break, I said; I see you every day and I need some
space. (I'd never uttered these words before, nor understood
them.) When he'd gone home I had a good cry. I had no
idea any more what I thought about anything. My thoughts
were racing, as was my heart. I felt unpleasantly unwell. I
was absolutely in turmoil.

A text arrived as I was making a cup of tea and on my
third handkerchief. It said: 'Please don't do this. I love you.
I like your laugh. We love each other.' It was true. I was in
love with him and it was scaring me. I wanted to hide from
it and to be safe.

Edward went to Germany the next morning and kept up
a steady drip of communication, without expecting me to
reply. He was just keeping in touch, keeping the line open,
he said; he wanted to give me the space that I needed, but
when things happened or when he had a thought, it was me
he wanted to tell. They were short messages, saying what he
was doing and what the city was like. He sent pictures of the
cakes he'd eaten, and said that he loved me, mentioning this

as an incidental extra fact, each time. In the evening he Skyped from his hotel room, and I saw his face, and it was sad and concerned. I felt a rush of love and guilt and shame. It couldn't have been helped – doubt was a stage I had to go through, but I felt bad, all the same. 'How are you?' he asked me gravely.

'I'm fine, darling,' I said. 'I'm sorry. I seem to be a basket case.' His continuing attentiveness could have been the worst thing possible for a woman who felt cornered, but it was strangely de-cornering. I didn't feel suffocated, but loved. I was loved. The crisis began to pass. We spent much of the evening video-calling, and ended up redrafting *Tales of the Riverbank*. We capsized Hammy Hamster's boat but he survived.

Lesson Ten: *don't expect people to be rational all the time. Humans aren't rational all the time, and especially not when there's a lot at stake, or when things are rapidly in flux. Let things play out properly and the dust settle before rushing to conclusions. Be prepared to say, 'I was wrong.'*

Late in the day that Edward flew home, the buzzer sounded at the flat and there he was. I went out onto the landing and saw him running up the stairs three at a time, holding a bunch of flowers. We had a long, long embrace standing on my doorstep, hearing each other's heartbeats, each other's breathing. I had a tremendous feeling of belonging, simultaneously reassuring and alarming. The alarm hadn't dissipated entirely. It still had little flare-ups. Did I dare give my heart, properly give it, or was I going to be on guard, on alert, half anticipating disaster for the rest of my life? 'Next time,' he said, 'I'd like you to come away with me. Would you like to? I have to go to Copenhagen next.' He had a work commitment there on the Monday, but we could go on Friday night, he said, and have the weekend together.

The day before we went, I looked at my small carry-on bag and saw the size of the challenge. There were what to pack (and how to be) questions, and three full nights ahead. We'd never spent a whole night together before, sharing our wake-up habits and navigating that sometimes tricky passage between an extended date and the morning's domestic ordinariness.

During our long weekend in Denmark, we learned things about one another. He learned that I'm not good at walking past a museum. I learned that he's not good at walking past a cake shop. I took photographs of almost everything. (He took one, of me standing in a square.) I learned that he isn't any good at lying in bed in the morning, not even on holiday. The day ahead excites him, and by 7 a.m. he was showered and reading. I'd seen books about popular science, history, polar exploration, piled on the bedside at his flat, but on holiday a weakness for 99p Kindle thrillers was revealed. When he got back into bed he whispered to me to sleep some more. 'Or would you like a cup of tea?' He hummed as he made it, and volunteered to test the biscuits. Later, when I admired a necklace at a crafts stall, he insisted on buying it. He protested that he needed nothing when I tried to buy him a present in exchange, though I managed to gift him a woolly hat. 'What about this?' I said, when I found it at another stall. It was hand-knitted, cotton-lined, made of a soft grey wool. He realised immediately that this was a part of my campaign against the red hat, and was highly amused. 'But this is actually great,' he conceded, putting it on and grinning at me. 'I do like grey.'

We discovered, on that weekend, that we're both schedulers, who like to study a map and plot a course. 'We can vary the plan as we go,' I said.

'As we come across new places and get distracted,' he added.

'And then we can change the plan,' I said.

'Exactly,' he agreed.

When we returned to the hotel in the late afternoon to rest, I discovered that he's a fan of pre-siesta sex. I also discovered, that evening in the restaurant, that he knows some Danish. Under pressure of questioning, he admitted that he could speak a little Finnish, but had better Japanese. He's one of those people who has a facility for languages, and can get by in two dozen. I teased him that it was another thing he should have listed on his dating profile. This had become a running joke. He said I should have mentioned that I like sci-fi; I would have got a lot more dates. I told him he should have mentioned that he grins during romcoms, and is ace at ironing. He said I should have mentioned my talent for anagrams. We took a crossword into a restaurant and puzzled other diners (Edward had enough Danish to translate our neighbours' reaction as 'What the hell?'). We both like to look at cryptic puzzles while we eat. Admittedly this is a tad eccentric. We're equally eccentric, and how freakishly lucky is that?

It was in Copenhagen that our togetherness first became self-evident; a fact. We were together in the world, now, not just as an idea, but physically. I had proof of this. I saw us in shop windows as we passed by, and our shadows stretching ahead of us on pavements. I saw Edward holding on to my hand. It was cold and windy so we spent a lot of time on the tourist bus, going round and round, talking about the buildings and random subjects, and hopping off for wintry sightseeing. The Little Mermaid was smaller than expected, but the weekend was much, much easier. We were both relaxed and light-hearted. Silences, when they came, were easy and contented. I began to feel that I'd known him for a hundred years.

Standing at passport control on the way back, I was struck by how everyday it seemed that we were travelling together. I looked at his serious face as he stood in the queue, and groped for the right word. What was the word? Safety. I felt safe, in multiple dimensions. I can't begin to tell you what a relief this was. A scene from *When Harry Met Sally* came to mind, in which Carrie Fisher, playing Sally's (Meg Ryan's) best friend, says to her boyfriend, about dating, specifically the relief of being able to abandon dating: 'Tell me I'll never have to be out there again.' He (Bruno Kirby) tells her, with affecting solemnity, 'You will never have to be out there again.' Thank you, Nora Ephron. One of the great romantic moments of cinema.

I'd have thoughts like this and then I'd wince, because feeling safe still felt presumptuous. But Lesson Eleven was this: *don't over-analyse everything to bloody death.*

What Happened Next

Some time has passed between then and now, since the end of the last chapter and the beginning of this one. Some time has passed since we went to Copenhagen, since I went through the tricky period of realising that I was in love and that it was okay to be. Fear of my own vulnerability held me back for a while, though of course if you're really properly to connect with someone and know them, mutual vulnerability is the one vital thing. It was genuinely difficult, though, for a while. The crust of suspicion and cynicism took its time to be shed. The strong defences that had built up over years had to be relaxed, had to stand down. T.S. Eliot in *The Waste Land* talks about spring being painful, lilacs pushing through dead land, the agony of dull roots being revived by spring rain, and it can be that physical, like an illness, like an attack, when you find yourself feeling again, and hoping, and loving. It hurts, when the rusted machinery of your heart cranks back into action. When finally it happened, after so much disappointment, it made me emotional. It made me panicky. It made me want to fight off those new feelings and be safe again. But we got through it. Edward saw what was happening and stood firm and waited. The storm came and went and the sky grew blue, and I held on harder to his hand afterwards, grateful that he'd weathered it. We're over the crossover zone, now. If we're no longer dating, it's only because we're past that point.

We're partners now. We're not only still together, but intend to be together for the rest of our lives. We talk about the future, and what we'll do in our old age, and how we'll live and where we might be. When people ask, 'So how did you two meet?' – which is something people want to know when you're in a new relationship and you're past 50 – I admit that I hesitate for a moment before answering. It took me a while to start being open about it. I used to say, 'Oh, through friends of friends.' Sometimes I still do. It's not that there's any stigma, exactly, but on the other hand I don't want to get into it. People are fascinated by ordinary-looking relationships emerging out of what the media informs them is a soup of depravity, and so they're desperate to hear the whole story. They're likely to take hold of your wrist, at a party, and lead you off somewhere quiet so you can tell them about the ins and outs, metaphorical and literal. Sometimes I smile to myself, imagining the two of us – Edward and me – as two old-timers, about 90 years old, way in the future, asked by young people for the story of how we got together, and me saying, in my elderly croaky voice, 'Well, it was a dating app I didn't often use because it was full of players and leg-over merchants.' It's not massively romantic, as a How We Met story. (Except, in a way it is, because of all the bloody adversity.)

Let's consider how the two of us would have been dealt with by an online algorithm. I'm not sure it would even have let us see one another, after dating site pre-selection, because we're so obviously incompatible. Let's also consider the wish list. I had a picture in my mind of the man I'd end up with, when I first signed up. He'd be a bit bohemian, maybe, perhaps an academic in a linen jacket and a neckerchief, maybe with a leather wristband and a satchel. It wasn't the only image I had of the man I might find, but it was certainly one of them. He didn't have a face and he often looked quite overweight – sturdy, anyway – but he had a certain style. He'd be good in the kitchen and he'd like to dance. He'd be gregarious and make me go to parties. I envisaged re-entering the world via his slipstream, after a long period of social awkwardness.

Not really any of the above has come to pass. Edward's not an academic, or sturdy or a neckerchief and wristband wearer, nor remotely bohemian. He's the most conservative dresser I've ever met, though at the same time strangely wacky. He's colour blind, which explains a lot. He wears loud checked shirts with clashing patterned jumpers. Sometimes he'll add a tie, a third dissonant feature. He wears odd socks. He has two pairs of shoes, because that's all he needs, and recoils at the idea of a man bag that isn't his manly black rucksack. He hates parties – which is secretly a relief – and has never been in a nightclub in his life and if he did he'd wear a suit (and a tie). Left to his own devices he'd live on pizzas, pasta and ice cream, and cold meat with potatoes. He has a very serious addiction to pudding, and afternoon tea, and Saturday morning pastries, and it's difficult to resist joining in. I've been putting on weight and have had to call a halt to the cake-fests, asking that he get his doughnut fix at the office instead. Foodie he is not, though in a restaurant he's fairly daring. At home he undercooks things and insists they got the full twenty-five minutes the recipe dictated, and glowers when they go back in the oven, which is funny.

There's plenty of on-paper incompatibility. I like the Rolling Stones and Edward likes the Beatles. I tease him for having Enya on his iPod; he teases me for having Fleetwood

Mac on mine, and for singing along. On the face of it we're travel-incompatible, too. Most of the countries on his bucket list are northern ones. Iceland. The Arctic Circle trip from southern Norway. Alaska, so that he can see bears catching salmon. I want to camp in a desert at night, and travel on a train through Indian hills, and I want to go to Africa. (We've agreed we'll try to do all of it, his list and mine.) Counter-intuitively, he can't bear to be cold. He hogs the duvet and insists that he doesn't. He has to be coaxed into the Mediterranean Sea with promises. He stands at hip depth, the place where anyone who knows about acclimatisation ought never to stand for long, while I shout, 'Plunge! Plunge!' and, 'It's warm when you get in!' It's like he's not even British. He'll only swim in heated pools, while I'm a human golden retriever, likely to jump into a puddle at a moment's notice.

We've been of cultural service to one another. I've become fascinated by new developments in astronomy. He knows more about art and world cinema than he used to, and has been initiated into the ways of Scandi crime drama. We've brought our differing professions and interests together into the mix. We're learning a language together, though he's much quicker to absorb its patterns than I am. We're learning more about history and natural history. We're studying maps and making plans. Furthermore, I've allowed my hair to turn from dark brown – its dyed equivalent to the dark brown of my youth – to its natural silvery grey. I embrace my age; I acknowledge it and am a survivor. It's a gift that love has given me.

My dog loves Edward. He's become our dog, slowly and surely. The dog prefers him to me, and looks to him for instructions and praise; there's a lot more wagging if Edward's holding the lead. I'll get used to it. My mother loves Edward, too: loves him sincerely and always asks about him on the phone. How is he and what's he been doing? Is he well? Sometimes I put him on to talk to her and they smile at one another in words. 'Such a lovely man,' she says to me, at least twice a week. 'You picked a good one there; you were so lucky.' She's been known to shake her head in wonder at the fact that I found him on a dating site (soupof-depravity.com) – as if I'd bought a crappy ring at a market and the jewels had turned out to be real. When they met for the first time, she was impressed by his height, his gentleness, his good manners, and by his having real handkerchiefs rather than tissues in his pockets. He reminded her of my dad in some ways, she said, sounding a little bit infatuated; Edward knows how to be impressive to mothers. We see his parents fairly often as they live close by, and we get along well, the four of us; there's always plenty to talk about. Chief Sensible Friend approves, too, which is a relief; we say it doesn't matter what our pals think of our partners, but actually it matters a lot. The posse are happy for me, now that they've stopped being tentative about the whole thing in case it didn't last. My sister, who lives far away, has met him and has given an enthusiastic thumbs up. Jack hasn't met him, but says he couldn't be more pleased. He's a little bit envious, at the same time, of the love that we've found and that has eluded him for a long time.

Edward still holds my hand in the street, every time we go out together. He strides along, so if we're late or have to go uphill the offer of a tow is genuinely useful. I've also learned that he can be gloriously silly. He can go off on a riff and develop it. Seventies children's television comes up quite often and I join in; I do Johnny Morris-style voices to nature documentaries, and vocalise the dog's thoughts. We've amassed a fund of private jokes and still do crosswords at the weekend. Though naturally a quiet man, Edward can become extremely talkative – and he's also a good listener. He has deep reserves of goodness. If I'm upset, he says, 'Tell me what I can do.' He steps forward to deal with trouble, and deals with it unflinchingly. He's also profoundly tactile. He pauses to put his arms around me when we're cooking, and holds me close to his chest and makes his Edward noise (*'hmmrrrmmrrrmm'*. He says it's his Ent noise). He snuggles up in bed and says how lovely it is to snuggle. He's the prince of back rubs. If I can't sleep, he tells me a story. He opens his arms and invites my head onto his shoulder.

It's possible that Edward could make his own list of ways in which I took him astray from the woman he had in mind when he signed up to online dating. But he doesn't really think like that. He's the most uncritical, non-judgemental person I know. When we met friends at outdoor seating for a beer, one chilly night, and he saw that I was cold, he tried to give me clothes of his own. Would I like his jacket? I must take his scarf. I murmured that I couldn't get my own coat to close up, because being with him and in the radius of his near-constant snacking was making me fat. I met his eyes when I said this, waiting for a reaction there that he wouldn't have time to hide. But instead he maintained the same loving eye contact and said, without a beat of time passing, 'Well, just buy a bigger coat.' (I didn't. I have given up biscuits.) We amuse each other with our assumptions and anecdotes and foibles. It's one of the ways in which we're still travelling towards one another. Being with someone new in your fifties: it prompts you to look at the whole sweep of your life. You see patterns there. You see the path behind you and the one ahead. You might see someone else's path and the two converging into one. We can see that path now.

When the owners of the flat I was renting gave me notice that they were going to sell, and I began to think about where I might move to, Edward decided that it was time he moved, too; that he had to get out of his tragic bachelor pad with the uncomfortable budget sofas and worn carpets and windowless boxroom kitchen. 'I should start looking for something to buy,' he said. 'Maybe you could help me look – if you'd like to.' I told him I would. I've always loved property hunting, studying floorplans and thinking about colours and furnishings and making homes homely. 'As you know, I could badly do with your advice on these things,' Edward said. (It was true.)

Do you remember, at the beginning of this story, my telling you that after my marriage failed I spent some time eating whole tubs of ice cream and crying over property search programmes? Home has always meant a lot to me, not just as a fact but as an idea. I talked a lot to long-suffering pals about not being able to paint walls, when I took the rental, after the divorce took 50 per cent of my house fund away. I became borderline obsessive about the wall-painting issue. Not being able to paint walls was a hard thing to have to accept. Living in someone else's flat, my landlord's flat – his spare flat, at that – was tough for my pride in my surroundings, and my sense of myself. I admire people who can rent their whole lives quite happily and don't have to deal with inner narratives about reward and punishment, but after everything I'd been through, not having a home that was mine for my old age felt like a punishment too far by the universe (though obviously it doesn't do to anthropomorphise the universe). So I was thrilled to be invited to help with Edward's flat search. We looked at some property listings online and discussed the pros and cons of what was available. It was going to be a tough search; he'd had the same divorce-related division of assets issue and so the budget wasn't large.

Then he said, 'Would you like to move in, when I find it?'

'What?' I said. 'Do you mean as a lodger? As house sharers? I'd pay rent?' That was genuinely what I thought he meant. He knew I was looking for somewhere to live.

'Well, it'd be great if you could help with the mortgage, but that wasn't what I meant.'

'I don't understand,' I said.

'I mean – shall we buy a flat together?'

My cheeks burned. I must have looked as if I were running a fever. 'Buy a flat *together*,' I said. 'You mean like – you mean …'

'Move in together. Live together. Be together,' he said. Having to spell it out.

'Together,' I said.

'We could go and see some flats,' he said. 'This weekend. And choose one. That suits us.'

'Together?' I was so excited I thought I would be sick. Genuinely. I thought I would vomit up my happiness, right then and there.

'Yes,' he said. 'What do you say?'

I said yes. And now we live together, in a flat that we chose. There are things in it that each of us brought from the past, but not many. Lots of those were given away and new things took their place. It's a modest little home but it's ours. It's ground floor with its own front door and there's a teeny tiny paved front yard for the dog to sit out in, and for us to sit out in on sunny days at our little bistro table, with cups of tea (or a beer, in the evening, while dinner's cooking). There's a small raised walled bed where I'm about to start killing a succession of plants, and a shed for the bikes and room for a barbecue. We might get a barbecue, so that Edward can burn chicken and I can stand by and applaud.

On days off we go out and about in the car we also bought together (his was gifted to his ex) and take the dog into the countryside and climb hills that almost kill me, to look at views that I take a million pictures of. Generally he takes only one, of me sitting on a rock scowling at him and telling him to wait because I'm not yet in position; that's the usual pattern. I'd assumed that he wasn't very fit, because when I enquired whether he did any sport he said that he didn't, and probably ought to, which is pretty much my answer if anyone asks – I'm always just about to start swimming again, and have been on the cusp of doing so for a decade. But it turns out that he has two bicycles, one of them a posh expensive one, and that not only does he go off and do thirty-mile cycle rides for fun, but that he's also done LEJOG, otherwise known as Land's End to John O'Groats. I'm not sure my *Pilates for Nanas* DVD is really up on the same sort of level. But never mind.

Thankfully the trips we do together are rarely physically challenging. We go to places on buses, and have been known to take a picnic. We take trains. We have outings (*expotitions*, because that's what Christopher Robin went on), to stately homes, where Edward's always unfailingly nice about my critiquing the décor. We visit historic sites and cathedral cities, and spend days in green places, rambling towards pubs that have good beer. In short, we're utterly, contentedly middle-aged. We read on the sofa together, one at each end. We'll interrupt each other, sometimes, to say, 'Hey, listen to this,' and read out a section that has grabbed us. It's what I asked the universe for, when I started online dating: a bookish, kind man who'd enjoy reading with me. Sometimes the universe gives you what you want. I like this idea. Sometimes it's satisfying to anthropo-morphise the universe.

In short, we are happy. I have my heartfix, and he has his. Love is more precious, in some ways, the second time around. We're more aware of how lucky we are, and because of that heightened awareness, we're more careful with the precious and the lucky, perhaps. We take care of one another, in every possible way. We don't argue, but if there's disagreement we sort it out quickly, and steer it towards laughter (usually at ourselves), and we don't let anything get in the way of our rapport.

We are happy, and it's amazing to be able to write those three words and not feel the need to qualify or footnote them. It's taken time and a lot of ups and downs to get here, to the point at which I'm able to use three words, but I can use them now, confidently, without fear and without creep-ing doubts. Another, happier phase of life has begun. The best part about this ending is that it isn't really the end.

693 Days

The *Guardian* column that led to this book wasn't the beginning of the process of writing. The diary came first. Every day that I was listed on dating sites, I wrote an entry in a journal which became a series of journals (they now form quite a pile), recording what was happening, who I was talking to or seeing and the conversations I was having. The *Guardian* column lagged quite some way behind events. I wouldn't have agreed to do it in real time; it wouldn't have been fair to any of us, and might even have altered the outcome.

There wasn't any initial intention to publish. I wrote because I was lonely and sad and heartbroken, and – having been made to feel profoundly unloved at the end of my marriage – I needed to know I was lovable, and needed to love in return. Contentment was the goal, rather than a relationship specifically. It wasn't at all obvious when I started that I would find someone. If the dating experiment was going to end with realising I was going to be single, possibly for the rest of my life, then that was okay. It had to be.

Undoubtedly I was naïve when I started. I went into online dating assuming that all my interactions there would be with men of about the same age and with the same interests. I assumed all those other people would be looking for undying love with life partners … and then I arrived and was pelted with questions about whether I wore stockings or not. Of course there were also encounters with good people (most were essentially good people, even if some of them were *behaving* badly; we need to distinguish between the two), but most of the time I was blanked, or propositioned, or challenged or scorned, or ignored or put in my place, or propositioned some more. Writing the journal helped navigate through the weirdness. When I stopped writing I found I had 215,000 words. Some passages have been reproduced here without any editing. In others I have paused and reflected on how I felt and how I acted, with the different eyes of hindsight.

I thought there might be a book in the diaries at about the halfway point, when it was all going very badly. This was a year into the search and long before I met Edward. I added a lot of soul-searching and bleak diagnosis to this possible manuscript, and my ex was mentioned quite a bit. In short, it wasn't publishable. The last line was something like: 'So that's why you should stay away from online dating, dear readers. Avoid it *like the plague*.'

It was hard work, finding Edward. It took 693 days, from first signing up to a dating site to the day of our first date, and I went at the project hammer and tongs. I rolled up my sleeves and did online dating thoroughly. When I moaned, as often I did, that I wasn't getting much of a response to my efforts, people would gently point out that in fact I seemed to be getting a lot of traffic and juggling a lot of email and requests to meet. Many of these, however, were the result of my own effort, in trawling sites and approaching men who wouldn't otherwise have seen someone of 50, or 51. Often, in the account that you've just read, when I say that 'I heard from' someone, it was contact made in response to my contacting them first.

I'm project-oriented by nature and so it took a lot of time. I wasn't going to let this thing beat me, and the worse it got the more determined I became. But I understand why people give up; I almost did, after all. Online dating, purely in its mechanisms, its opportunities, its failure to punish rudeness and abuse – which all go on behind its own securely closed doors – doesn't promote or reward courtesy, empathy, fidelity or tolerance. I'm not saying it should. Obviously 'it' doesn't have any moral character; it's just a listing and messaging system. Theoretically it's a neutral space, but nonetheless an argument could be made that it brings out the worst in some of us, our restless unsatisfiable worst. Certainly it encourages the idea that perfection must be out there, the perfect ten: it's going to take hard work to find them, perhaps, because they're currently in Finland, or Bolivia, or because – and this is the killer – they haven't actually joined up yet, but they will, some time soon, some day. That's not a state of mind I can envy.

One thing that makes online dating hard to generalise about is that there isn't a predictable link between the amount of effort put in and the result. You could meet the first guy who asked you out and move in with him a year later, as happened to someone I know. You could write to six people every night for two years and get nowhere: I thought that was going to be my story. When the columns were published in the *Guardian*, I'd often be berated online for not giving a man enough of a chance, or too much of one. People made these judgements based on very few facts, and if you're having a go at online dating, sometimes you will find your friends behave in similar fashion. 'You've stopped seeing him – what's wrong with him?' (As if he's a vacuum cleaner and fixable.) Or, 'You said no to a date, what the hell for?'

Don't waste too much time explaining the ups and downs of online dating to your social circle. It can distort the way you see the process, and the people on offer, and even yourself. Tell them, 'When there's news I'll let you know, but there's no news at the moment.' Say, 'Yes, I've had a few dates, but nothing serious; it's been sociable and fun but I'm not seeing anyone, no.' (You might have to lie about it being fun.) Mothers, especially, might need to be fed these soothing useful phrases. I went round Europe hitchhiking when I was 18, and didn't confess to my mum that I hadn't done it by train until many years later. 'Oh God,' she said, when eventually I told her. 'I'm so glad you didn't tell me at the time; I would've had a fit.' It's the same with online dating. Don't talk about it. It's *Fight Club*. We don't talk about *Fight Club*.

If you decide to ignore this advice and opt for keeping people informed, be prepared to be told you're too picky. Hold fast to your pickiness, I say. It's vital to trust your pickiness. Your search for love isn't a recruitment process. You don't need to refer to legislation and worry about fairness, and explain why you can't hire someone, why they're not getting the job. It isn't a job. There's no more personal process than finding someone to whom you will give full access, to your heart, to your body, to your future. It's about complex feelings, not qualifications. This may sound like the bleedin' obvious, but I've had to make this speech to people at least three times.

On the other hand, don't dismiss someone after one date just because 'there wasn't a spark'. I don't know how this whole spark narrative got started, but it's everywhere. If it's used as an excuse and there was really another reason, I can see the point: it's the classic 'It's not you, it's me' in another guise. If it's that the person was horrible, or talked about the Kardashians for forty-five minutes, or picked their nose while talking to you, then fair enough. Use the spark excuse with my blessing. But don't get into an expectation that a spark must present itself in an otherwise nice evening spent with a nice person, and that if there isn't an electricity episode, there's no point having a second nice evening with the nice person with whom you got on really well. 'We had such a good time, and he was really nice but there was no spark,' is an irritating comment to hear. The persistent mythology of the spark has a lot to answer for.

I'm not arguing that everyone you meet ought to be given an allowance of a minimum three dates, on principle. What I'm distinguishing between is style and content. Don't be too hasty in judging a person's date demeanour or the flavour of their initial communications with you, because shy or nervous people take time to show themselves. Sometimes people are afraid, or ill or distracted by a problem or have no confidence or think you're there on sufferance. Great people have off days.

EIGHT RULES FOR ONLINE DATING – AND SOME HARD-EARNED ADVICE

The plan to woo by written word wasn't completely wrong-headed. A little bit of emailing or a long phone conversation before meeting is helpful. It would be sad to fall for Trevor, for instance, based on his lovely smile, his love of theatre and his manners, and only realise in a post-coital chat that he was the man who didn't want a woman who was his intellectual equal. But *Don't get into a protracted email cycle with people*: that's **Rule One** of dating, and the one I broke the most.

Rule Two is: *Don't underestimate other people's capacity for snap judgements*. Sometimes all it takes to bring things to an untimely end is for someone to get their first proper view of your arse encased in jeans. They have inflexible arse-size-shape criteria, and that's that.

Watch out for people like Martin, the email-lover who talked the talk and walked away. He could be Cyrano de Bergerac but he wasn't really free. **Rule Three** is: *Don't assume everybody is equally single*.

Rule Four is also pertinent here: *People are often prepared to lie to get out of a tight spot*. Martin told me he didn't want to meet me because he was afraid he'd break my heart. It wasn't true. He just felt massively cornered.

Rule Five is: *Don't assume we all have the same intentions and integrity*. I know of women who've been wooed by men who then dropped them without comment. They met and slept with men they met online, and never heard from them again. One of the women asked the man who'd done this to her why he'd done it. 'He said that actually having sex on the first date meant he *wasn't* interested,' she said. 'He wanted to get sex out of it at least.'

Rule Six is: *Don't ever feel pressurised into having sex*. The person communicating that pressure is not your friend: it's that simple.

Rule Seven is: *It's normal online dating practice to ignore someone's messages if you don't fancy them*. The first nine times this happened I was convinced there was a glitch in the system, and wrote to one of the Admins.

Rule Eight is: *Just because you are in the grip of something it doesn't mean the other person is*. I don't have to tell you that I broke this rule with Andrew. I was convinced for weeks that Andrew and I had the spark, and misled myself about the reason for his keenness to talk. Andrew, it turns out, talks to everybody and anybody. Andrew lives alone, and when unleashed on the society of a neighbourhood coffee shop, with its congregation of regulars, has trouble stopping talking. It didn't even occur to him that I might be a prospect.

I still see Andrew sometimes, though I rarely go to that coffee shop any more. He doesn't change. He talks about change and seems to be stuck. The last time I talked to him, his eyes kept straying to the denim-clad bottom of a young woman who was organising her coat, bag and laptop at the next table. He said that he was thinking about relocating to somewhere in Asia, because in Asia a woman would be happy to look after him and also the house, without expecting much in return. I wasn't sure if he was joking or not. I asked if he was seeing anyone. 'Depends how you define it,' he said. 'As you know, I don't do relationships.' How would I know, and what on earth did he mean? 'Jesus Christ,' I said to myself as I walked home. 'You really dodged a bullet, there.'

General advice to women: Watch out for men who are dating in the open sense: seeing a lot of people at once and auditioning, perhaps permanently. Watch out for men who use the word *femininity* pejoratively, or who use the term 'red pill'. Watch out for men who think women have a duty to keep young and beautiful, at the expense of being, thinking, doing, reading, eating, travelling, experiencing. I don't advise hooking up with one of these guys, if you intend to live past 60. I don't know about you – perhaps you take pleasure in being high maintenance, and if so, carry on, do your thing; whatever floats your boat. I intend to be even lower maintenance than I am now, in my sixties. I intend to do a lot of being, thinking, doing, reading, eating, travelling, experiencing, in my sixties. The world of my sixties is principally going to be about not giving a shit what anyone thinks of what I look like. I am going to grant Edward full equality in this. My prediction is that he'll become stringy (on a diet of buns) and I'll become stout (despite giving up sugar), and that we'll love each other for ever.

Advice to men: Don't send out mass mail-outs, but if you do, at least try to disguise them. Be specific. Don't write a string of generic phrases. We're looking for a little glimpse of you, in a blind dating world. Don't leave most of the fields blank on your dating site listing and then say, 'If you want to know more, just ask.' Yes, of course I want to know more than your age and where you live, you pillock: how do you think romance works? Don't mention sex before meeting someone. Don't assume women will want to engage in your on-screen porn scenario. Don't add lots of teenage-girl kisses and hugs to your initial approach (total turn-off). Don't send dick pics. Don't be a dick.

I very nearly gave up the search. I thought it was me and that my experience was unusual. I assumed I was alone in having so many travails, until the column appeared, whereupon my mailbox filled up with women saying, 'Me too, oh God, me too,' and 'I have had near identical issues.' At times, online dating was just too hard. It rocked my confidence. It caused deep new wells of anxiety to be dug. I went repeatedly into people-pleaser mode (for some of us, it's hard-wired) and hated myself for it. Honestly, what's the point if that's how it makes you feel? The process is supposed to be about happiness, but a dating site is a machine, one that could trample you and break your bones. It's a system that can facilitate very bad behaviour, for those who want to behave badly. Why put yourself through that? You might as well stay at home with your dog and read books and drink tea, and twiddle your toes in contented singledom. At least there's integrity in that, and self-esteem.

Well. The answer, for me, comes back to the outcome. I found Edward at the end of my long road, and so I can't do anything but recommend it.

If you were thinking of trying online dating, I'd say go ahead, but cautiously and fully armoured. You will almost certainly have knockbacks and you might also hear from oddballs with 'niche' desires. That's okay: you're not under any obligation to explain yourself. There are times when it's okay to make the V sign to the screen and move on, and blow a raspberry at the same time. Even after a dating disaster, a summary rejection, keep the door open. Keep a foothold in possibility. Keep the door open but don't expect too much. Have dignity and be your authentic self. Be pithy rather than gushing, and wait and see. Be your real age. Post recent photographs, including one that really looks like you; you want someone who will fall in love with your morning face. You don't want someone who falls in love with Gilda, only to be disappointed to wake up with Rita Hayworth (though they'd be idiots, obviously). Don't pedal too much. Don't plead. Remind yourself that this is supposed to be fun. You're not a commodity; you're the client, and others' judgement is essentially irrelevant. Don't get over-invested before meeting. Don't email twenty times. Don't find yourself in an email/Skype relationship from which you have to extricate yourself. Break the ice, make an arrangement, then meet somebody. If the other person's consistently too tired or busy to talk or to meet, take the hint: they are virtually wearing a T-shirt with *I DO NOT WANT YOU* written on it; they're virtually digging an escape tunnel. If it goes wrong, the mantra is *YOUR LOSS, BUDDY*. (This is all advice I wish I'd taken.) Looking back at the dating diary now, I'm often amazed at things I did and said, half entertained and half clammy with regret. There may seem a high cost to online dating, but I'm here to tell you something I never expected to be able to say: that if you stand firm and you're lucky, there's also a prize.

As some people were unreticent about saying, when the column came to an end, there's suspiciously good news at the end of this quest: it's too happy an ending to believe and Edward's too good to be true. When I told him some people didn't believe in him, he said, 'Tell them I don't believe in them either.' He knew about the column. He knows about this book. His first reaction was, 'That's brave.' His second was, 'Do you mind if I don't read it?' (No. No, I don't. I really, really don't, sweetheart.)

A Final Dedication

This book is retrospectively dedicated to you, Edward.

You're unlikely ever to read this, but thank you, thank you for the happy ending, for the heartfix, which I didn't really believe was possible when I embarked on this quest. You're the kindest, most thoughtful, most loving of men, and your love, friendship, care and adoration are sincerely and enthusiastically returned. I love you. I'm so happy to be sharing my life with you.